RADICAL
SOCIOLOGY

RADICAL
SOCIOLOGY

An Introduction

Edited by
DAVID HOROWITZ

Canfield Press   San Francisco

A Department of Harper & Row, Publishers, Inc.
New York   Evanston   London

Cover Design: Doug Luna

RADICAL SOCIOLOGY: AN INTRODUCTION
Copyright © 1971 by David Horowitz

Standard Book Number: 06-383865-6

Library of Congress Catalog Card Number: 72-160833

71   72   73   74   10   9   8   7   6   5   4   3   2   1

PREFACE

Virtually all sociology texts now available to students and teachers are attempts to understand the structures and institutions of society with an eye to making them function better. The present text is unique in that it attempts to understand these structures and institutions, mainly of modern American society, in order to change them into something fundamentally different, and in many ways antithetic, to what they are now. All contemporary sociology texts regard the social order from the perspective of the privileged few on, or near, the top of the social and economic ladder: their "scientific" objective is the effective management of society and the reduction of its tensions and conflicts.

The present text, by contrast, adopts a perspective more in harmony with the interests of those further down the social hierarchy: it sees social conflict as a reflection of the imbalances of property and power at the heart of the present social order, and their intensification as possible preludes to the overthrow of its inequitable, racist and imperial framework. It is in this sense a "radical" textbook, unorthodox in its methodology and approach, and untypical in its concern with the consequences of accumulated power and wealth, and its disinterest in the academically fashionable (profitable) problems of social administration.

This is a basic — but not a simple — text, organized to introduce the student to a radical approach to the study of society. The order of sections and selections represents a logical progression of subject matter and is designed to facilitate the understanding of a sociological model and perspective which has no established place in the university curriculum, but whose superiority to orthodox models in comprehending the present social system and its crisis, will be evident at once.

David Horowitz
Berkeley, 1971

CONTENTS

RADICAL
SOCIOLOGY

GENERAL INTRODUCTION: Sociology and Society

Like other intellectual disciplines directly concerned with contemporary American society and its conflicts, academic sociology is in a state of profound crisis. Like other crises, the sociological crisis has had its ascending stages. The indictment of the sociological establishment began with the charge that its models, which pictured modern American society as basically harmonious, pluralist, and post-"ideological," were hopelessly distant from the American reality and were irrelevant to America's tensions and conflicts. This indictment was quickly extended by the realization that the models and techniques which sociologists were developing (often on lucrative government and corporation contracts) were being placed in the service of the ruling powers of the social status quo, and that they were themselves integral parts of the system of social oppression and institutional aggression which the radicals condemned. Confrontation within the discipline inevitably followed.

In September, 1968, the solemnity of the American Sociological Convention at the Sheraton Hotel in Boston was shattered by a spokesman for the radical sociology caucus, who had followed the Secretary of Health, Education and Welfare, to the speaker's platform.

"These remarks," began Martin Nicolaus, "are not addressed to the Secretary of Health, Education and Welfare. . . . The department of which the man is head is more accurately described as the agency which watches over the inequitable distribution of preventable disease, over the funding of domestic propaganda and indoctrination, and over the preservation of a cheap and docile reserve labor force to keep everybody else's wages down. He is Secretary of disease, propaganda, and scabbing.

"This may be put too strongly for you—for you—but it all depends on where you look from, where you stand. If you stand inside the Sheraton Hotel these terms are offensive, but if you gentlemen and ladies would care to step across the street into Roxbury [the black ghetto] you might get a different perspective and a different vocabulary. If you will look at the social world through the eyes of those who are at the bottom of it, through the eyes of your subject population (and if you will endow those eyes with the same degree of clearsightedness you profess to encourage among yourselves), then you will get a different conception of the social science to which you are devoted. That is to say that this assembly here tonight is a kind of life. It is not a coming together of those who study and know—or promote study and knowledge of—social reality. It is a conclave of high and low priests, scribes, intellectual valets, and their innocent victims, engaged in the mutual affirmation of a falsehood, in common consecration of a myth."

The myth, according to Nicolaus, was that professional sociology is a value-free discipline: "Sociology is not now and never has been any kind of objective seeking-out of social truth or reality. Historically, the profession is an outgrowth of nineteenth-century European traditionalism and conservatism, wedded to twentieth-century American corporation liberalism.

"That is to say that the eyes of sociologists, with few but honorable (or honorable but few) exceptions have been turned downward, and their palms upward. Eyes down to study the activities of the lower classes, of the subject population—those activities which created problems for the smooth exercise of governmental hegemony. . . ."

The fact that sociological knowledge and expertise was put in the service of the guardians of the status quo and the beneficiaries of its privilege was of course, no accident. "It is no secret and no original discovery that the major and dominant sectors of sociology today are sold—computers, codes and questionnaires—to the people who have enough money to afford this ornament, and who see a useful purpose being served by keeping hundreds of intelligent men and women occupied in the pursuit of harmless trivia and off the streets. I am not asserting that every individual researcher sells his brain for a bribe—although many of us know of research projects where that has happened literally—but merely that the dominant structure of the profession, in which all of its members are to some extent socialized, is a structure in which service to the ruling class of this society is the highest form of honor and achievement. (The speaker's table today is an illustration.) The honored sociologist, the bi-status sociologist, the book-a-year sociologist, the sociologist who always wears the livery—the suit and tie—of his masters: this is the type of sociologist who sets the tone and the ethic of the profession, and it is this type of sociologist who is nothing more or less than a house servant in the corporate establishment, a white intellectual Uncle Tom not only for this government and ruling class, but for any government and ruling class—which explains to my mind why Soviet sociologists and American sociologists are finding after so many years of isolation that, after all, they have something in common."

The upsurge of radical energies within the university, of which Nicolaus's speech provides a particularly articulate expression, has been widely misunderstood or—more accurately—misrepresented as "anti-intellectual" in motive and direction. In fact, the shoe fits the other foot. It is the academic establishment, the so-called profession of scholars, that has betrayed its intellectual mission by acquiescing in, and in many cases actively abetting, the open transformation of the university into an elaborate service station for the dominant forces of wealth and power in society.

Senator Fulbright, an enlightened conservative, has drawn attention to the incalculable damage inflicted on the academic ideal by the very guardians of its inner sanctorum: "Research in chemical and biological warfare" he noted in April, 1969, "is not one of those activities that can be regarded as appropriate to an 'idealistic' institution. Nor is Pentagon-sponsored field research in counter-insurgency an appropriate activity for social scientists who ought to be acting as independent and critical commentators on their government's policies. Far from being victims of anti-intellectualism as some of these scholars complain when their activities are criticized, they themselves are perpetuating a virulent form of anti-intellectualism. They do so by contributing to the corruption of their universities, the militarization of American society, and that persistent degradation of values which goes by the polite name of credibility gap."

From a radical perspective, Senator Fulbright's indictment is far too narrow, of course, but it catches the main point. Far from forming a disinterested basis for the pursuit of knowledge, the academic organization of research and learning, under the trusteeship of corporate wealth, legitimates the existing social order and actively serves its most powerful interests. This fact should surprise no one, except perhaps academic sociologists who have been maintaining the pluralistic, "post-Marxian" character of American society for more than a generation.

The urgency of the radical critique of the university is only partly spurred by intellectual concern, even as Fulbright's own indictment is only partly motivated by the plight of pure intellect. A more profound reason for radical rebellion in the academy is the wasted potential of the university as a quasi-democratized institution which could provide a powerful weapon in the struggle against the reign of inequality and social privilege in the American social order, and against the escalating crimes of its expanding overseas empire.

"Unlike knowledge about trees and stones," as Nicolaus put it in his Boston speech, "knowledge about people directly affects what we are, what we do, what we may hope for. The corporate rulers of this society would not be spending as much money as they do for knowledge, if knowledge did not confer power. So far, sociologists have been schlepping this knowledge from the people, giving knowledge to the rulers. What if the machinery were reversed? What if the habits, problems, secrets, and unconscious motivations of the wealthy and powerful were daily scrutinized by a thousand systematic researchers; were hourly pried into, analyzed, and cross-referenced; were tabulated and published in a hundred inexpensive mass-circulation journals and written so that even the fifteen-year-old high school dropout could understand them and predict the actions of his landlord, manipulate and control him? Would the war in Vietnam have been possible if the structure, function, and motion of the U.S. imperial establishment had been a matter of detailed public knowledge ten years ago?" Far from working to develop the knowledge that would help to liberate the vast majority from its servitude to the privileged few, "sociology has worked to create and increase the inequitable distribution of knowledge; it has worked to make the power structure relatively more powerful and knowledgeable, and thereby to make the subject population relatively more impotent and ignorant."

The task of a radical sociology is to reverse this process, to study the structure of social oppression and to bring this knowledge, and the power that it conveys, to the powerless and exploited social majority. But to do this it is necessary first to develop an appropriate theory and methodology. The theoretical models that service an unjust status quo cannot also serve the effort to understand the social process, its governing relations, and the measures necessary to revolutionize them.

The "political" significance of abstract sociological models becomes clear if one considers for a moment the perspective of a privileged minority which dominates society and reaps its major benefits. Such a minority naturally prefers to sustain its rule by persuasion rather than coercion. Yet, to persuade the majority of its stake in a status quo in which it is suffering manifest injustice is far from simple.

To accomplish this task it is necessary first to obscure the class division of society and then to appeal to the common human bonds shared by the whole of society, privileged and unprivileged alike. It is necessary to stress the common benefits that accrue to all individuals in society from "peace," "harmony," and "social conciliation" as opposed to "anarchy" and civil war.

Classes, particularly economic classes, are dismissed in such a presentation as artificial constructs, while individuals who possess significant social opportunities, within the rules of the prevailing order, are identified as the true constituent elements of the social order. Maintaining stability and order (and with them the inequitable status quo) appears, in this ruling class conception of society, to be manifestly in the general interest; and if a ruling class were to sponsor academic pursuits, then the problem of maintaining stability would be a central focus of its sociology.

In point of fact, academic sociology as currently practiced in the institutions of higher learning in America, sponsored by corporate and foundation wealth, adheres to this pattern of reasoning rather closely. When it views the social order from what might be called a macro-social perspective (i.e., one that takes the social whole as the subject of analysis), the perspective of academic sociologists is predominantly "functionalist," adopting a theoretical approach that develops its analysis around the central problem of the maintenance of the social order and its equilibrium.*

But the basic orientation of academic sociologists is *micro-social* in character: academic sociologists are chiefly concerned with individuals, groups, and institutions as they are influenced by or integrated into the prevailing social order. A typical modern "dictionary" of sociology, for example, defines "social system" as "a social group or set of interacting persons conceived of as distinct from the particular persons who compose it." A family, a boy scout troop, and American capitalism are all social systems in this conceptual framework (though this particular "dictionary" fails even to characterize capitalism as a "social" system).

In contrast, radical sociology begins with a perspective in which the social system is the distinctive pattern of economic, political, and cultural relationships according to which a group organizes the production and distribution of goods and services

---

*For a theoretical analysis of Parsonian functionalism and its social/political bias, see Alvin Gouldner, *The Coming Crisis of Western Sociology*, Basic Books, 1970.

necessary to sustain itself, and by which it ensures the maintenance of its basic structures. Feudalism, slavery, and capitalism are all social systems in this sense, and the main task of the sociologist is to understand the specific institutional bases of these systems, their modi operandi, and the principles of their development. In short, radical sociology begins with the specific, historically conditioned organization of the basic activities which sustain a social order, and it proceeds from there. It is easy to see that such a perspective is "radical" in the usual sense, in that it leads directly to the question of how a social order may be reconstructed in order to better serve the needs of its members, rather than how its members and institutions may be adjusted and accommodated to the need to maintain social stability and order.

The critical importance of this shift in perspective can be better appreciated, perhaps, by means of a concrete example. Robert A. Nisbet, a leading academic sociologist, is the author of a recent introductory textbook which announces its intention to provide a "conceptual" approach that avoids the empirical orientation, usual to such texts, in which "the reader is merely taken on a kind of tour of such institutions in society as family, school, community, church, industry, political government, and social class, among others." In short, Nisbet claims to avoid the conservative, micro-social bias which pervades the academic sociological field.

The title of Nisbet's text, *The Social Bond,* identifies the concept through which he proposes to approach the study of society: "Just as modern chemistry concerns itself with what it calls the chemical bond, seeking the forces that make atoms stick together as molecules, so does sociology investigate the forces that enable biologically derived human beings to stick together in the 'social molecules' in which we actually find them from the moment, quite literally, of their conception." Sociology is defined as the study of how human beings are stuck together in the social relationships *"in which we actually find them"*—the conservatism of the sociological project as viewed by the academic establishment could not be more explicit. Here methodology is clearly ideology.

Nisbet's methodological perspective is conservative in another, more characteristic, way—namely in its effort to generalize sociological theory and concepts. The abstraction inherent in the notion of "social bond," as a generalized concept applicable to all societies, groups, and even relationships, introduces a profoundly conservative bias into any analysis that employs it in as fundamental a way as Nisbet proposes. For if concepts are generalized so as to have no distinctive reference to specific social orders, then the inevitable result is to universalize social problems (the problem of authority, for example, exists in the family, in the classroom, in the doctor's office, in the factory, in capitalist society, and indeed in virtually any social system conceivable). Such abstraction has the effect of making any social problem a "human problem" (or a problem of human beings in any social group) rather than a problem stemming from a particular historical organization of the productive and distributive apparatus of society and from a particular allocation of social wealth and labor. In short, to base an analysis on the common factors and relationships that permeate any human society is to take the focus of analysis away from the specifics of the given social order, with its particular forms of privilege and oppression and its particular possibilities of development and reconstruction. In the end, such scientistic modes of abstraction lead to a rapid regression towards the abstract individual, that is, towards the conservative point of origin: "The fundamental and inescapable subject matter of sociology," writes Nisbet, "and of all the social sciences—is human beings and how and why they behave as they do." Thus, sociology (and economics and political science) is reduced ultimately to individual psychology.

The gulf between this behavioral perspective (which represents the dominant academic trend) and the perspective of a radical like Marx is so wide as to make the latter virtually incomprehensible to the former. What else is one to make of Nisbet's interpretation of Marx's doctrine of social class in the following terms: "The scientific utility of the Marxian doctrine of social class is cause for debate. This doctrine states very succinctly that men's productive (economic) relations determine the class structure of every social order and that all major social, cultural, and intellectual differences among groups in a population are the consequence of class differences. Putting the matter bluntly and in a degree of specific detail that is largely implicit in Marx himself but has been made *explicit* in countless writings by followers of Marx, we may say that social class determines the way men will live and think in society. In the long run social class will be the most powerful determinant of life style as well as of political allegiance, economic, religious, familial, and educational disposition, and of consciousness generally. It is in this sense that Marxists have used the word 'ideology'—to refer to the sum total of beliefs and attitudes about world and society which, it is held, derive ultimately from the social class people belong to."

The odd but significant feature of this quoted paragraph is that there is not one correct statement about Marx's class theory in it. Indeed, Nisbet's account of Marx's alleged theory of ideology doesn't even make sense. Marx did not say that everyone's beliefs and attitudes flow from his class position. Marx said that the ruling ideas of an epoch are the ideas of the ruling class. If other sectors of the population had ideas corresponding to their class positions and interests, then they would change the social order to their own benefit, which is precisely why the ruling or dominant social ideas have to conform to the ideas and needs of the ruling class. To put it bluntly: if society is ruled by a minority with special privileges, the ideas that the majority have about the social order must be distorted or biased towards the perspective of the ruling minority, or else the social order would be unstable. Marx's proposition is not only not the nonsense that Nisbet makes of it, but it is virtually self-evident.

Where Nisbet's formulation goes astray is in his insistence on treating Marx as though he were a behavioral scientist. Marx was not concerned with the determinants of individual behavior, but with the determinants of the social order and its development. He was concerned with the social roles which individuals are *compelled* to assume by the relations of production and distribution that have been established, as it were, behind their backs and mediated in capitalist societies through the market. The latter point was grasped by Max Weber: "The capitalist economy of the present day is an immense cosmos into which the individual is born, and which presents itself to him, at least as an individual, as an unalterable order of things in which he must live. It forces the individual insofar as he is involved in the system of market relationships, to conform to capitalistic rules of action." What Marx argues is that these *relationships* are determinant for the matrix of social possibilities. He does not argue as Nisbet suggests that there are no aspects of individual human behavior, that fall outside them. In short, as Weber correctly observes, "The manufacturer who in the long run acts counter to these norms will just as inevitably be eliminated from the economic scene as the worker who cannot or will not adapt himself to them will be thrown into the streets without a job."*

Weber's own class analysis, however, retreats to the orthodox vantage point. His class concept (class is defined by him as "the availability of typical life chances") bases the analytic perspective on the individual operating in the cosmos, whereas the Marxian perspective and analysis starts from the cosmos itself. This "cosmos," which is both social and economic, is determined in capitalist society by the institution of private property in the means of production. It does not matter whether an individual capital owner is a socialist or a Republican, a Catholic or an atheist. What matters is that the capital-owning class *by the very fact of its ownership,* determines the basic pattern of resource allocation and economic/social development and that its social existence, its existence *as a class* is dependent on the maintenance of these institutional relationships. Hence, it may well be that liberal ideas (for example, those associated with Progressivism or the New Deal, which once appeared to be inimical to the ruling class) become dominant politically: but the content of the ideas will have been changed in the process of their social acceptance to accommodate the continued dominance of the business order and the property principle. Only a revolution which transforms the pri-

*Max Weber, *The Protestant Ethic and the Spirit of Capitalism*, New York: Scribner's, 1948.

mary economic power relation can alter these secondary relations and phenomena. It is because this recognition is the central focus and orienting perception of any radical sociology that such a sociology threatens the sociological establishment, which is supported and rewarded by the powers of the status quo.

The fact of academic sociology's subservience to power, however, does not lead necessarily to the conclusion that academic sociologists have nothing to contribute, analytically, towards the understanding of the social process. If that were the case, their services would hardly be so much in demand by the prevailing powers, nor would their efforts be so liberally funded and rewarded. From the generalizing concern with social behavior and organization there flows a considerable amount of insight into the elements that social orders have in common and into the ways in which organizations and institutions operate and maintain themselves—in short, into the management and maintenance of social systems in general. Such insights and the techniques which are developed from them are naturally of interest to the managers and trustees of the social framework.

What is not to be found in orthodox social analysis, however, is any insight into the specific features of the prevailing capitalist social structure and the determining effect of these features on social priorities and on the configurations of power, politics, and social conflict that dominate contemporary historical development. For this kind of insight it is necessary to build the analysis on the historically conditioned class relations that arise from the effort to maintain and expand the material infrastructure of the social order. In short, it is necessary to adopt the theoretical vantage point first established by Marx.

Although Marx is certainly the father of the analytic viewpoint expressed in the selections of this volume—as he is of virtually all "radical" analyses of capitalism in the sense defined earlier—it would be incorrect to describe many of the authors as Marxists in the strict sense of the word. The term "Marxism" itself has only limited utility as the description of an analytic school by now, although its political vitality remains undiminished. For Marxism as the ideology of several successful revolutions in the twentieth century has itself become codified and canonized in ways inimical to its development as a social theory. As a result, the only really significant Marxist theory in the last fifty years has been the work of "heretics" while the number of orthodox Marxisms has multiplied severalfold. The term "radical sociology" may appear, at first, as a somewhat nondescriptive replacement to cover the perspective shared by these writers, but if it is taken in the sense of going to the root relationships of the historically conditioned—and therefore changeable—social order, it seems adequate enough.

The present volume does not pretend to set forth a comprehensive radical analysis of contemporary society, or even a comprehensive model on which a radical analysis could be built. What it does seek is to present the student with a selection of first-rate analyses that, taken together, will illustrate the basic principles for forming such models and perspectives.

This task, while modest enough, is performed by no existing textbook. The mere fact that this is the case illustrates the ideological nature of the so-called free academy in its present incarnation. That is why the most far-sighted elements in the current upsurge of student activism on the campus aim not merely to make token changes in university forms and procedures, but to radically restructure the academic enterprise itself, to make it democratic in composition, administration, and finance, and therefore truly radical in its social outlook and contribution. But that, of course, is only possible via a social revolution.

1/Economy
and Society

A moment's reflection will serve to establish that there is no such distinct intellectual perspective as "sociology," if what is meant by this term is a discipline which can be formally separated from economics, political science, and the other social sciences that have been accorded departmental and professional status in the present university system. For none of these areas is functionally independent of the others. Economic activity is social activity. Moreover, it is by far the most time-consuming and essential portion of human social activity. For these reasons, economic activity, as Marx argues in The German Ideology, is primary among all social activities. The needs which economic activity fills are basic needs, such as food and shelter; they are the premise of all other activities, social and otherwise.

To say that economic activity is the conditioning (or determining) basis of social activity in the sense that without sustenance and shelter no other activity is possible, is virtually a truism, though its self-evidence does not prevent academic social theorists from failing to recognize its significance in their work. Marx, of course, went beyond this simple proposition to an exploration of the framework imposed by the necessities of material production upon all other social productions (including social consciousness and culture). In producing for their material needs, human beings enter into definite social relations of ownership and cooperation, and these relations, Marx observed, are themselves conditioned by the forces and technology of production. "It follows... that a certain mode of production, or industrial stage, is always combined with a certain mode of co-operation, or social stage, and this mode of co-operation is itself a 'productive force.' Further, that the multitude of productive forces accessible to men determines the nature of society, hence that the 'history of humanity' must always be treated in relation to the history of industry and exchange." In short, Marx posited a necessary, determinate relationship between the stages of ownership (the so-called relations of production) and the stages of industrial or technological development (the means or forces of production). Since social relations tended to be relatively conservative in their development and since technology was relatively dynamic, there was an inherent tendency to conflict between them (or what Marx would have called an internal contradiction). At certain nodal points in human history, these conflicts or contradictions broke towards a dramatic resolution, a "higher stage" of social development in which the relations and means of production were once more brought into relative harmony. This was the germ of Marx's theory of social change.

Marx summarized his insights in a memorable passage in the preface to A Contribution to the Critique of Political Economy: "In the social production of their life, men enter into definite relations that are indispensable and independent of their will, relations of production which correspond to a definite stage of development of their material productive forces. The sum total of these relations of production constitutes the economic structure of society, the real foundation, on which rises a legal and political superstructure and to which correspond definite forms of social consciousness. The mode of production of material life conditions the social, political and intellectual life process in general. It is not the consciousness of men that determines their being, but, on the contrary, their social being that determines their consciousness. At a certain stage of their development, the material productive forces of society come in conflict with the existing relations of production, or—what is but a legal expression for the same thing—with the property relations within which they have been at work hitherto. From the forms of development of the productive forces, these relations turn into their fetters. Then begins an epoch of social revolution. With the change of the economic foundations the entire immense superstructure is more or less rapidly transformed."

Brilliant as this formulation is—there is surely nothing in all sociological literature as pregnant with insight or as ambitious in its theoretical program—the thesis has not stood the test of time, at least not as an attempt to tie the whole complex development of society and the state to a specific form of the development of the forces of production, thus opening the whole of human history to "scientific explanation" in the nineteenth-century sense. Industrial development under quasi-feudal superstructures in late nineteenth-century Germany and Japan, and under non-bourgeois, collectivist superstructures in post-1917 Russia and elsewhere, have pretty well demonstrated that the positing of a determinate relationship between industrial and social stages of development was too optimistic.

This is not to say, however, that the basic Marxian notion of a dependent relationship between the organization of the productive forces and the pattern of the social order is not still the foundation of any meaningful social analysis. It is only to say that we must accept a more modest program in establishing the relationships between the two than the nineteenth-century would have found satisfactory. It is necessary to shift the focus of analysis even more sharply towards the social organization and economic basis of power.

Thus, this more modest program entails a shift to a theoretical focus that is even more "Marxist" in the traditional sense. For if the technical organization of production (division of labor, instruments of production) does not always coincide with a definite social organization of production and, in particular, with a system of property ownership, then the latter becomes the central nexus—at once social and economic—on which an analysis of society and its development must be based.

* * *

"The material framework of modern civilization is the industrial system, and the directing force which animates this framework is business enterprise." This may sound like Marx, but it is the opening sentence of Thorstein Veblen's The Theory of Business Enterprise, published in 1904. Veblen developed his analysis of society around the central conflict between the "industrial system" and the "business system," the former being based on science and the latter on what Veblen called the "pecuniary principle," or the quest for monetary gain. It will immediately be seen that Veblen's "industrial system" corresponds roughly to Marx's forces of production, while the business system is an analogue for Marx's relations of production. The different categories do, of course, entail a difference in perspective, a shift of focus from the relations between basic social classes to the system of incentives and goals which directs social energies. Both theories, however, recognize the pivotal significance of the "private" or "business" organization of the economy in a market system. For it is the corporate ownership/organization of the means of production that determines the allocation of social resources and the uses to which industrial technology is put. The dominance of pecuniary or market values over use values and social values is the fundamental characteristic of capitalist economies and accounts for their increasing irrationality and chronic social crisis: the coexistence of poverty and affluence, and the perverse channeling of the national wealth into environmentally and socially destructive activities.

In his brief but lucid essay on the state, Paul Sweezy covers the key points of the Marxian analytic approach to this basic social institution and illuminates the differences between this approach and the approach of orthodox social science. The abstractions of Sweezy's summary are given substance in Richard Hofstader's account of the ideology of the founding fathers and the American constitution. Hofstader, a non-Marxist historian, provides a portrait of the social origins, attitudes, and achievements of the founding fathers which validates the Marxist and Veblenian approaches and shows how important the historical dimension is to the construction of any adequate sociological theory.

C. Wright Mills *was a latter-day sociological maverick, whose writings constitute one of the few oases of realism amid the arid sands of postwar academic sociology. In* The Power Elite, *which appeared in 1956 and which cost Mills his academic respectability, he returned the question of power to its central place as a sociological concern: "The power elite is composed of men whose positions enable them to transcend the ordinary environments of ordinary men and women; they are in positions to make decisions having major consequences. Whether they do or do not make such decisions is less important than the fact that they do occupy such pivotal positions: their failure to act, their failure to make decisions, is itself an act that is often of greater consequence than the decisions they do make. For they are in command of the major hierarchies and organizations of modern society. They rule the big corporations. They run the machinery of the state and claim its prerogatives. They direct the military establishment. They occupy the strategic command posts of the social structure, in which are now centered the effective means of the power and the wealth and the celebrity which they enjoy."*

Mills's model of a tri-partite power structure, corporate-political-military, is ultimately unconvincing. He himself shows the political directorate to be dependent on, or an extension of, the corporate rich. On the other hand, the case for a "military ascendancy," while fashionable with many liberals, has never mustered significant evidence to support it. But if Mills's analysis of the relationship between elites in the power structure seems inadequate, his description of the corporate rich exhibits no such deficiency. A striking portrait of money power, it shows that nearly two hundred years after the Declaration of Independence, and the Constitutional conventions, the stratification of American society, though modified, remains intact, and that government of, by, and for the people is as distant a prospect as ever.

ECONOMY AND SOCIETY

KARL MARX and FREDERICK ENGELS

The premises from which we begin are not arbitrary ones, not dogmas, but real premises from which abstraction can only be made in the imagination. They are the real individuals, their activity and the material conditions under which they live, both those which they find already existing and those produced by their activity. These premises can thus be verified in a purely empirical way.

The first premise of all human history is, of course, the existence of living human individuals. Thus the first fact to be established is the physical organization of these individuals and their consequent relation to the rest of nature. Of course, we cannot here go either into the actual physical nature of man, or into the natural conditions in which man finds himself— geological, orohydrographical, climatic and so on. The writing of history must always set out from these natural bases and their modifiction in the course of history through the action of man.

Men can be distinguished from animals by consciousness, by religion or anything else you like. They themselves begin to distinguish themselves from animals as soon as they begin to *produce* their means of subsistence, a step which is conditioned by their physical organization. By producing their means of subsistence men are indirectly producing their actual material life.

The way in which men produce their means of subsistence depends first of all on the nature of the actual means they find in existence and have to reproduce. This mode of production

From *The German Ideology* by Karl Marx and Frederick Engels. Reprinted by permission of International Publishers Company.

must not be considered simply as being the reproduction of the physical existence of the individuals. Rather it is a definite form of activity of these individuals, a definite form of expressing their life, a definite *mode of life* on their part. As individuals express their life, so they are. What they are, therefore, coincides with their production, both with *what* they produce and with *how* they produce. The nature of individuals thus depends on the material conditions determining their production.

This production only makes its appearance with the increase of population. In its turn this presupposes the intercourse of individuals with one another. The form of this intercourse is again determined by production.

The relations of different nations among themselves depend upon the extent to which each has developed its productive forces, the division of labour and internal intercourse. This statement is generally recognized. But not only the relation of one nation to others, but also the whole internal structure of the nation itself depends on the stage of development reached by its production and its internal and external intercourse. How far the productive forces of a nation are developed is shown most manifestly by the degree to which the division of labour has been carried. Each new productive force, in so far as it is not merely a quantitative extension of productive forces already known, (for instance the bringing into cultivation of fresh land), brings about a further development of the division of labour.

The division of labour inside a nation leads at first to the separation of industrial and commercial from agricultural labour, and hence to the separation of town and country and a clash of interests between them. Its further development leads to the separation of commercial from industrial labour. At the same time through the division of labour there develop further, inside these various branches, various divisions among the individuals co-operating in definite kinds of labour. The relative position of these individual groups is determined by the methods employed in agriculture, industry and commerce (patriarchalism, slavery, estates, classes). These same conditions are to be seen (given a more developed intercourse) in the relations of different nations to one another.

The various stages of development in the division of labour

are just so many different forms of ownership; i.e. the existing stage in the division of labour determines also the relations of individuals to one another with reference to the material, instrument, and product of labour.

The first form of ownership is tribal ownership. It corresponds to the undeveloped stage of production, at which a people lives by hunting and fishing, by the rearing of beasts or, in the highest stage, agriculture. In the latter case it presupposes a great mass of uncultivated stretches of land. The division of labour is at this stage still very elementary and is confined to a further extension of the natural division of labour imposed by the family. The social structure is therefore limited to an extension of the family; patriarchal family chieftains; below them the members of the tribe; finally slaves. The slavery latent in the family only develops gradually with the increase of population, the growth of wants, and with the extension of external relations, of war or of trade.

The second form is the ancient communal and State ownership which proceeds especially from the union of several tribes into a city by agreement or by conquest, and which is still accompanied by slavery. Beside communal ownership we already find movable, and later also immovable, private property developing, but as an abnormal form subordinate to communal ownership. It is only as a community that the citizens hold power over their labouring slaves, and on this account alone, therefore, they are bound to the form of communal ownership. It is the communal private property which compels the active citizens to remain in this natural form of association over against their slaves. For this reason the whole structure of society based on this communal ownership, and with it the power of the people, decays in the same measure as immovable private property evolves. The division of labour is already more developed. We already find the antagonism of town and country; later the antagonism between those states which represent town interests and those which represent country, and inside the towns themselves the antagonism between industry and maritime commerce. The class relation between citizens and slaves is now completely developed.

This whole interpretation of history appears to be contradicted by the fact of conquest. Up till now violence, war, pillage, rape and slaughter, etc. have been accepted as the driving force of history. Here we must limit ourselves to the chief points and take therefore only a striking example—the destruction of an old civilization by a barbarous people and the resulting formation of an entirely new organization of society. (Rome and the barbarians; Feudalism and Gaul; the Byzantine Empire and the Turks). With the conquering barbarian people war itself is still, as hinted above, a regular form of intercourse, which is the more eagerly exploited as the population increases, involving the necessity of new means of production to supersede the traditional and, for it, the only possible, crude mode of production. In Italy it was, however, otherwise. The concentration of landed property (caused not only by buying-up and indebtedness but also by inheritance, since loose living being rife and marriage rare, the old families died out and their possessions fell into the hands of a few) and its conversion into grazing-land (caused not only by economic forces still operative today but by the importation of plundered and tribute-corn and the resultant lack of demand for Italian corn) brought about the almost total disappearance of the free population. The very slaves died out again and again, and had constantly to be replaced by new ones. Slavery remained the basis of the whole productive system. The plebeians, mid-way between freemen and slaves, never succeeded in becoming more than a proletarian rabble. Rome indeed never became more than a city; its connection with the provinces was almost exclusively political and could therefore easily be broken again by political events.

With the development of private property, we find here for the first time the same conditions which we shall find again, only on a more extensive scale, with modern private property. On the one hand the concentration of private property, which began very early in Rome (as the Licinian agrarian law proves), and proceeded very rapidly from the time of the civil wars and especially under the Emperors; on the other hand, coupled with this, the transformation of the plebeian small peasantry into a proletariat, which, however, owing to its intermediate position between propertied citizens and slaves, never achieved an independent development.

The third form of ownership is feudal or estate-property. If antiquity started out from the town and its little territory, the Middle Ages started out from the country. This different starting-point was determined by the sparseness of the population at that time, which was scattered over a large area and which received no large increase from the conquerors. In contrast to Greece and Rome, feudal development therefore extends over a much wider field, prepared by the Roman conquests and the spread of agriculture at first associated with it. The last centuries of the declining Roman Empire and its conquest by the barbarians destroyed a number of productive forces; agriculture had declined, industry had decayed for want of a market, trade had died out or been violently suspended, the rural and urban population had decreased. From these conditions and the mode of organization of the conquest determined by them, feudal property developed under the influence of the Germanic military constitution. Like tribal and communal ownership, it is based again on a community; but the directly producing class standing over against it is not, as in the case of the ancient community, the slaves, but the enserfed small peasantry. As soon as feudalism is fully developed, there also arises antagonism to the towns. The hierarchical system of land ownership, and the armed bodies of retainers associated with it, gave the nobility power over the serfs. This feudal organization was, just as much as the ancient communal ownership, an association against a subjected producing class; but the form of association and the relation to the direct producers were different because of the different conditions of production.

This feudal organization of land-ownership had its counterpart in the towns in the shape of corporative property, the feudal organization of trades. Here property consisted chiefly in the labour of each individual person. The necessity for association against the organized robber-nobility, the need for communal covered markets in an age when the industrialist was at the same time a merchant, the growing competition of the escaped serfs swarming into the rising towns, the feudal structure of the whole country: these combined to bring about the guilds. Further, the gradually accumulated capital of individual craftsmen and their stable numbers, as against the growing population, evolved the relation of journeyman and apprentice, which brought into being in the towns a hierarchy similar to that in the country.

Thus the chief form of property during the feudal epoch consisted on the one hand of landed property with serf-labour chained to it, and on the other of individual labour with small capital commanding the labour of journeymen. The organization of both was determined by the restricted conditions of production—the small-scale and primitive cultivation of the land, and the craft type of industry. There was little division of labour in the heyday of feudalism. Each land bore in itself the conflict of town and country and the division into estates was certainly strongly marked; but apart from the differentiation of princes, nobility, clergy and peasants in the country, and masters, journeymen, apprentices and soon also the rabble of casual labourers in the towns, no division of importance took place. In agriculture it was rendered difficult by the strip-system, beside which the cottage industry of the peasants themselves emerged as another factor. In industry there was no division of labour at all in the individual trades themselves, and very little between them. The separation of industry and commerce was found already in existence in older towns; in the newer it only developed later, when the towns entered into mutual relations.

The grouping of larger territories into feudal kingdoms was a necessity for the landed nobility as for the towns. The organization of the ruling class, the nobility, had, therefore, everywhere a monarch at its head.

The fact is, therefore, that definite individuals who are productively active in a definite way enter into these definite social and political relations. Empirical observation must in each separate instance bring out empirically, and without any mystification and speculation, the connection of the social and political structure with production. The social structure and the State are continually evolving out of the life-process of definite individuals, but of individuals, not as they may appear in their own or other people's imagination, but as they really are; i.e. as they are effective, produce materially, and are active under definite material limits, presuppositions and conditions independent of their will.

The production of ideas, of conceptions, of consciousness, is at first directly interwoven with the material activity and the material intercourse of men, the language of real life. Conceiving, thinking, the mental intercourse of men, appear at this stage as the direct efflux of their material behaviour. The same applies to mental production as expressed in the language of the politics, laws, morality, religion, metaphysics of a people. Men are the producers of their conceptions, ideas, etc.—real, active men, as they are conditioned by a definite development of their productive forces and of the intercourse corresponding to these, up to its furthest forms. Consciousness can never be anything else than conscious existence, and the existence of men is their actual life-process. If in all ideology men and their circumstances appear upside down as in a *camera obscura*, this phenomenon arises just as much from their historical life-process as the inversion of objects on the retina does from their physical life-process.

In direct contrast to German philosophy which descends from heaven to earth, here we ascend from earth to heaven. That is to say, we do not set out from what men say, imagine, conceive, nor from men as narrated, thought of, imagined, conceived, in order to arrive at men in the flesh. We set out from real, active men, and on the basis of their real life-process we demonstrate the development of the ideological reflexes and echoes of this life-process. The phantoms formed in the human brain are also, necessarily, sublimates of their material life-process, which is empirically verifiable and bound to material premises. Morality, religion, metaphysics, all the rest of ideology and their corresponding forms of consciousness, thus no longer retain the semblance of independence. They have no history, no development; but men, developing their material production and their material intercourse, alter, along with this their real existence, their thinking and the products of their thinking. Life is not determined by consciousness, but consciousness by life. In the first methods of approach the starting-point is consciousness taken as the living individual; in the second it is the real living individuals themselves, as they are in actual life, and consciousness is considered solely as *their* consciousness.

This method of approach is not devoid of premises. It starts out from the real premises and does not abandon them for a moment. Its premises are men, not in any fantastic isolation or abstract definition, but in their actual, empirically perceptible process of development under definite conditions. As soon as this active life-process is described, history ceases to be a collection of dead facts as it is with the empiricists (themselves still abstract), or an imagined activity of imagined subjects, as with the idealists.

Where speculation ends—in real life—there real, positive science begins: the representation of the practical activity, of the practical process of development of men. Empty talk about consciousness ceases, and real knowledge has to take its place. When reality is depicted, philosophy as an independent branch of activity loses its medium of existence. At the best its place can only be taken by a summing-up of the most general results, abstractions which arise from the observation of the historical development of men. Viewed apart from real history, these abstractions have in themselves no value whatsoever. They can only serve to facilitate the arrangement of historical material, to indicate the sequence of its separate strata. But they by no means afford a recipe or schema, as does philosophy, for neatly trimming the epochs of history. On the contrary, our difficulties begin only when we set about the observation and the arrangement—the real depiction—of our historical material, whether of a past epoch or of the present. The removal of these difficulties is governed by premises which it is quite impossible to state here, but which only the study of the actual life-process and the activity of the individuals of each epoch will make evident. We shall select here some of these abstractions, which we use to refute the ideologists, and shall illustrate them by historical examples.

Since we are dealing with the Germans, who do not postulate anything, we must begin by stating the first premise of all human existence, and therefore of all history, the premise namely that men must be in a position to live in order to be able to "make history." But life involves before everything else eating and drinking, a habitation, clothing and many other things. The first historical act is thus the production of the means to satisfy these needs, the production of material life itself. And indeed this is an historical act, a fundamental condition of all history, which today, as thousands of years ago, must daily and hourly be fulfilled merely in order to sustain human life. Even when the sensuous world is reduced to a minimum, to a stick as with Saint Bruno, it presupposes the action of producing the stick. The first necessity therefore in any theory of history is to observe this fundamental fact in all its significance and all its implications and to accord it its due importance.

The second fundamental point is that as soon as a need is satisfied, (which implies the action of satisfying, and the acquisition of an instrument), new needs are made; and this production of new needs is the first historical act. Here we recognize immediately the spiritual ancestry of the great historical wisdom of the Germans who, when they run out of positive material and when they can serve up neither theological nor political nor literary rubbish, do not write history at all, but invent the "prehistoric era." They do not, however, enlighten us as to how we proceed from this nonsensical "prehistory" to history proper; although, on the other hand, in their historical speculation they seize upon this "prehistory" with especial eagerness because they imagine themselves safe there from interference on the part of "crude facts," and, at the same time, because there they can give full rein to their speculative impulse and set up and knock down hypotheses by the thousand.

The third circumstances which, from the very first, enters into historical development, is that men, who daily remake their own life, begin to make other men, to propagate their kind: the relation between man and wife, parents and children, the FAMILY. The family which to begin with is the only social relationship, becomes later, when increased needs create new social relations and the increased population new needs, a subordinate one (except in Germany), and must then be treated and analysed according to the existing empirical data,* not according to "the concept of the family," as is the custom in Germany. These three aspects of social activity are not of course to be taken as three different stages, but just, as I have said, as three aspects or, to make it clear to the Germans, three "moments," which have existed simultaneously since the dawn of history and the first men, and still assert themselves in history today.

The production of life, both of one's own in labour and of fresh life in procreation, now appears as a double relationship: on the one hand as a natural, on the other as a social relationship. By social we understand the co-operation of several individuals, no matter under what conditions, in what manner and to what end. It follows from this that a certain mode of production, or industrial stage, is always combined with a certain mode of co-operation, or social stage, and this mode of co-operation is itself a "productive force." Further, that the multitude of productive forces accessible to men determines the nature of society, hence that the "history of humanity" must always be studied and treated in relation to the history of industry and exchange. But it is also clear how in Germany it is impossible to write this sort of history, because the Germans

*The building of houses. With savages each family has of course its own cave or hut like the separate family tent of the nomads. This separate domestic economy is made only the more necessary by the further development of private property. With the agricultural peoples a communal domestic economy is just as impossible as a communal cultivation of the soil. A great advance was the building of towns. In all previous periods, however, the abolition of individual economy, which is inseparable from the abolition of private property, was impossible for the simple reason that the material conditions governing it were not present. The setting-up of a communal domestic economy presupposes the development of machinery, of the use of natural resources and of many other productive forces—e.g. of water-supplies, of gas-lighting, steam-heating, etc., the removal of the antagonism of town and country. Without these conditions a communal economy would not in itself form a new productive force; lacking any material basis and resting on a purely theoretical foundation, it would be a mere freak and would end in nothing more than a monastic economy.—What was possible can be seen in the formation of towns and the erection of communal buildings for various definite purposes (prisons, barracks, etc.). That the abolition of individual economy is inseparable from the abolition of the family is self-evident.

lack not only the necessary power of comprehension and the material but also the "evidence of their senses," for across the Rhine you cannot have any experience of these things since history has stopped happening. Thus it is quite obvious from the start that there exists a materialistic connection of men with one another, which is determined by their needs and their mode of production, and which is as old as men themselves. This connection is ever taking on new forms, and thus presents a "history" independently of the existence of any political or religious nonsense which would hold men together on its own.

Only now, after having considered four moments, four aspects of the fundamental historical relationships, do we find that man also possesses "consciousness"; but, even so, not inherent, not "pure" consciousness. From the start the "spirit" is afflicted with the curse of being "burdened" with matter, which here makes its appearance in the form of agitated layers of air, sounds, in short of language. Language is as old as consciousness, language is practical consciousness, as it exists for other men, and for that reason is really beginning to exist for me personally as well; for language, like consciousness, only arises from the need, the necessity, of intercourse with other men. Where there exists a relationship, it exists for me: the animal has no "relations" with anything, cannot have any. For the animal, its relation to others does not exist as a relation. Consciousness is therefore from the very beginning a social product, and remains so as long as men exist at all. Consciousness is at first, of course, merely consciousness concerning the immediate sensuous environment and consciousness of the limited connection with other persons and things outside the individual who is growing self-conscious. At the same time it is consciousness of nature, which first appears to men as a completely alien, all-powerful and unassailable force, with which men's relations are purely animal and by which they are overawed like beasts; it is thus a purely animal consciousness of nature (natural religion).

We see here immediately: this natural religion or animal behaviour towards nature is determined by the form of society and *vice versa*. Here, as everywhere, the identity of nature and man appears in such a way that the restricted relation of men to nature determines their restricted relation to one another, and their restricted relation to one another determines men's restricted relation to nature, just because nature is as yet hardly modified historically; and, on the other hand, man's consciousness of the necessity of associating with the individuals around him is the beginning of the consciousness that he is living in society at all. This beginning is as animal as social life itself at this stage. It is mere herd-consciousness, and at this point man is only distinguished from sheep by the fact that with him consciousness takes the place of instinct or that his instinct is a conscious one.

This sheep-like or tribal consciousness receives its further development and extension through increased productivity, the increase of needs, and, what is fundamental to both of these, the increase of population. With these there develops the division of labour, which was originally nothing but the division of labour in the sexual act, then that division of labour which develops spontaneously or "naturally" by virtue of natural predisposition (e.g. physical strength), needs, accidents, etc., etc. Division of labour only becomes truly such from the moment when a division of material and mental labour appears. From this moment onwards consciousness *can* really flatter itself that it is something other than consciousness of existing practice, that it is *really* conceiving something without conceiving something *real;* from now on consciousness is in a position to emancipate itself from the world and to proceed to the formation of "pure" theory, theology, philosophy, ethics, etc. But even if this theory, theology, philosophy, ethics, etc. comes into contradiction with the existing relations, this can only occur as a result of the fact that existing social relations have come into contradiction with existing forces of production; this, moreover, can also occur in a particular national sphere of relations through the appearance of the contradiction, not within the national orbit, but between this national consciousness and the practice of other nations, i.e. between the national and the general consciousness of a nation.

Moreover, it is quite immaterial what consciousness starts to do on its own: out of all such muck we get only the one inference that these three moments, the forces of production, the state of society, and consciousness, can and must come into contradiction with one another, because the division of labour implies the possibility, nay the fact that intellectual and material activity—enjoyment and labour, production and consumption—devolve on different individuals, and that the only possibility of their not coming into contradiction lies in the negation in its turn of the division of labour. It is self-evident, moreover, that "spectres," "bonds," "the higher being," "concept," "scruple," are merely the idealistic, spiritual expression, the conception apparently of the isolated individual, the image of very empirical fetters and limitations, within which the mode of production of life, and the form of intercourse coupled with it, move.

With the division of labour, in which all these contradictions are implicit, and which in its turn is based on the natural division of labour in the family and the separation of society into individual families opposed to one another, is given simultaneously the distribution, and indeed the unequal distribution, (both quantitative and qualitative), of labour and its products, hence property: the nucleus, the first form, of which lies in the family, where wife and children are the slaves of the husband. This latent slavery in the family, though still very crude, is the first property, but even at this early stage it corresponds perfectly to the definition of modern economists who call it the power of disposing of the labour-power of others. Division of labour and private property are, moreover, identical expressions: in the one the same thing is affirmed with reference to activity as is affirmed in the other with reference to the product of the activity.

Further, the division of labour implies the contradiction between the interest of the separate individual or the individual family and the communal interest of all individuals who have intercourse with one another. And indeed, this communal interest does not exist merely in the imagination, as "the general good," but first of all in reality, as the mutual interdependence of the individuals among whom the labour is divided. And finally, the division of labour offers us the first example of how, as long as man remains in natural society, that is as long as a cleavage exists between the particular and the common interest, as long therefore as activity is not voluntarily, but naturally, divided, man's own deed becomes an alien power opposed to him, which enslaves him instead of being controlled by him. For as soon as labour is distributed, each man has a particular, exclusive sphere of activity, which is forced upon him and from which he cannot escape. He is a hunter, a fisherman, a shepherd, or a critical critic, and must remain so if he does not want to lose his means of livelihood; while in communist society, where nobody has one exclusive sphere of activity but each can become accomplished in any branch he wishes, society regulates the general production and thus makes it possible for me to do one thing today and another tomorrow, to hunt in the morning, fish in the afternoon, rear cattle in the evening, criticize after dinner, just as I have a mind, without ever becoming hunter, fisherman, shepherd or critic.

This crystallization of social activity, this consolidation of what we ourselves produce into an objective power above us, growing out of our control, thwarting our expectations, bringing to naught our calculations, is one of the chief factors in historical development up till now. And out of this very contradiction between the interest of the individual and that of the community the latter takes an independent form as the STATE, divorced from the real interests of individual and community, and at the same time as an illusory communal life, always based, however, on the real ties existing in every family and tribal conglomeration (such as flesh and blood, language, division of labour on a larger scale, and other interests) and especially, as we shall enlarge upon later, on the classes, already determined by the division of labour, which in every such mass of men separate out, and of which one dominates all the others. It follows from this that all struggles within the State, the struggle between democracy, aristocracy and monarchy, the struggle for the franchise, etc., etc., are merely the illusory forms in which the real struggles of the different classes are fought out among one another (of this the German theoreticians have not the faintest inkling, although they have received a sufficient introduction to the subject in *The German-French Annals* and *The Holy Family*).

Further, it follows that every class which is struggling for mastery, even when its domination, as is the case with the proletariat, postulates the abolition of the old form of society in its entirety and of mastery itself, must first conquer for itself political power in order to represent its interest in turn as the general interest, a step to which in the first moment it is forced. Just because individuals seek *only* their particular interest, i.e. that not coinciding with their communal interest (for the "general good" is the illusory form of communal life), the latter will be imposed on them as an interest "alien" to them, and "independent" of them, as in its turn a particular, peculiar "general interest"; or they must meet face to face in this antagonism, as in democracy. On the other hand too, the *practical* struggle of these particular interests, which constantly *really* run counter to the communal and illusory communal interests, make *practical* intervention and control necessary through the illusory "general-interest" in the form of the State. The social power, i.e. the multiplied productive force, which arises through the co-operation of different individuals as it is determined within the division of labour, appears to these individuals, since their co-operation is not voluntary but natural, not as their own united power but as an alien force existing outside them, of the origin and end of which they are ignorant, which they thus cannot control, which on the contrary passes through a peculiar series of phases and stages independent of the will and the action of man, nay even being the prime governor of these.

The "estrangement" (to use a term which will be comprehensible to the philosophers) can, of course, only be abolished given two *practical* premises. For it to become an "intolerable" power, i.e. a power against which men make a revolution, it must necessarily have rendered the great mass of humanity "propertyless," and produced, at the same time, the contradiction of an existing world of wealth and culture, both of which conditions presuppose a great increase in productive power, a high degree of its development. And, on the other hand, this development of productive forces (which itself implies the actual empirical existence of men in their *world-historical,* instead of local, being) is absolutely necessary as a practical premise: firstly, for the reason that without it only *want* is made general, and with want the struggle for necessities and all the old filthy business would necessarily be reproduced; and secondly, because only with this universal development of productive forces is a *universal* intercourse between men established, which produces in all nations simultaneously the phenomenon of the "propertyless" mass (universal competition), makes each nation dependent on the revolutions of the others, and finally has put *world-historical,* empirically universal individuals in place of local ones. Without this, (1) Communism could only exist as a local event; (2) the forces of intercourse themselves could not have developed as universal, hence intolerable powers: they would have remained homebred superstitious conditions; and (3) Each extension of intercourse would abolish local communism. Empirically, communism is only possible as the act of the dominant peoples "all at once" or simultaneously, which presupposes the universal development of productive forces and the world-intercourse bound up with them. How otherwise could property have had a history at all, have taken on different forms, and landed property, for instance, according to the different premises given, have proceeded in France from parcellation to centralization in the hands of a few, in England from centralization in the hands of a few to parcellation, as is actually the case today? Or how does it happen that trade, which after all is nothing more than the exchange of products of various individuals and countries, rules the whole world through the relation of supply and demand—a relation which, as an English economist says, hovers over the earth like the Fate of the Ancients, and with invisible hand allots fortune and misfortune to men, sets up empires and overthrows empires, causes nations to rise and to disappear—while with the abolition of the basis of private property, with the communistic regulation of production (and, implicit in this, the destruction of the alien relation between men and what they themselves produce), the power of the relation of supply and demand is dissolved into nothing, and men get exchange, production, the mode of their mutual relation, under their own control again?

Communism is for us not a stable state which is to be established, an *ideal* to which reality will have to adjust itself. We call communism the *real* movement which abolishes the present state of things. The conditions of this movement result from the premises now in existence. Besides, the world-market is presupposed by the mass of propertyless workers—labour-power cut off as a mass from capital or from even a limited satisfaction—and therefore no longer by the mere precariousness of labour, which, not giving an assured livelihood, is often lost through competition. The proletariat can thus only exist *world-historically,* just as communism, its movement, can only have a "world-historical" existence. World-historical existence of individuals, i.e. existence of individuals which is directly linked up with world history.

The form of intercourse determined by the existing productive forces at all previous historical stages, and in its turn determining these, is *civil* society. This, as is clear from what we have said above, has as its premises and basis the simple family and the multiple, the so-called tribe, the more precise determinants of which are enumerated in our remarks above. Already here we see how this civil society is the true source and theatre of all history, and how nonsensical is the conception of history held hitherto, which neglects the real relationships and confines itself to high-sounding dramas of princes and states. Civil society embraces the whole material intercourse of individuals within a definite stage of the development of productive forces. It embraces the whole commercial and industrial life of this stage and, in so far, transcends the State and the nation, though, on the other hand again, it must assert itself towards foreign peoples as nationality, and inwardly must organize itself as State. The word "civil society" emerged in the eighteenth century, when property relationships had already extricated themselves from the ancient and medieval communal society. Civil society as such only develops with the bourgeoisie; the social organization evolving directly out of production and commerce, which in all ages forms the basis of the State and of the rest of the idealistic superstructure, has, however, always been designated by the same name.

In history up to the present it is certainly an empirical fact that separate individuals have, with the broadening of their activity into world-historical activity, become more and more enslaved under a power alien to them (a pressure which they have conceived of as a dirty trick on the part of the so-called universal spirit), a power which has become more and more enormous and, in the last instance, turns out to be the *world-market*. But it is just as empirically established that, by the overthrow of the existing state of society by the communist revolution (of which more below) and the abolition of private property which is identical with it, this power, which so baffles the German theoreticians, will be dissolved; and that then the liberation of each single individual will be accomplished in the measure in which history becomes transformed into world-history. From the above it is clear that the real intellectual wealth of the individual depends entirely on the wealth of his real connections. Only then will the separate individuals be liberated from the various national and local barriers, be brought into practical connection with the material and intellectual production of the whole world and be put in a position to acquire the capacity to enjoy this all-sided production of the whole earth (the creations of man). Universal dependence, this natural form of the world-historical co-operation of individuals, will be transformed by this communist revolution into the control and conscious mastery of these powers, which, born of the action of men on one another, have till now overawed and governed men as powers completely alien to them. Now this view can be expressed again in speculative-idealistic, i.e. fantastic, terms as "spontaneous generation of the species," ("society as the subject"), and thereby the series of inter-related individuals can be conceived as a single individual, which accomplishes the mystery of generating itself. It is clear here that individuals certainly make one another, physically and mentally, but do not make themselves either in the non-sense of Saint Bruno, nor in the sense of the "unique," of the "made" man.

Our conception of history depends on our ability to expound the real process of production, starting out from the simple material production of life, and to comprehend the form of intercourse connected with this and created by this (i.e. civil society in its various stages), as the basis of all history; further, to show it in its action as State; and so, from this starting-point, to explain the whole mass of different theoretical products and forms of consciousness, religion, philosophy, ethics etc., etc., and trace their origins and growth, by which means, of course, the whole thing can be shown in its totality (and therefore, too, the reciprocal action of these various sides on one another). It has not, like the idealistic view of history, in every period to look for a category, but remains constantly on the real ground of history; it does not explain practice from the idea but explains the formation of ideas from material practice; and accordingly it comes to the conclusion that all forms and products of consciousness cannot be dissolved by mental criticism, by resolution into "self-consciousness" or transformation into "apparitions," "spectres," "fancies," etc., but only the practical overthrow of the actual social relations which gave rise to this idealistic humbug; that not criticism but revolution is the driving force of history, also of religion, of philosophy and all other types of theory. It shows that history does not end by being resolved into "self-consciousness" as "spirit of the spirit," but that in it at each stage there is found a material result: a sum of productive forces, a historically created relation of individuals to nature and to one another, which is handed down to each generation from its predecessor; a mass of productive forces, different forms of capital, and conditions, which, indeed, is modified by the new generation on the one hand, but also on the other prescribes for it its conditions of life and gives it a definite development, a special character. It shows that circumstances make men just as much as men make circumstances.

This sum of productive forces, forms of capital and social forms of intercourse, which every individual and generation finds in existence as something given, is the real basis of what the philosophers have conceived as "substance" and "essence of man," and what they have deified and attacked: a real basis which is not in the least disturbed, in its effect and influence on the development of men, by the fact that these philosophers revolt against it as "self-consciousness" and "the unique."

These conditions of life, which different generations find in existence, decide also whether or not the periodically recurring revolutionary convulsion will be strong enough to overthrow the basis of all existing forms. And if these material elements of a complete revolution are not present (namely, on the one hand the existence of productive forces, on the other the formation of a revolutionary mass, which revolts not only against separate conditions of society up till then, but against the very "production of life" till then, the "total activity" on which it was based), then, as far as practical development is concerned, it is absolutely immaterial whether the "idea" of this revolution has been expressed a hundred times already; as the history of communism proves.

In the whole conception of history up to the present this real basis of history has either been totally neglected or else considered as a minor matter quite irrelevant to the course of history. History must therefore always be written according to an extraneous standard; the real production of life seems to be beyond history, while the truly historical appears to be separated from ordinary life, something extra-superterrestrial. With this the relation of man to nature is excluded from history and hence the antithesis of nature and history is created. The exponents of this conception of history have consequently only been able to see in history the political actions of princes and States, religious and all sorts of theoretical struggles, and in particular in each historical epoch have had to share the *illusion of that epoch*. For instance, if an epoch imagines itself to be actuated by purely "political" or "religious" motives, although "religion" and "politics" are only forms of its true motives, the historian accepts this opinion. The "idea," the "conception" of these conditioned men about their real practice, is transformed into the sole determining, active force, which controls and determines their practice. When the crude form in which the division of labour appears with the Indians and Egyptians calls forth the caste-system in their State and religion, the historian believes that the caste-system is the power which has produced this crude social form. While the French and the English at least hold by the political illusion, which is moderately close to reality, the Germans move in the realm of the "pure spirit," and make religious illusion the driving force of history.

The Hegelian philosophy of history is the last consequence, reduced to its "finest expression," of all this German historiography, for which it is not a question of real, nor even of political, interests, but of pure thoughts, which inevitably appear, even to Saint Bruno, as a series of "thoughts" that devour one another and are finally swallowed up in "self-consciousness" and equally inevitably, and more logically, the course of history appears to the Blessed Max Stirner, who knows not a thing about real history, as a mere tale of "knights," robbers and ghosts, from whose visions he can, of course, only save himself by "unholiness." This conception is truly religious: it postulates religious man as the primitive man, and in its imagination puts the religious production of fancies in the place of the real production of the means of subsistence and of life itself. This whole conception of history, together with its dissolution and the scruples and qualms resulting from it, is a purely *national* affair of the Germans and has only *local* interest for the Germans, as for instance the important question treated several times of late: how really we "pass from the realm of God to the realm of man"—as if this "realm of God" had ever existed anywhere save in the imagination, and the learned gentlemen, without being aware of it, were not constantly living in the "realm of man" to which they are now seeking the way; and as if the learned pastime (for it is nothing more) of explaining the mystery of this theoretical bubble-blowing did not on the contrary lie in demonstrating its origin in actual earthly conditions.

* * *

The ideas of the ruling class are in every epoch the ruling ideas: i.e. the class, which is the ruling material force of society, is at the same time its ruling intellectual force. The class which has the means of material production at its disposal, has control at the same time over the means of mental production, so that thereby, generally speaking, the ideas of those who lack the means of mental production are subject to it. The ruling ideas are nothing more than the ideal expression of the dominant material relationships, the dominant material relationships grasped as ideas; hence of the relationships which make the one class the ruling one, therefore the ideas of its dominance. The individuals composing the ruling class possess among other things consciousness, and therefore think. In so far, therefore, as they rule as a class and determine the extent and compass of an epoch, it is self-evident that they do this in their whole range, hence among other things rule also as thinkers, as producers of ideas, and regulate the production and distribution of the ideas of their age: thus their ideas are the ruling ideas of the epoch. For instance, in an age and in a country where royal power, aristocracy and bourgeoisie are contending for mastery and where, therefore, mastery is shared, the doctrine of the separation of powers proves to be the dominant idea and is expressed as an "eternal law." The division of labour, which we saw above as one of the chief forces of history up till now, manifests itself also in the ruling class as the division of mental and material labour, so that inside this class one part appears as the thinkers of the class (its active, conceptive ideologists, who make the perfecting of the illusion of the class about itself their chief source of livelihood), while the others' attitude to these ideas and illusions is more passive and receptive, because they are in reality the active members of this class and have less time to make up illusions and ideas about themselves. Within this class this cleavage can even develop into a certain opposition and hostility between the two parts, which, however, in the case of a practical collision, in which the class itself is endangered, automatically comes to nothing, in which case there also vanishes the semblance that the ruling ideas were not the ideas of the ruling class and had a power distinct from the power of this class. The existence of revolutionary ideas in a particular period presupposes the existence of a revolutionary class; about the premises for the latter sufficient has already been said above.

If now in considering the course of history we detach the ideas of the ruling class from the ruling class itself and attribute to them an independent existence, if we confine ourselves to saying that these or those ideas were dominant, without bothering ourselves about the conditions of production and the producers of these ideas, if we then ignore the individuals and world conditions which are the source of the ideas, we can say, for instance, that during the time that the aristocracy was dominant, the concepts honour, loyalty, etc., were dominant, during the dominance of the bourgeoisie the concepts freedom, equality, etc. The ruling class itself on the whole imagines this to be so. This conception of history, which is common to all historians, particularly since the eighteenth century, will necessarily come up against the phenomenon that increasingly abstract ideas hold sway, i.e. ideas which increasingly take on the form of universality. For each new class which puts itself in the place of one ruling before it, is compelled, merely in order to carry through its aim, to represent its interest as the common interest of all the members of society, put in an ideal form; it will give its ideas the form of universality, and represent them as the only rational, universally valid ones. The class making a revolution appears from the very start, merely because it is opposed to a *class,* not as a class but as the representative of the whole of society; it appears as the whole mass of society confronting the one ruling class. It can do this because, to start with, its interest really is more connected with the common interest of all other non-ruling classes, because under the pressure of conditions its interest has not yet been able to develop as the particular interest of a particular class. Its victory, therefore, benefits also many individuals of the other classes which are not winning a dominant position, but only in so far as it now puts these individuals in a position to raise themselves into the ruling class. When the French bourgeoisie overthrew the power of the aristocracy, it thereby made it possible for many proletarians to raise themselves above the proletariat, but only in so far as they became bourgeois. Every new class, therefore, achieves its hegemony only on a broader basis than that of the class ruling previously, in return for which the opposition of the non-ruling class against the new ruling class later develops all the more sharply and profoundly. Both these things determine the fact that the struggle to be waged against this new ruling class, in its turn, aims at a more decided and radical negation of the previous conditions of society than could all previous classes which sought to rule.

This whole semblance, that the rule of a certain class is only the rule of certain ideas, comes to a natural end, of course, as soon as society ceases at last to be organized in the form of class-rule, that is to say as soon as it is no longer necessary to represent a particular interest as general or "the general interest" as ruling.

BUSINESS AND LAW

THORSTEIN VEBLEN

INTRODUCTORY

The material framework of modern civilization is the industrial system, and the directing force which animates this framework is business enterprise. To a greater extent than any other known phase of culture, modern Christendom takes its complexion from its economic organization. This modern economic organization is the "Capitalistic System" or "Modern Industrial System," so called. Its characteristic features, and at the same time the forces by virtue of which it dominates modern culture, are the machine process and investment for a profit.

The scope and method of modern industry are given by the machine. This may not seem to hold true for all industries, perhaps not for the greater part of industry as rated by the bulk of the output or by the aggregate volume of labor expended. But it holds true to such an extent and in such a pervasive manner that a modern industrial community cannot go on except by the help of the accepted mechanical appliances and processes. The machine industries—those portions of the industrial system in which the machine process is paramount—are in a dominant position; they set the pace for the rest of the industrial system. In this sense the present is the age of the machine process. This dominance of the machine process in industry marks off the present industrial situation from all else of its kind.

In a like sense the present is the age of business enterprise. Not that all industrial activity is carried on by the rule of investment for profits, but an effective majority of the industrial forces are organized on that basis. There are many items of great volume and consequence that do not fall within the immediate scope of these business principles. The housewife's work, e.g., as well as some appreciable portion of the work on farms and in some handicrafts, can scarcely be classed as business enterprise. But those elements in the industrial world that take the initiative and exert a far-reaching coercive guidance in matters of industry go to their work with a view to profits on investment, and are guided by the principles and exigencies of business. The business man, especially the business man of wide and authoritative discretion, has become a controlling force in industry, because, through the mechanism of investments and markets, he controls the plants and processes, and these set the pace and determine the direction of movement for the rest. His control in those portions of the field that are not immediately under his hand is, no doubt, somewhat loose and uncertain; but in the long run his discretion is in great measure decisive even for these outlying portions of the filed, for he is the only large self-directing economic factor. His control of the motions of other men is not strict, for they are not under coercion from him except through the coercion exercised by the exigencies of the situation in which their lives are cast; but as near as it may be said of any human power in modern times, the large business man controls the exigencies of life under which the community lives. Hence, upon him and his fortunes centers the abiding interest of civilized mankind.

For a theoretical inquiry into the course of civilized life as it runs in the immediate present, therefore, and as it is running into the proximate future, no single factor in the cultural situation has an importance equal to that of the business man and his work.

This of course applies with peculiar force to an inquiry into the economic life of a modern community. In so far as the theorist aims to explain the specifically modern economic phenomena, his line of approach must be from the business man's standpoint, since it is from that standpoint that the course of these phenomena is directed. A theory of the modern economic situation must be primarily a theory of business traffic, with its motives, aims, methods, and effects.

BUSINESS ENTERPRISE

The motive of business is pecuniary gain, the method is essentially purchase and sale. The aim and usual outcome is an accumulation of wealth. Men whose aim is not increase of possessions do not go into business, particularly not on an independent footing.

* * *

Under modern circumstances, where industry is carried on on a large scale, the discretionary head of an industrial enterprise is commonly removed from all personal contact with the body of customers for whom the industrial process under his control purveys goods or services. The mitigating effect which personal contact may have in dealings between man and man is therefore in great measure eliminated. The whole takes on something of an impersonal character. One can with an easier conscience and with less of a sense of meanness take advantage of the necessities of people whom one knows of only as an indiscriminate aggregate of consumers. Particularly is this true when, as frequently happens in the modern situation, this body of consumers belongs in the main to another, inferior class, so that personal contact and cognizance of them is not only not contemplated, but is in a sense impossible. Equity, in excess of the formal modicum specified by law, does not so readily assert its claims where the relations between the parties are remote and impersonal as where one is dealing with one's necessitous neighbors who live on the same social plane. Under these circumstances the adage cited above loses much of its axiomatic force. Business management has a chance to proceed on a temperate and sagacious calculation of profit and loss, untroubled by sentimental considerations of human kindness or irritation or of honesty.

The broad principle which guides producers and merchants, large and small, in fixing the prices at which they offer their wares and services is what is known in the language of the railroads as "charging what the traffic will bear." Where a given enterprise has a strict monopoly of the supply of a given article or of a given class of services this principle applies in the unqualified form in which it has been understood among those who discuss railway charges. But where the monopoly is less strict, where there are competitors, there the competition that has to be met is one of the factors to be taken account of in determining what the traffic will bear; competition may even become the most serious factor in the case if the enterprise in question has little or none of the character of a monopoly. But it is very doubtful if there are any successful business ventures within the range of the modern industries from which the monopoly element is wholly absent. They are, at any rate, few and not of great magnitude. And the endeavor of all such enterprises that look to a permanent continuance of their business is to establish as much of a monopoly as may be. Such a monopoly position may be a legally established one, or one due to location or the control of natural resources, or it may be a monopoly of a less definite character resting on custom and prestige (good-will). This latter class of monopolies are not commonly classed as such; although in character and degree the advantage which they give is very much the same as that due to a differential advantage in location or in the command of resources. The end sought by the systematic advertising of the larger business concerns is such a monopoly of custom and prestige. This form of monopoly is sometimes of great value, and is frequently sold under the name of good-will, trademarks, brands, etc. Instances are known where such monopolies of custom, prestige, prejudice, have been sold at prices running up into the millions.

The great end of consistent advertising is to establish such differential monopolies resting on popular conviction. And the advertiser is successful in this endeavor to establish a profitable popular conviction, somewhat in proportion as he correctly apprehends the manner in which a popular conviction on any given topic is built up. The cost, as well as the pecuniary value and the magnitude, of this organized fabrication of popular convictions is indicated by such statements as that the proprietors of a certain well-known household remedy, reputed among medical authorities to be of entirely dubious value, have for a series of years found their profits in spending several million dollars annually in advertisements. This case is by no means unique.

* * *

Attention is here called to this matter of advertising and the necessity of it in modern competitive business for the light which it throws on "cost of production" in the modern system, where the process of production is under the control of business men and is carried on for business ends. Competitive advertising is an unavoidable item in the aggregate costs of industry. It does not add to the serviceability of the output, except it be incidentally and unintentionally. What it aims at is the sale of the output, and it is for this purpose that it is useful. It gives vendibility, which is useful to the seller, but has no utility to the last buyer. Its ubiquitous presence in the costs of any business enterprise that has to do with the production of goods for the market enforces the statement that the "cost of production" of commodities under the modern business system is cost incurred with a view to vendibility, not with a view to serviceability of the goods for human use.

* * *

The outcome of this recital, then, is that wherever and in so far as business ends and methods dominate modern industry the relation between the usefulness of the work (for other purposes than pecuniary gain) and the remuneration of it is remote and uncertain to such a degree that no attempt at formulating such a relation is worth while. This is eminently and obviously true of the work and gains of business men, in whatever lines of business they are engaged. This follows as a necessary consequence of the nature of business management.

Work that is, on the whole, useless or detrimental to the community at large may be as gainful to the business man and to the workmen whom he employs as work that contributes substantially to the aggregate livelihood. This seems to be peculiarly true of the bolder flights of business enterprise. In so far as its results are not detrimental to human life at large, such unproductive work directed to securing an income may seem to be an idle matter in which the rest of the community has no substantial interests. Such is not the case. In so far as the gains of these unproductive occupations are of a substantial character, they come out of the aggregate product of the other occupations in which the various classes of the community engage. The aggregate profits of the business, whatever its character, are drawn from the aggregate output of goods and services; and whatever goes to the maintenance of the profits of those who contribute nothing substantial to the output is, of course, deducted from the income of the others, whose work tells substantially.

There are, therefore, limits to the growth of the industrially parasitic lines of business just spoken of. A disproportionate growth of parasitic industries, such as most advertising and much of the other efforts that go into competitive selling, as well as warlike expenditure and other industries directed to turning out goods for conspicuously wasteful consumption, would lower the effective vitality of the community to such a degree as to jeopardize its chances of advance or even its life. The limits which the circumstances of life impose in this respect are of a selective character, in the last resort. A persistent excess of parasitic and wasteful efforts over productive industry must bring on a decline. But owing to the very high productive efficiency of the modern mechanical industry, the margin available for wasteful occupations and wasteful expenditures is very great. The requirements of the aggregate livelihood are so far short of the possible output of goods by modern methods as to leave a very wide margin for waste and parasitic income. So that instances of such a decline, due to industrial exhaustion, drawn from the history of any earlier phase of economic life, carry no well-defined lesson as to what a modern industrial community may allow itself in this respect.

While it is in the nature of things unavoidable that the management of industry by modern business methods should involve a large misdirection of effort and a very large waste of goods and services, it is also true that the aims and ideals to which this manner of economic life gives effect act forcibly to offset all this incidental futility. These pecuniary aims and ideals have a very great effect, for instance, in making men work hard and unremittingly, so that on this ground alone the business system probably compensates for any wastes involved in its working. There seems, therefore, to be no tenable ground for thinking that the working of the modern business system involves a curtailment of the community's livelihood. It makes up for its wastefulness by the added strain which it throws upon those engaged in the productive work.

* * *

BUSINESS PRINCIPLES
IN LAW AND POLITICS

Popular welfare is bound up with the conduct of business; because industry is managed for business ends, and also because there prevails throughout modern communities a settled habit of rating the means of livelihood and the amenities of life in pecuniary terms. But apart from their effect in controlling the terms of livelihood from day to day, these principles are also in great measure decisive in the larger affairs of life, both for the individual in his civil relations and for the community at large in its political concerns. Modern (civilized) institutions rest, in great part, on business principles. This is the meaning, as applied to the modern situation, of the current phrases about the Economic Interpretation of History, or the Materialistic Theory of History.

Because of this settled habit of seeing all the conjunctures of life from the business point of view, in terms of profit and loss, the management of the affairs of the community at large falls by common consent into the hands of business men and is guided by business considerations. Hence modern politics is business politics, even apart from the sinister application of the phrase to what is invidiously called corrupt politics. This is true both of foreign and domestic policy. Legislation, police surveillance, the administration of justice, the military and diplomatic service, all are chiefly concerned with business relations, pecuniary interests, and they have little more than an incidental bearing on other human interests. All this apparatus is also charged with the protection of life and personal liberty, but its work in this bearing has much of a pecuniary order.

* * *

The state, that is to say, the government, was once an organization for the control of affairs in the interest of princely or dynastic ends. In internal affairs statecraft was occupied with questions of the dynastic succession, the endeavors and intrigues of the political magnates, fiscal administration directed to finding adequate support for the princely power, and the like. In external politics the objective end was dynastic prestige and security, military success, and the like. Such is still in part the end of political endeavor in those countries, as e.g., Germany, Austria, or Italy, where the transition to a constitutional government has not been completed. But since the advent of constitutional government and parliamentary representation, business ends have taken the lead of dynastic ends in statecraft, very much in the same measure as the transition to constitutional methods has been effectually carried through. A constitutional government is a business government. It is particularly through the business expedient of parliamentary voting on the budget that any constitutional executive, e.g., is kept within constitutional bounds; and the budget is voted with a main view to its expediency for business ends. The expediency of business enterprise is not questioned, whereas the expediency of an increase of princely power and dignity, with the incidental costs, may be questioned.

Modern governmental policies, looking as they do to the furthering of business interests as their chief care, are of a "mercantile" complexion. They aim to foster trade, as did the mercantile policies of the sixteenth and seventeenth centuries, although since "trade" has come to include much else than foreign commerce, the modern policies look to business in the more comprehensive sense which the term now necessarily has.

But these modern mercantile policies, with their tariffs, treaties, interstate commerce regulations, and maxims prohibiting all "restraint of trade," are after all not of the same nature as the mercantile policies of the old French and German statesmen, which they superficially resemble. The old "mercantile system," as it prevailed on the Continent of Europe, was conceived in the interest of the prince, the furthering of commercial advantage being a means to princely power and dignity. The modern mercantilism under constitutional rule, on the other hand, looks to the prince or to the government as a means to the end of commercial gain. With the transition to constitutional rule and methods, the discretion and autonomy in the case has passed from the hands of the prince into those of the business men, and the interests of the business men have superseded those of the crown.

Representative government means, chiefly, representation of business interests. The government commonly works in the interest of the business men with a fairly consistent singleness of purpose. And in its solicitude for the business men's interests it is borne out by current public sentiment, for there is a naïve, unquestioning persuasion abroad among the body of the people to the effect that, in some occult way, the material interests of the populace coincide with the pecuniary interests of those business men who live within the scope of the same set of governmental contrivances. This persuasion is an article of popular metaphysics, in that it rests on an uncritically assumed solidarity of interests, rather than on an insight into the relation of business enterprise to the material welfare of those classes who are not primarily business men. This persuasion is particularly secure among the more conservative portion of the community, the business men, superior and subordinate, together with the professional classes as contrasted with those vulgar portions of the community who are tainted with socialistic or anarchistic notions. But since the conservative element comprises the citizens of substance and weight, and indeed the effective majority of law-abiding citizens, it follows that, with the sanction of the great body of the people, even including those who have no pecuniary interests to serve in the matter, constitutional government has, in the main, become a department of the business organization and is guided by the advice of the business men. The government has, of course, much else to do besides administering the general affairs of the business community; but in most of its work, even in what is not ostensibly directed to business ends, it is under the surveillance of the business interests. It seldom happens, if at all, that the government of a civilized nation will persist in a course of action detrimental or not ostensibly subservient to the interests of the more conspicuous body of the community's business men. The degree in which a government fails to adapt its policy to these business exigencies is the measure of its senility.

The ground of sentiment on which rests the popular approval of a government for business ends may be summed up under two heads: patriotism and property. Both of these terms stand for institutional facts that have come down out of a past which differed substantially from the present situation. The substance of both is of the nature of unreasoning sentiment, in the sense that both are insisted on as a matter of course, as self-legitimating grounds of action which, it is felt, not only give expedient rules of conduct, but admit of no question as to their ulterior consequences or their value for the life-purposes of the community. The former of these fundamental institutional habits of thought (perhaps better, habits of mind) runs back to the discipline of early barbarism, through the feudal days of fealty to the earlier days of clan life and clannish animosity. It has therefore the deep-rooted strength given by an extremely protracted discipline of predation and servitude. Under modern conditions it is to be rated as essentially an institutional survival, so ingrained in the populace as to make any appeal to it secure of a response irrespective of the material merits of the contention in whose behalf the appeal is made.

By force of this happy knack of clannish fancy the common man is enabled to feel that he has some sort of metaphysical share in the gains which accrue to the business men who are citizens of the same "commonwealth"; so that whatever policy furthers the commercial gains of those business men whose domicile is within the national boundaries is felt to be beneficial to all the rest of the population.

The second institutional support of business politics, viz. property, is similarly an outgrowth of the discipline of the past, and similarly, though perhaps in a less degree, out of touch with the discipline of the more recent cultural situation. In the form in which it prevails in the current popular animus, the principle of ownership comes down from the days of handicraft industry and petty trade, as pointed out above. As it is of less ancient and less unbroken descent, so it seems also to be a less secure cultural heritage than the sense of patriotic solidarity. It says that the ownership of property is the material foundation of human well-being, and that this natural right of ownership is sacred, after the manner in which individual life, and more especially national life, is sacred. The habits of life and thought inculcated by joint work under the manorial system and by joint rules under the handicraft system have apparently contributed much to the notion of a solidarity of economic interests, having given the notion such a degree of consistency as has enabled it to persist in the face of a visible discrepancy of interests in later, capitalistic times. Under this current, business régime, business gains are the basis of individual wealth, and the (pseudo) notion of joint acquisition has taken the place of the manorial notion of joint work. The institutional animus of ownership, as it took shape under the discipline of early modern handicraft, awards the ownership of property to the workman who has produced it. By a dialectical conversion of the terms, this metaphysical dictum is made to fit the circumstances of later competitive business by construing acquisition of property to mean production of wealth; so that a business man is looked upon as the putative producer of whatever wealth he acquires. By force of this sophistication the acquisition of property by any person is held to be, not only expedient for the owner, but meritorious as an action serving the common good. Failure to bargain shrewdly or to accumulate more goods than one has produced by the work of one's own hands is looked upon with a feeling of annoyance, as a neglect, not only of opportunity, but of duty. The pecuniary conscience commonly does not, of course, go to quixotic lengths in a public-spirited insistence on everybody's acquiring more than an aliquot part of the aggregate wealth on hand, but it is felt that he best serves the common good who, other things equal, diverts the larger share of the aggregate wealth to his own possession. His acquiring a defensible title to it makes him the putative producer of it.

The natural-rights basis of ownership is by this paralogism preserved intact, and the common man is enabled to feel that the business men in the community add to the aggregate wealth at least as much as they acquire a title to; and the successful business men are at least as well persuaded that such is their relation to the aggregate wealth and to the material well-being of the community at large. So that both the business men whose gains are sought to be enhanced by business politics and the populace by whose means the business gains are secured work together in good faith toward a well-advised business end—the accumulation of wealth in the hands of those men who are skilled in pecuniary matters.

The manner in which business interests work out in government policy may be shown by following up their bearing upon one phase of this policy. An extreme expression of business politics, and at the same time a characteristic trait of the higher levels of national life in Christendom, is the current policy of war and armaments. Modern business is competitive, emulative, and the direction of business enterprise is in the hands of men who are single-minded in their competitive conduct of affairs. They neither are inclined, nor will business competition permit them, to neglect or overlook any expedient that may further their own advantage or hinder the advantage of their rivals. Under the modern situation, as it has taken shape since the industrial revolution, business competition has become international, covering the range of what is called the world market. In this international competition the machinery and policy of the state are in a peculiar degree drawn into the service of the larger business interests; so that, both in commerce and industrial enterprise, the business men of one nation are pitted against those of another and swing the forces of the state, legislative, diplomatic, and military, against one another in the strategic game of pecuniary advantage. The business interests domiciled within the scope of a given government fall into a loose organization in the form of what might be called a tacit ring or syndicate, proceeding on a general understanding that they will stand together as against outside business interests. The nearest approach to an explicit plan and organization of such a business ring is the modern political party, with its platform, tacit and avowed. Parties differ in their detail aims, but those parties that have more than a transient existence and superficial effect stand for different lines of business policy, agreeing all the while in so far that they all aim to further what they each claim to be the best, largest, most enduring business interests of the community. The ring of business interests which secures the broadest approval from popular sentiment is, under constitutional methods, put in charge of the government establishment. This popular approval may be secured on the ground of a sound business platform or (in part) on some ground extraneous to business policy proper, such as a wave of national animosity, a popular candidate, a large grain crop, etc. But the only secure basis of an enduring party tenure of the government machinery is a business policy which falls in with the interests or the prejudices of the effective majority.

In international competition the *ultima ratio* is, as ever, warlike force, whether the issue be between princes of the grace of God or princes of ownership. It is a favorite maxim of modern politics that trade follows the flag. This is the business man's valuation of national policy and of the ends of national life. So stated, the maxim probably inverts the sequence of facts, but it is none the less a fair expression of the close relation there is between business endeavor and the modern military policies. Diplomacy, if it is to be effective for whatever end, must be backed by a show of force and of a readiness to use it. The definitive argument of those who speak for armaments (in England and America) is that the maintenance of business interests requires the backing of arms. On the Continent of Europe this argument commonly comes second, while patriotic fancy and animosity take first place.

Armaments serve trade not only in the making of general terms of purchase and sale between the business men of civilized countries, but they are similarly useful in extending and maintaining business enterprise and privileges in the outlying regions of the earth. The advanced nations of Christendom are proselyters, and there are certain valuable perquisites that come to the business men of those proselyting nations who advance the frontiers of the pecuniary culture among the backward populations. There is commonly a handsome margin of profit in doing business with these, pecuniarily unregenerate, populations, particularly when the traffic is adequately backed with force. But, also commonly, these peoples do not enter willingly into lasting business relations with civilized mankind. It is therefore necessary, for the purposes of trade and culture, that they be firmly held up to such civilized rules of conduct as will make trade easy and lucrative. To this end armament is indispensable.

But in the portioning out of the trade perquisites that fall to the proselyters any businss community is in danger of being overreached by alien civilizing powers. No recourse but force is finally available in disputes of this kind, in which the aim of the disputants is to take advantage of one another as far as they can. A warlike front is therefore necessary, and armaments and warlike demonstrations have come to be a part of the regular apparatus of business, so far as business is concerned with the world market.

In so far as it is guided by the exigencies of trade, the objective end of warlike endeavor is the peace and security necessary to an orderly development of business. International business relations, it is well said, make for peace; in the sense, of course, that they enforce the pacification of recalcitrant barbarians and lead to contention between civilized nations for a revision of the peace terms. When a modern government goes to war for trade purposes, it does so with a view to reëstablishing peace on terms more lucrative to its business men.

The above inquiry into the nature and causes of the wars of nations has resulted in little else than a recital of commonplaces; the facts and their connection are matters of common notoriety, and probably no one would hazard a quotation of the slight and obvious inferences drawn in the course of the recital. The excuse for this discursive review of the motives and aims of a war policy is that it gives a basis for an outlook on the present and immediate future of business enterprise.

The experience of Continental Europe in the matter of armaments during the last half-century, and of all the greater nations during the last two decades, argues that when warlike emulation between states of somewhat comparable force has once got under way it assumes a cumulative character; so that a scale of expenditure for armaments which would at the outset have seemed absurdly impossible comes presently to be accepted as a matter of course. Hitherto the cumulative augmentation of war expenditures and of war animus shows no sign of slackening. One after another, the states that have offered some show of peaceable inclinations have been drawn into the international game of competitive armaments, as they have one after another become ambitious to push the enterprises of their business men in the international markets. An armament is serviceable only if it is relatively large; its absolute magnitude is a matter of no particular consequence for competitive politics. It is its comparative size that counts. Hence the greater the several armaments, the greater the political need of greater armaments, and the prompter the resentment of injuries and the livelier the felt need of offending and of taking offense. A progressively larger proportion of the nation's forces are withdrawn from industry and devoted to warlike ends. In this cumulative diversion of effort to warlike ends a point is presently reached beyond which the question of armament is no longer. What amount of warlike expenditure is needed to extend or maintain business traffic? but rather, What amount will the nation's resources bear? But the progression does not stop at that point; witness the case of Italy, France, and Germany, where the war drain has visibly impaired the industrial efficiency of the several nations concerned, but where the burden still goes on growing, with no stopping-place in sight. England and, more particularly, America are not so near exhaustion, because they have larger resources to draw on as well as a culture and a population more efficient for industrial work. But there is no evident reason why these two should not likewise enter on a policy of emulative exhaustion, and so sacrifice their aggregate industrial and business interest to the furtherance of the "great game."

The question may suggest itself. Why should not the business community, who have a large discretion in international politics and whose aggregate gains are cut into by excessive war expenditures, call a halt when the critical point is reached? There is more than one reason for their failure to do so. War and preoccupation with warlike enterprise breed a warlike animus in the community, as well as a habit of arbitrary, autocratic rule on the part of those in authority and an unquestioning, enthusiastic subservience on the part of the subjects. National animosity and national pride demand more and more of military standing, at the same time that the growing official class needs increasing emoluments and a larger field of employment and display. The cultural effects of the discipline of warfare and armament are much the same whether it is undertaken for dynastic or for business ends; in either case it takes on a dynastic complexion and breeds the temperament, ideals, and institutional habits proper to a dynastic system of politics. The farther it goes the more it comes to make use of business interests as a means rather than an end, as, e.g., in modern Germany, France, and Italy, and in the Continental states of the sixteenth and seventeenth centuries. The crown, court, bureaucracy, military establishment, and nobility, under whatever designations, gradually come to their own again in such a situation, and affairs again come to run on questions of the maintenance and dignity of these superior elements of the population. The objective end of protracted warlike endeavor necessarily shifts from business advantage to dynastic ascendancy and courtly honor. Business interests fall to the position of fiscal ways and means, and business traffic becomes subservient to higher ends, with a fair chance of ultimate exhaustion or collapse through the bankruptcy of the state.

Business enterprise is an individual matter, not a collective one. So long as the individual business man sees a proximate gain for himself in meeting the demands for war funds and materials to maintain the courtly and official establishments that go with military politics, it is not in the nature of the business man to draw back. It is always his profits, not his livelihood, that is involved; the question which touches his profits is the relative gainfulness of alternative lines of investment open to him. So long as the pecuniary inducements held out by the state, in bidding for funds or supplies, overbalance the inducements offered by alternative lines of employment, the business men will supply these demands, regardless of what the ulterior substantial outcome of such a course may be in the end. Funds and business enterprise are now of so pronounced an international or cosmopolitan character that any business man may, even without fully appreciating the fact, lend his aid to the fisc of a hostile power as readily as to a friendly power or to the home government; whereby an equable and comprehensive exhaustion of the several communities involved in the concert of nations is greatly facilitated. Barring accidents and untoward cultural agencies from outside of politics, business, or religion, there is nothing in the logic of the modern situation that should stop the cumulative war expenditures short of industrial collapse and consequent national bankruptcy, such as terminated the carnival of war and politics that ran its course on the Continent in the sixteenth and seventeenth centuries.

THE STATE

PAUL SWEEZY

There is a tendency on the part of modern liberal theorists to interpret the state as an institution established in the interests of society as a whole for the purpose of mediating and reconciling the antagonisms to which social existence inevitably gives rise. This is a theory which avoids the pitfalls of political metaphysics and which serves to integrate in a tolerably satisfactory fashion a considerable body of observed fact. It contains, however, one basic shortcoming, the recognition of which leads to a theory essentially Marxian in its orientation. A critique of what may be called the class-mediation conception of the state is, therefore, perhaps the best way of introducing the Marxian theory.

The class-mediation theory assumes, usually implicitly, that the underlying class structure, or what comes to the same thing, the system of property relations is an immutable datum, in this respect like the order of nature itself. It then proceeds to ask what arrangements the various classes will make to get along with each other, and finds that an institution for mediating their conflicting interests is the logical and necessary answer. To this institution powers for maintaining order and settling quarrels are granted. In the real world what is called the state is identified as the counterpart of this theoretical construction.

The weakness of this theory is not difficult to discover. It lies in the assumption of an immutable and, so to speak, self-maintaining class structure of society. The superficiality of this assumption is indicated by the most cursory study of history.*

---

*Many theorists recognize this up to a point, but they believe that what was true of past societies is not true of modern society. In other words, capitalism is regarded as the final end-product of social evolution.

Excerpts from *Theory of Capitalist Development* by Paul M. Sweezy. © 1942 by Paul M. Sweezy. Reprinted by permission of Monthly Review Press.

The fact is that many forms of property relations with their concomitant class structures have come and gone in the past, and there is no reason to assume that they will not continue to do so in the future. The class structure of society is no part of the natural order of things; it is the product of past social development, and it will change in the course of future social development.

Once this is recognized it becomes clear that the liberal theory goes wrong in the manner in which it initially poses the problem. We cannot ask: Given a certain class structure, how will the various classes, with their divergent and often conflicting interests, manage to get along together? We must ask: How did a particular class structure come into being and by what means is its continued existence guaranteed? As soon as an attempt is made to answer this question, it appears that the state has a function in society which is prior to and more fundamental than any which present-day liberals attribute to it. Let us examine this more closely.

A given set of property relations serves to define and demarcate the class structure of society. From any set of property relations one class or classes (the owners) reap material advantages; other classes (the owned and the non-owners) suffer material disadvantages. A special institution capable and willing to use force to whatever degree is required is an essential to the maintenance of such a set of property relations. Investigation shows that the state possesses this characteristic to the fullest degree, and that no other institution is or can be allowed to compete with it in this respect. This is usually expressed by saying that the state, and the state alone, exercises sovereignty over all those subject to its jurisdiction. It is, therefore, not difficult to identify the state as the guarantor of a given set of property relations.

If now we ask, where the state comes from, the answer is that it is the product of a long and arduous struggle in which the class which occupies what is for the time the key positions in the process of production gets the upper hand over its rivals and fashions a state which will enforce that set of property relations which is in its own interest. In other words any particular state is the child of the class or classes in society which benefit from the particular set of property relations which it is the state's obligation to enforce. A moment's reflection will carry the conviction that it could hardly be otherwise. As soon as we have dropped the historically untenable assumption that the class structure of society is in some way natural or self-enforcing, it is clear that any other outcome would lack the prerequisites of stability. If the disadvantaged classes were in possession of state power, they would attempt to use it to establish a social order more favorable to their own interests, while a sharing of state power among the various classes would merely shift the locale of conflict to the state itself.

That such conflicts within the state, corresponding to fundamental class struggles outside, have taken place in certain transitional historical periods is not denied. During those long periods, however, when a certain social order enjoys a relatively continuous and stable existence, the state power must be monopolized by the class or classes which are the chief beneficiaries.

As against the class-mediation theory of the state, we have here the underlying idea of what has been called the class-domination theory. The former takes the existence of a certain class structure for granted and sees in the state an institution for reconciling the conflicting interests of the various classes; the latter, on the other hand, recognizes that classes are the product of historical development and sees in the state an instrument in the hands of the ruling classes for enforcing and guaranteeing the stability of the class structure itself.

It is important to realize that, so far as capitalist society is concerned, 'class domination' and 'the protection of private property' are virtually synonymous expressions. Hence when we say with Engels that the highest purpose of the state is the protection of private property, we are also saying that the state is an instrument of class domination. This is doubtless insufficiently realized by critics of the Marxian theory who tend to see in the notion of class domination something darker and more sinister than 'mere' protection of private property. In other words they tend to look upon class domination as something reprehensible and the protection of private property as something meritorious. Consequently, it does not occur to them to identify the two ideas. Frequently, no doubt, this is because they have in mind not capitalist property, but rather private property as it would be in a simple commodity-producing society where each producer owns and works with his own means of production. Under such conditions there are no classes at all and hence is no class domination. Under capitalist relations, however, property has an altogether different significance, and its protection is easily shown to be identical with the preservation of class dominance. Capitalist private property does not consist in things—things exist independently of their ownership—but in a social relation between people. Property confers upon its owners freedom from labor and the disposal over the labor of others, and this is the essence of all social domination whatever form it may assume. It follows that the protection of property is fundamentally the assurance of social domination to owners over non-owners. And this, in turn, is precisely what is meant by class domination, which it is the primary function of the state to uphold.

The recognition that the defense of private property is the first duty of the state is the decisive factor in determining the attitude of genuine Marxist socialism towards the state. 'The theory of the Communists,' Marx and Engels wrote in the *Communist Manifesto,* 'can be summed up in the single sentence: Abolition of private property.' Since the state is first and foremost the protector of private property, it follows that the realization of this end cannot be achieved without a head-on collision between the forces of socialism and the state power.*

*The treatment of the relation between the state and property has of necessity been extremely sketchy. In order to avoid misunderstanding, the following note should be added. The idea that the state is an organization for the maintenance of private property was by no means an invention of Marx and Engels. On the contrary, it constituted the cornerstone of the whole previous development of political thought from the breakdown of feudalism and the origins of the modern states. Bodin, Hobbes, Locke, Rousseau, Adam Smith, Kant, and Hegel—to mention but a few outstanding thinkers of the period before Marx—clearly recognized this central function of the state. They believed private property to be the necessary condition for the full development of human potentialities, the *sine*

The fact that the first concern of the state is to protect the continued existence and stability of a given form of society does not mean that it performs no other functions of economic importance. On the contrary, the state has always been a very significant factor in the functioning of the economy within the framework of the system of property relations which it guarantees.

* * *

First, the state power is invoked to solve problems which are posed by the economic development of the particular form of society under consideration, in this case capitalism. In the earlier period a shortage of labor power, in the later period over-exploitation of the laboring population were the subjects of state action. In each case the solution of the problem required state intervention. Many familiar examples of a similar character readily come to mind.

Second, we should naturally expect that the state power under capitalism would be used first and foremost in the interests of the capitalist class since the state is dedicated to the preservation of the structure of capitalism and must therefore be staffed by those who fully accept the postulates and objectives of this form of society. This is unquestionably true, but it is not inconsistent to say that state action may run counter to the immediate economic interests of some or even all of the capitalists provided only that the overriding aim of preserving the system intact is promoted. The legal limitation of the working day is a classic example of state action of this sort. The intensity of class antagonism engendered by over-exploitation of the labor force was such that it became imperative for the capitalist class to make

qua non of genuine freedom. Marx and Engels added that freedom based on private property is freedom for an exploiting class, and that freedom for _all_ presupposes the abolition of private property, that is to say the achievement of a classless society. Nevertheless, Marx and Engels did not forget that the realization of a classless society (abolition of private property) is possible only on the basis of certain definite historical conditions; without the enormous increase in the productivity of labor which capitalism had brought about, a classless society would be no more than an empty Utopia.

concessions even at the cost of immediate economic advantages.* For the sake of preserving domestic peace and tranquility, blunting the edge of class antagonisms, and ultimately avoiding the dangers of violent revolution, the capitalist class is always prepared to make concessions through the medium of state action. It may, of course, happen that the occasion for the concessions is an actual materialization of the threat of revolution.† In this case their purpose is to restore peace and order so that production and accumulation can once again go forward uninterruptedly.

Let us summarize the principles underlying the use of the state as an economic instrument within the framework of capitalism. In the first place, the state comes into action in the economic sphere in order to solve problems which are posed by the development of capitalism. In the second place, where the interests of the capitalist class are concerned, there is a strong predisposition to use the state power freely. And, finally, the state may be used to make concessions to the working class provided that the consequences of not doing so are sufficiently dangerous to the stability and functioning of the system as a whole.

It should be noted that none of these conclusions lends support to the revisionist view that socialism can be achieved through a series of piecemeal reforms. On the contrary, they grow out of and supplement the basic principle that the state exists in the first instance for the protection of capitalist property relations. Reforms may modify the functioning of capitalism but never threaten its foundation. Rosa Luxemburg stated the true Marxian position succinctly in the following words:

*This example makes clear the concession character of state action favoring the working class, since it could not possibly be maintained that the workers had a share in state power in England at the time the main factory acts were passed. In this connection it is sufficient to recall that the Reform Act of 1832 contained high property qualifications for voting and it was not until 1867 that the franchise was next extended. By this time the most important victories in the struggle for factory legislation had already been won.

†For example, Marx remarked that in France, 'the February [1858] revolution was necessary to bring into the world the 12 hours' law.' Capital 1, p. 328.

> *'Social control' . . . is concerned not with the limitation of capitalist property, but on the contrary with its protection. Or, speaking in economic terms, it does not constitute an attack on capitalist exploitation but rather a normalization and regularization of this exploitation.*

Marx never said anything to contradict this, and to cite his chapter on the working day, as revisionists frequently do, in support of the gradualist standpoint is simply to betray a misunderstanding of his entire theoretical system.

Up to this point nothing has been said about the form of government in capitalist society. Is it possible that the principles of state action which have been examined do not hold in a fully democratic capitalist society? (By 'fully democratic' we mean no more than what exists today in most of the English-speaking world: parliamentarism combined with universal suffrage and organizational freedom in the political sphere.)

If Marxist theory answers this question in the negative, this must not be interpreted to mean that the question of democracy is regarded as of no importance, but only that democracy does not alter the basic significance of the state in relation to the economy. The existence of democracy is, of course, a matter of prime importance particularly to the working class. Only under a democratic form of government can the working class organize freely and effectively for the achievement of its ends, whether they happen to be socialist or merely reformist in character. It is for this reason that one of the first demands of the labor movement in all non-democratic countries has always been the establishment of democratic forms of government. Moreover, for the ruling class democracy has always constituted a potential threat to the stability of its position and has consequently been granted grudgingly, with limitations, and usually only under severe pressure. Marx stated the main issues very forcibly in discussing the democratic French constitution of 1848:

> *The most comprehensive contradiction of this constitution consisted in the following: the classes whose social slavery the constitution is to perpetuate, proletariat, peasants, petty*

bourgeois, it puts in possession of political power through universal suffrage. And from the class whose old social power it sanctions, the bourgeoisie, it withdraws the political guarantees of this power. It forces its rule into democratic conditions, which at every moment help the hostile classes to victory and jeopardize the very foundations of bourgeois society.

Democracy brings the conflicts of capitalist society into the open in the political sphere; it restricts the freedom of the capitalists to use the state in their own interests; it reinforces the working class in demanding concessions; finally, it even increases the possibility that the working class will present demands which threaten the system itself and so must be rejected by the capitalists and their state functionaries regardless of the consequences. . . . There is, in other words, nothing in the nature of democracy to make us change our view of the fundamental functions and limits of state action in capitalist society. Again, we must insist that the revisionists, in holding the opposed view, that socialism can be gradually substituted for capitalism by the methods of capitalist democracy, were in reality abandoning Marx altogether.

The fallacy of the revisionist position was never more clearly pointed out than by Rosa Luxemburg in her polemic against Bernstein and Schmidt in 1899:

> *According to Conrad Schmidt, the achievement of a social democratic majority in parliament should be the direct way to the gradual socialization of society . . . Formally, to be sure, parliamentarism does express the interests of the entire society in the state organization. On the other hand, however, it is still capitalist society, that is to say, a society in which capitalist interests are controlling . . . The institutions which are democratic in form are in substance instruments of the dominant class interests. This is most obvious in the fact that so soon as democracy shows a disposition to deny its class character and to become an instrument of the real interests of the people, the democratic forms themselves are sacrificed by the bourgeoisie and their representatives in the state. The*

idea of a social democratic majority appears therefore as a calculation which, entirely in the spirit of bourgeois liberalism, concerns itself with only one side—the formal side—of democracy but which leaves out of account the other side, its real content.

The spread of fascism in the last two decades, particularly in those countries where working-class organization had reached its greatest development, has done much to weaken the belief in the possibility of a gradual transition to socialism through the methods provided by capitalist democracy. Otto Bauer, one of the outstanding representatives of the Second International and long leader of the Austrian socialists, expressed a widespread view when he wrote, in 1936, that the experience of fascism 'destroys the illusion of reformist socialism that the working class can fill the forms of democracy with socialist content and develop the capitalist into a socialist order without a revolutionary jump.' Rosa Luxemburg's warning that in an extremity 'the democratic forms themselves are sacrificed by the bourgeoisie and their representatives in the state' has turned out to be well-founded.

THE FOUNDING FATHERS:
An Age of Realism

RICHARD HOFSTADER

Long ago Horace White observed that the Constitution of the United States "is based upon the philosophy of Hobbes and the religion of Calvin. It assumes that the natural state of mankind is a state of war, and that the carnal mind is at enmity with God." Of course the Constitution was founded more upon experience than any such abstract theory; but it was also an event in the intellectual history of Western civilization. The men who drew up the Constitution in Philadelphia during the summer of 1787 had a vivid Calvinistic sense of human evil and damnation and believed with Hobbes that men are selfish and contentious. They were men of affairs, merchants, lawyers, planter-businessmen, speculators, investors. Having seen human nature on display in the market place, the courtroom, the legislative chamber, and in every secret path and alleyway where wealth and power are courted, they felt they knew it in all its frailty. To them a human being was an atom of self-interest. They did not believe in man, but they did believe in the power of a good political constitution to control him.

This may be an abstract notion to ascribe to practical men, but it follows the language that the Fathers used. General Knox, for example, wrote in disgust to Washington after the Shays Rebellion that Americans were, after all, "men—actual men possessing all the turbulent passions belonging to that animal." Throughout the secret discussions at the Constitutional Convention it was clear that this distrust of man was first and foremost a distrust of the common man and democratic rule. As the Revolution took away the restraining hand of the British government, old colonial grievances of farmers, debtors, and squatters against merchants, investors, and large landholders had flared up anew; the lower orders took advantage of new democratic constitutions in several states, and the possessing classes were frightened. The members of the Constitutional Convention were concerned to create a government that could not only regulate commerce and pay its debts but also prevent currency inflation and stay laws, and check such uprising as the Shays Rebellion.

Cribbing and confining the popular spirit that had been at large since 1776 were essential to the purposes of the new Constitution. Edmund Randolph, saying to the Convention that the evils from which the country suffered originated in "the turbulence and follies of democracy," and that the great danger lay in "the democratic parts of our constitutions"; Elbridge Gerry, speaking of democracy as "the worst of all political evils"; Roger Sherman, hoping that "the people . . . have as little to do as may be about the government"; William Livingston, saying that "the people have ever been and ever will be unfit to retain the exercise of power in their own hands"; George Washington, the presiding officer, urging the delegates not to produce a document of which they themselves could not approve simply in order to "please the people"; Hamilton, charging that the "turbulent and changing" masses "seldom judge or determine right" and advising a permanent governmental body to "check the imprudence of democracy"; the wealthy young planter Charles Pinckney, proposing that no one be president who was not worth at least one hundred thousand dollars—all these were quite representative of the spirit in which the problems of government were treated.

Democratic ideas are most likely to take root among discontented and oppressed classes, rising middle classes, or perhaps some sections of an old, alienated, and partially disinherited aristocracy, but they do not appeal to a privileged class that is still amplifying its privileges. With a half-dozen exceptions at the most, the men of the Philadelphia Convention were sons of men who had considerable position and wealth, and as a group they had advanced well beyond their fathers. Only one of them, William Few of Georgia, could be said in any sense to represent the yeoman farmer class which constituted the overwhelming majority of the free population. In the late eighteenth century "the better kind of people" found themselves set off from the mass by a hundred visible, tangible, and audible distinctions of dress, speech, manners, and education. There was a continuous lineage of upper-class contempt, from pre-Revolutionary Tories like Peggy Hutchinson, the Governor's daughter, who wrote one day: "The dirty mob was all about me as I drove into town," to a Federalist like Hamilton, who candidly disdained the people. Mass unrest was often received in the spirit of young Gouverneur Morris: "The mob begin to think and reason. Poor reptiles! . . . They bask in the sun, and ere noon they will bite, depend upon it. The gentry begin to fear this." Nowhere in America or Europe—not even among the great liberated thinkers of the Enlightenment—did democratic ideas appear respectable to the cultivated classes. Whether the Fathers looked to the cynically illuminated intellectuals of contemporary Europe or to their own Christian heritage of the idea of original sin, they found quick confirmation of the notion that man is an unregenerate rebel who has to be controlled.

And yet there was another side to the picture. The Fathers were intellectual heirs of seventeenth-century English republicanism with its opposition to arbitrary rule and faith in popular sovereignty. If they feared the advance of democracy, they also had misgivings about turning to the extreme right. Having recently experienced a bitter revolutionary struggle with an external power beyond their control, they were in no mood to follow Hobbes to his conclusion that any kind of government must be accepted in order to avert the anarchy and terror of a state of nature. They were uneasily aware that both military dictatorship and a return to monarchy were being seriously discussed in some quarters—the former chiefly among unpaid and discontented army officers, the latter in rich and fashionable Northern circles. John Jay, familiar with sentiment among New York's mercantile aristocracy, wrote to Washington, June 27, 1786, that he feared that "the better kind of people (by which I mean the people who are orderly and industrious, who are content with their situations, and not uneasy in their circumstances) will be led, by the insecurity of property, the loss of confidence in their rulers, and the want of public faith and rectitude, to consider the charms of liberty as imaginary and delusive." Such men, he thought, might be prepared for "almost any change that may promise them quiet and security." Washington, who had already repudiated a suggestion that he become a military dictator, agreed, remarking that "we are apt to run from one extreme to the other."

Unwilling to turn their backs upon republicanism, the Fathers also wished to avoid violating the prejudices of the people. "Notwithstanding the oppression and injustice experienced among us from democracy," said George Mason, "the genius of the people is in favor of it, and the genius of the people must be consulted." Mason admitted "that we had been too democratic," but feared that "we should incautiously run into the opposite extreme." James Madison, who has quite rightfully been called the philosopher of the Constitution, told the delegates: "It seems indispensable that the mass of citizens should not be without a voice in making the laws which they are to obey, and in choosing the magistrates who are to administer them." James Wilson, the outstanding jurist of the age, later appointed to the Supreme Court by Washington, said again and again that the ultimate power of government must of necessity reside in the people. This the Fathers commonly accepted, for if government did not proceed from the people, from what other source could it legitimately come? To adopt any other premise not only would be inconsistent with everything they had said against British rule in the past but would open the gates to an extreme concentration of power in the future. Hamilton saw the sharp distinction in the Convention when he said that "the members most tenacious of republicanism were as loud as any in declaiming the vices of democracy." There was no better expression of the dilemma of a man who has no faith in the people but insists that government be based upon them than that of Jeremy Belknap, a New England clergyman, who wrote to a friend: "Let it stand as a principle that government originates from the people; but let the people be taught . . . that they are not able to govern themselves."

If the masses were turbulent and unregenerate, and yet if government must be founded upon their suffrage and consent, what could a Constitution-maker do? One thing that the Fathers did not propose to do, because they thought it impossible, was to change the nature of man to conform with a more ideal system. They were inordinately confident that they knew what man always had been and what he always would be. The eighteenth-century mind had great faith in universals. Its method, as Carl Becker has said, was "to go up and down the field of history looking for man in general, the universal man, stripped of the accidents of time and place." Madison declared that the causes of political differences and of the formation of factions were "sown in the nature of man" and could never be eradicated. "It is universally acknowledged," David Hume had written, "that there is a great uniformity among the actions of men, in all nations and ages, and that human nature remains still the same, in its principles and operations. The same motives always produce the same actions. The same events always follow from the same causes."

Since man was an unchangeable creature of self-interest, it would not do to leave anything to his capacity for restraint. It was too much to expect that vice could be checked by virtue; the Fathers relied instead upon checking vice with vice. Madison once objected during the Convention that Gouverneur Morris was "forever inculcating the utter political depravity of men and the necessity of opposing one vice and interest to another vice and interest." And yet Madison himself in the *Federalist* number 51 later set forth an excellent statement of the same thesis:*

*Cf. the words of Hamilton to the New York ratifying convention: "Men will pursue their interests. It is as easy to change human nature as to oppose the strong current of selfish passions. A wise legislator will gently divert the channel, and direct it, if possible, to the public good."

> *Ambition must be made to counteract ambition. . . . It may be a reflection on human nature that such devices should be necessary to control the abuses of government. But what is government itself, but the greatest of all reflections on human nature? If men were angels, no government would be necessary. . . . In framing a government which is to be administered by men over men, the great difficulty lies in this: you must first enable the government to control the governed; and in the next place oblige it to control itself.*

Political economists of the laissez-faire school were saying that private vices could be public benefits, that an economically beneficent result would be providentially or "naturally" achieved if self-interest were left free from state interference and allowed to pursue its ends. But the Fathers were not so optimistic about politics. If, in a state that lacked constitutional balance, one class or one interest gained control, they believed, it would surely plunder all other interests. The Fathers, of course, were especially fearful that the poor would plunder the rich, but most of them would probably have admitted that the rich, unrestrained, would also plunder the poor. Even Gouverneur Morris, who stood as close to the extreme aristocratic position as candor and intelligence would allow, told the Convention: "Wealth tends to corrupt the mind and to nourish its love of power, and to stimulate it to oppression. History proves this to be the spirit of the opulent."

What the Fathers wanted was known as "balanced government," an idea at least as old as Aristotle and Polybius. This ancient conception had won new sanction in the eighteenth century, which was dominated intellectually by the scientific work of Newton, and in which mechanical metaphors sprang as naturally to men's minds as did biological metaphors in the Darwinian atmosphere of the late nineteenth century. Men had found a rational order in the universe and they hoped that it could be transferred to politics, or, as John Adams put it, that governments could be "erected on the simple principles of nature." Madison spoke in the most precise Newtonian language when he said that such a "natural" government must be so constructed "that its several constituent parts may, by their mutual relations, be the means of keeping each other in their proper places." A properly designed state, the Fathers believed, would check interest with interest, class with class, faction with faction, and one branch of government with another in a harmonious system of mutual frustration.

In practical form, therefore, the quest of the Fathers reduced primarily to a search for constitutional devices that would force various interests to check and control one another. Among those who favored the federal Constitution three such devices were distinguished.

The first of these was the advantage of a federated government in maintaining order against popular uprisings or majority rule. In a single state a faction might arise and take complete control by force; but if the states were bound in a federation, the central government could step in and prevent it. Hamilton quoted Montesquieu: "Should a popular insurrection happen in one of the confederate states, the others are able to quell it." Further, as Madison argued in the *Federalist* number 10, a majority would be the most dangerous of all factions that might arise, for the majority would be the most capable of gaining complete ascendancy. If the political society were very extensive, however, and embraced a large number and variety of local interests, the citizens who shared a common majority interest "must be rendered by their number and local situation, unable to concert and carry into effect their schemes of oppression." The chief propertied interests would then be safer from "a rage for paper money, for an abolition of debts, for an equal division of property, or for any other improper or wicked project."

The second advantage of good constitutional government resided in the mechanism of representation itself. In a small direct democracy the unstable passions of the people would dominate lawmaking; but a representative government, as Madison said, would "refine and enlarge the public views by passing them through the medium of a chosen body of citizens." Representatives chosen by the people were wiser and more deliberate than the people themselves in mass assemblage. Hamilton frankly anticipated a kind of syndical paternalism in which the wealthy and dominant members of every trade or industry would represent the others in politics. Merchants, for example, were "the natural representatives" of their employees and of the mechanics and artisans they dealt with. Hamilton expected that Congress, "with too few exceptions to have any influence on the spirit of the government, will be composed of landholders, merchants, and men of the learned professions."

The third advantage of the government the Fathers were designing was pointed out most elaborately by John Adams in the first volume of his *Defence of the Constitutions of Government of the United States of America,* which reached Philadelphia while the Convention was in session and was cited with approval by several delegates.* Adams believed that the aristocracy and the democracy must be made to neutralize each other. Each element should be given its own house of the legislature, and over both houses there should be set a capable, strong, and impartial executive armed with the veto power. This split assembly would contain within itself an organic check and would be capable of self-control under the governance of the executive. The whole system was to be capped by an independent judiciary. The inevitable tendency of the rich and the poor to plunder each other would be kept in hand.

It is ironical that the Constitution, which Americans venerate so deeply, is based upon a political theory that at one crucial point stands in direct antithesis to the main stream of American democratic faith. Modern American folklore assumes that democracy and liberty are all but identical, and when democratic writers take the trouble to make the distinction, they usually assume that democracy is necessary to liberty. But the Founding Fathers thought that the liberty with which they were most concerned was menaced by democracy. In their minds liberty was linked not to democracy but to property.

What did the Fathers mean by liberty? What did Jay mean

---

*"Mr. Adams' book," wrote Benjamin Rush, often in the company of the delegates, "has diffused such excellent principles among us that there is little doubt of our adopting a vigorous and compounded Federal Legislature. Our illustrious Minister in this gift to his country has done us more service than if he had obtained alliances for us with all the nations of Europe."

when he spoke of "the charms of liberty"? Or Madison when he declared that to destroy liberty in order to destroy factions would be a remedy worse than the disease? Certainly the men who met at Philadelphia were not interested in extending liberty to those classes in America, the Negro slaves and the indentured servants, who were most in need of it, for slavery was recognized in the organic structure of the Constitution and indentured servitude was no concern of the Convention. Nor was the regard of the delegates for civil liberties any too tender. It was the opponents of the Constitution who were most active in demanding such vital liberties as freedom of religion, freedom of speech and press, jury trial, due process, and protection from "unreasonable searches and seizures." These guarantees had to be incorporated in the first ten amendments because the Convention neglected to put them in the original document. Turning to economic issues, it was not freedom of trade in the modern sense that the Fathers were striving for. Although they did not believe in impeding trade unnecessarily, they felt that failure to regulate it was one of the central weaknesses of the Articles of Confederation, and they stood closer to the mercantilists than to Adam Smith. Again, liberty to them did not mean free access to the nation's unappropriated wealth. At least fourteen of them were land speculators. They did not believe in the right of the squatter to occupy unused land, but rather in the right of the absentee owner or speculator to pre-empt it.

The liberties that the constitutionalists hoped to gain were chiefly negative. They wanted freedom from fiscal uncertainty and irregularities in the currency, from trade wars among the states, from economic discrimination by more powerful foreign governments, from attacks on the creditor class or on property, from popular insurrection. They aimed to create a government that would act as an honest broker among a variety of propertied interests, giving them all protection from their common enemies and preventing any one of them from becoming too powerful. The Convention was a fraternity of types of absentee ownership. All property should be permitted to have its proportionate voice in government. Individual property interests might have to be sacrificed at times, but only for the community of propertied interests. Freedom for property would result in liberty for men—perhaps not for all men, but at least for all worthy.

What encouraged the Fathers about their own era, however, was the broad dispersion of landed property. The small land-owning farmers had been troublesome in recent years, but there was a general conviction that under a properly made Constitution a *modus vivendi* could be worked out with them. The possession of moderate plots of property presumably gave them a sufficient stake in society to be safe and responsible citizens under the restraints of balanced government. Influence in government would be proportionate to property: merchants and great landholders would be dominant, but small property-owners would have an independent and far from negligible voice. It was "politic as well as just," said Madison, "that the interests and rights of every class should be duly represented and understood in the public councils," and John Adams declared that there could be "no free government without a democratical branch in the constitution."

The farming element already satisfied the property requirements for suffrage in most of the states, and the Fathers generally had no quarrel with their enfranchisement. But when they spoke of the necessity of founding government upon the consent of "the people," it was only these small property-holders that they had in mind. For example, the famous Virginia Bill of Rights, written by George Mason, explicitly defined those eligible for suffrage as all men "having sufficient evidence of permanent common interest with and attachment to the community"—which meant, in brief, sufficient property.

However, the original intention of the Fathers to admit the yeoman into an important but sharply limited partnership in affairs of state could not be perfectly realized. At the time the Constitution was made, Southern planters and Northern merchants were setting their differences aside in order to meet common dangers—from radicals within and more powerful nations without. After the Constitution was adopted, conflict between the ruling classes broke out anew, especially after powerful planters were offended by the favoritism of Hamilton's policies to Northern commercial interests. The planters turned to the farmers to form an agrarian alliance, and for more than half a century this powerful coalition embraced the bulk of the articulate interests of the country. As time went on, therefore, the main stream of American political conviction deviated more and more from the antidemocratic position of the Constitution-makers. Yet, curiously, their general satisfaction with the Constitution together with their growing nationalism made Americans deeply reverent of the founding generation, with the result that as it grew stronger, this deviation was increasingly overlooked.

There is common agreement among modern critics that the debates over the Constitution were carried on at an intellectual level that is rare in politics, and that the Constitution itself is one of the world's masterpieces of practical statecraft. On other grounds there has been controversy. At the very beginning contemporary opponents of the Constitution foresaw an apocalyptic destruction of local government and popular institutions, while conservative Europeans of the old regime thought the young American Republic was a dangerous leftist experiment. Modern critical scholarship, which reached a high point in Charles A. Beard's *An Economic Interpretation of the Constitution of the United States,* started a new turn in the debate. The antagonism, long latent, between the philosophy of the Constitution and the philosophy of American democracy again came into the open. Professor Beard's work appeared in 1913 at the peak of the Progressive era, when the muckraking fever was still high; some readers tended to conclude from his findings that the Fathers were selfish reactionaries who do not deserve their high place in American esteem. Still more recently, other writers, inverting this logic, have used Beard's facts to praise the Fathers for their opposition to "democracy" and as an argument for returning again to the idea of a "republic."

In fact, the Fathers' image of themselves as moderate republicans standing between political extremes was quite accurate. They were impelled by class motives more than pietistic writers like to admit, but they were also controlled, as Professor Beard himself has recently emphasized, by a statesmanlike sense of moderation and a scrupulously republican philosophy. Any attempt, however, to tear their ideas out of the eighteenth-century context is sure to make them seem starkly reactionary. Consider, for example, the favorite maxim of John Jay: "The people who own the country ought to govern it." To the Fathers this was simply a swift axiomatic statement of the stake-in-society theory of political rights, a moderate conservative position under eighteenth-century conditions of property distribution in America. Under modern property relations this maxim demands a drastic restriction of the base of political power. A large portion of the modern middle class—and it is the strength of this class upon which balanced government depends—is propertyless; and the urban proletariat, which the Fathers so greatly feared, is almost one half the population. Further, the separation of ownership from control that has come with the corporation deprives Jay's maxim of twentieth-century meaning even for many propertied people. The six hundred thousand stockholders of the American Telephone & Telegraph Company not only do not acquire political power by virtue of their stock-ownership, but they do not even acquire economic power: they cannot control their own company.

From a humanistic standpoint there is a serious dilemma in the philosophy of the Fathers, which derives from their conception of man. They thought man was a creature of rapacious self-interest, and yet they wanted him to be free—free, in essence, to contend, to engage in an umpired strife, to use property to get property. They accepted the mercantile image of life as an eternal battleground, and assumed the Hobbesian war of each against all; they did not propose to put an end to this war, but merely to stabilize it and make it less murderous. They had no hope and they offered none for any ultimate organic change in the way men conduct themselves. The result was that while they thought self-interest the most dangerous and unbrookable quality of man, they necessarily underwrote it in trying to control it. They succeeded in both respects: under the competitive capitalism of the nineteenth century America continued to be an arena for various grasping and contending interests, and the federal government continued to provide a stable and acceptable medium within which they could contend; further, it usually showed the wholesome bias on behalf of property which the Fathers expected. But no man who is as well abreast of modern science as the Fathers were of eighteenth-century science believes any longer in unchanging human nature. Modern humanistic thinkers who seek for a means by which society may transcend eternal conflict and rigid adherence to property rights as its integrating principles can expect no answer in the philosophy of balanced government as it was set down by the Constitution-makers of 1787.

THE CORPORATE RICH

C. WRIGHT MILLS

Sixty glittering, clannish families do not run the American economy, nor has there occurred any silent revolution of managers who have expropriated the powers and privileges of such families. The truth that is in both these characterizations is less adequately expressed as 'America's Sixty Families' or 'The Managerial Revolution,' than as the managerial reorganization of the propertied classes into the more or less unified stratum of the corporate rich.

As families and as individuals, the very rich are still very much a part of the higher economic life of America; so are the chief executives of the major corporations. What has happened, I believe, is the reorganization of the propertied class, along with those of higher salary, into a new corporate world of privilege and prerogative. What is significant about this managerial reorganization of the propertied class is that by means of it the narrow industrial and profit interests of specific firms and industries and families have been translated into the broader economic and political interests of a more genuinely class type. Now the corporate seats of the rich contain all the powers and privileges inherent in the institutions of private property.

The recent social history of American capitalism does not reveal any distinct break in the continuity of the higher capitalist class. There are, to be sure, accessions in each generation, and there is an unknown turnover rate; the proportions of given types of men differ from one epoch to the next. But over the last half a century, in the economy as in the political order, there has been a remarkable continuity of interests, vested in

From *The Power Elite* by C. Wright Mills. © 1956 by Oxford University Press. Reprinted by permission.

the types of higher economic men who guard and advance them. The main drift of the upper classes, composed of several consistent trends, points unambiguously to the continuation of a world that is quite congenial to the continuation of the corporate rich. For in this stratum are now anchored the ultimate powers of big property whether they rest legally upon ownership or upon managerial control.

The old-fashioned rich were simply the propertied classes, organized on a family basis and seated in a locality, usually a big city. The corporate rich, in addition to such people, include those whose high 'incomes' include the privileges and prerogatives that have come to be features of high executive position. The corporate rich thus includes members of the big-city rich of the metropolitan 400, of the national rich who possess the great American fortunes, as well as chief executives of the major corporations. The propertied class, in the age of corporate property, has become a corporate rich, and in becoming corporate has consolidated its power and drawn to its defense new men of more executive and more political stance. Its members have become self-conscious in terms of the corporate world they represent. As men of status they have secured their privileges and prerogatives in the most stable private institutions of American society. They are a corporate rich because they depend directly, as well as indirectly, for their money, their privileges, their securities, their advantages, their powers on the world of the big corporations. All the old-fashioned rich are now more or less of the corporate rich, and the newer types of privileged men are there with them. In fact, no one can become rich or stay rich in America today without becoming involved, in one way or another, in the world of the corporate rich.

1

During the 'forties and 'fifties, the national shape of the income distribution became less a pyramid with a flat base than a fat diamond with a bulging middle. Taking into account price changes and tax increases, proportionately more families in 1929 than in 1951 (from 65 to 46 per cent) received family incomes of less than $3,000; fewer then than now received between $3,000 and $7,500 (from 29 to 47 per cent); but about the same proportions (6 and 7 per cent) in both 1929 and 1951 received $7,500 or more.*

Many economic forces at work during the war, and the war-preparations boom that has followed it, have made some people on the very bottom levels rise into what used to be the middle-range income levels, and some of those who used to be in the middle-range of income levels became upper-middle or upper. The changed distribution of real income has thus affected the middle and lower levels of the population, with which, of course, we are not here directly concerned. Our interest is in the higher levels; and the forces at work on the income structure have not changed the decisive facts of the big money.

At the very top of the mid-century American economy, there are some 120 people who each year receive a million dollars or more. Just below them, another 379 people appropriate between a half a million and a million. Some 1,383 people get from $250,000 to $499,999. And below all these, there is the broader base of 11,490 people who receive from $100,000 to $249,999.

Altogether, then, in 1949, there were 13,822 people who de-

*This shift—which of course is even more decisive as between say 1936 and 1951—is generally due to several economic facts: (1) There has been rather full employment—which during the war and its aftermath brought virtually all who wanted to work into the income-receiving classes. (2) There has been a great doubling up of income within families. In 1951, less than 16 per cent of the families at each of the two extremes, under $2,000 and over $15,000, consisted of families in which the wife also worked; but in the income range of $3,000 to $9,999, the proportion of working wives increased progressively with family income from 16 to 38 per cent. (3) During the 'twenties and 'thirties, large proportions of the very poor were farmers, but now fewer people are farmers and for those on the farm a prosperity has been backed up by various kinds of government subsidy. (4) Union pressure—which since the late 'thirties has forced a constant increase in wages. (5) Welfare programs of the government coming out of the 'thirties have put a floor under incomes—by wage minimums, social security for aged, and pensions for the unemployed and disabled veterans. (6) Underneath the whole prosperity of the 'forties and 'fifites, of course, is the structural fact of the war economy.

clared incomes of $100,000 or more to the tax collector. Let us draw the line of the openly declared corporate rich at that level: $100,000 a year and up. It is not an entirely arbitrary figure. For there is one fact about the fat diamond that remains true regardless of how many people are on each of its levels: on the middle and higher levels especially, the greater the yearly income, the greater the proportion of it from property, and the smaller the proportion from salaries, entrepreneurial withdrawal, or wages. The rich of the higher incomes, in short, are still of the propertied class. The lower incomes derive from wages.*

One hundred thousand dollars a year is the income level on which property enters the income picture in a major way: two-thirds (67 per cent) of the money received by the 13,702 people in the declared $100,000 and up to $999,999 bracket comes from property—from dividends, capital gains, estates, and trusts. The remaining one-third is split between chief executives and top entrepreneurs.

The higher you go up into these upper reaches, the more does property count, and the less does income for services performed. Thus 94 per cent of the money of the 120 people receiving a million dollars or more in 1949 came from property, 5 per cent from entrepreneurial profits, 1 per cent from salaries. Among these 120 people, there was considerable variation in the type of property from which their money came. But, regardless of the legal arrangements involved, those with big incomes receive it overwhelmingly from corporate property. That is the first reason that all the rich are now corporate rich, and that is the key economic difference between the rich and the more than 99 per cent of the population who are well below the $100,000 income level.

*Some 86 per cent of the money received by people paying taxes on less than $10,000 in 1949 came from *salaries and wages;* 9 per cent, from business or partnership profits; only 5 per cent from property owned.
As a proportion of money received, *entrepreneurial withdrawals* bulk largest among those receiving from $10,000 to $99,999 per year—34 per cent of the income gotten by people on this income level is business profits; 41 per cent, salaries and wages; and 23 per cent from property. (Two per cent is 'miscellaneous income,' annuities or pensions.)

In these tax-declared high-income classes, people come and go; every year the exact number of people varies. In 1929, when taxes were not so high as to make it so dangerous as now to declare high incomes, there were about 1,000 more such declarations than in 1949—a total of 14,816 declared incomes of $100,000 or more. In 1948 there were 16,280; in 1939 only 2,921. But on the highest levels there remains throughout the years a hard core of the very wealthy. Four-fifths of the 75 people who appropriated one million dollars or more in 1924, for example, got one million or more in at least one other year between 1917 and 1936. The chances are good that those who make it in one year will make it in another year or two.* Farther down the pyramid, only 3 or 4 per cent of the population during the decade after World War II have held as much as $10,000 in liquid assets.

2

Since virtually all statistics of income are based on declarations to tax collectors, they do not fully reveal the 'income' differences between the corporate rich and other Americans. In fact, one

*Such figures are, of course, only crude indications of the meaning of the big money, as they do not take into account the element of inflation. The number of corporate rich for any given year, as well as the number of million-dollar incomes, is related to the tax rate and to the profit level of the corporate world. Periods of low taxes and high profits are periods in which the declared million-dollar incomes flourish: in the ideal year of 1929, 513 people, estates, or trusts, told the government they had received incomes of one million or more. The average of these million-dollar incomes was $2.36 million, and after taxes the average million-dollar man had 1.99 million left. In the slump year of 1932, there were still 20 people who reported incomes of one million or more; by 1939, when three-fourths of all the families in the United States had incomes of less than $2,000 a year, there was 45 such million-dollar incomes reported. With the war, however, the number of million-dollar incomes increased as did the general level of income. In 1949 when both profits and taxes were high, the average income of the 120 people who told the government they had received one million or more was 2.13 million; after taxes they were left with $910,000. In 1919, however, when taxes and profits were high although profits were falling a bit, only 65 people earned one million or more, averaging 2.3 million before taxes, but only $825,000 after taxes.

major difference has to do with privileges that are deliberately created for the exclusion of 'income' from tax records. These privileges are so pervasive that we find it hard to take seriously the great publicity given to the 'income revolution,' which is said to have taken place over the last twenty years. A change, as we have just reported, has taken place in the total income distribution of the United States; but we do not find it very convincing to judge from declared income tax records that the share the rich receive of all the wealth in the country has decreased.

Tax rates being high, the corporate rich are quite nimble in figuring out ways to get income, or the things and experiences that income provides, in such a way as to escape taxation. The manner in which the corporate rich pay their taxes is more flexible and provides more opportunities for shrewd interpretations of the law than is true for the middle and lower classes. People of higher income figure their own tax deductions, or more usually have them figured by the experts they hire. Perhaps those whose income derives from property or from entrepreneurial and professional practice are as honest—or as dishonest—as poorer people on wages and salary, but they are also economically bolder, they have greater opportunities and greater skill, and, even more importantly, they have access to the very best skills available for such matters: accomplished lawyers and skillful accountants who specialize in taxation as a science and a game. In the nature of the case, it would be impossible to prove with exactitude, but it is difficult not to believe that as a general rule the higher the income and the more varied its sources, the greater the likelihood of the shrewd tax return. Much declared money is tricked, legally and illegally, from the tax collector; much illegal money is simply not declared.

Perhaps the most important tax loophole in retaining current income is the long-term capital gain. When a military man writes a best-seller or has it written fro him, when a businessman sells his farm or a dozen pigs, when an executive sells his stock—the profit received is not considered as income but as capital gain, which means that the profit to the individual after taxes is approximately twice what it would have been if that same amount of money had been received as a salary or a dividend. Individuals claiming long-term capital gains pay taxes on only 50 per cent of that gain. The half that is taxed is taxed at a progressive rate applicable to a person's total income; but the maximum tax on such gains is 52 per cent. This means that at no time can the tax paid on these capital gains be more than 26 per cent of the total gain received; and it will be smaller if the total income, including the gain, leaves the individual in a lower income tax bracket. But when the flow of money is turned around the other way, a capital *loss* of over $1,000 (those under $1,000 may be deducted from ordinary income) can be spread backward or forward in a five-year span to offset capital gains.

Aside from capital gains, the most profitable tax loophole is perhaps the 'depletion allowance' on oil and gas wells and mineral deposits. From 5 to 27% per cent of the gross income received on an oil well, but not exceeding 50 per cent of the net income from the property, is tax-free each year. Moreover, all the costs of drilling and developing an oil well can be deducted as they occur—instead of being capitalized and depreciated over the years of the well's productive life. The important point of privilege has less to do with the percentage allowed than with the continuation of the device long after the property is fully depreciated.

Those with enough money to play around may also off-set taxes by placing money in tax-free municipal bonds; they may split their income among various family members so that the taxes paid are at a lower rate than the combined income would have required. The rich cannot give away to friends or relatives more than a life-time total of $30,000 plus $3,000 each year without paying a gift tax; although, in the name of both husband and wife, a couple can give twice that amount. The rich man can also make a tax-deductible gift (up to 20 per cent of yearly income that is given to recognized charities is not taxed as income) that will provide him security for the rest of his life. He can donate to a named charity the principal of a fund, but continue to receive the income from it.* He thus makes an

*For example, a man can give $10,000 worth of stock to a theological seminary, which—because of tax savings—actually costs him only $4,268.49. In ten years,

immediate deduction on his income tax return; and he cuts that part of his estate that is subject to inheritance taxes.

There are other techniques that help the rich preserve their money after they are dead in spite of high estate taxes. For example, it is possible to set up a trust for a grandchild, and stipulate that the *child* receive the income from the trust as long as he is alive, although the property legally belongs to the grandchild. It is only at the death of the child (instead of both the original owner *and* the child) that an estate tax is paid.

A family trust saves taxes—both current income tax and estate tax levied upon death—for income of the trust fund is taxed separately. In addition, the trust provides the property holder with continuous professional management, eliminates the worries of responsibility, keeps the property intact in one manageable sum, builds the strongest possible legal safeguards to property, and, in effect, enables the owner to continue to control his property after he is dead.*

There are many kinds of trusts, and the law is rather complicated and strict in their application; but in one type of short-term trust 'what you do is Indian-give ownership of property to a trustee—and actually give away its income—for some set period (of more than 10 years). Then if the trust meets all other requirements, you're clear of tax on that income.'

---

let us assume, the stock increases in market value to $16,369.49, and the man receives $6,629 in income payments which is 50 per cent more than the cost of his gift. When the man dies, of course, the seminary will own the stock and receive its earnings.

*'Take the case of a married man,' a magazine for executives carefully explains, 'who has a taxable income of $30,000, including a $1,000 return on a $25,000 investment. After taxes, that $1,000 of income is worth only $450. Accumulating it each year for 10 years at compound interest of 4 per cent would produce, at the most, a fund of about $5,650 for his family. But suppose the man transfers the $25,000 investment to a short-term trust. If the arrangements meets certain requirements, the trust will pay a tax of about $200 on each $1,000 of income, leaving $800. in 10 years, that could build up to about $9,600—a gain of 70 per cent over what could have been accumulated without a trust . . . [This is not allowed in all states.] At the termination of the trust, the man would get back his $25,000, plus unrealized appreciation. The accumulated income would go to the trust beneficiary, someone within his family in a light tax status.'

Twenty-five years ago, there were no more than 250 foundations in the entire United States; today there are thousands. Generally, a foundation is defined as 'any autonomous, non-profit legal entity that is set up to "serve the welfare of mankind." It administers wealth that is transferred to it through tax-free gifts or bequests.' Actually, the setting up of foundations has often become a convenient way of avoiding taxes, 'operating as private banks for their donors; not infrequently, the "mankind" they have served turned out to be a few indigent relatives.' The Revenue Act of 1950 tried 'to plug up some of the bigger loopholes' but 'dubious foundations still have an advantage—the tax collector has a hard time getting information about them . . . revenue men complain they haven't time or manpower to check more than a tiny fraction of the reports already filed by foundations. They have to steer largely by instinct in deciding which ones to investigate,' and even the 1950 law does not require that all pertinent data concerning them be furnished to the government.

In recent years, more businesses have been creating foundations, thus making a bid for local and national good will, while encouraging research in their own industries. The corporation so engaged does not have to pay taxes on the 5 per cent of its profits that it yearly gives to its foundation. Very rich families also can keep control of their business after a death in the family by giving large shares of the company stock to a foundation (Ford is unusual in this respect only in the magnitude of the sums involved). The size of the inheritance tax, which might otherwise force a sale of stock to outsiders in order to pay the taxes, is reduced. 'If a man's chief concern is to raise a tax-free umbrella over part of his income and to give some jobs to needy retainers,' an alert business magazine advises its executive readers, 'he should by all means set up his own foundation, no matter how small. Then he may even prefer to have the overhead eat up all the income.'

For virtually every law taxing big money, there is a way those with big money can avoid it or minimize it. But such legal and illegal maneuvers are only part of the income privileges of the corporate rich: working hand-in-hand with the rules and regulations of the government, the corporations find ways directly to supplement the income of the executive rich. These various forms of feathering the nest now make it possible for executive members of the corporate rich to live richly on seemingly moderate incomes, while paying taxes lower than the law seemingly intends as fair and just. Among such privileged arrangements are following:

Under the deferred pay contract, the corporation signs up for a given salary for a number of years, and further agrees to pay an annual retainer after retirement as long as the executive doesn't go to work for any competing firm. The executive's loyalty is thus linked to the company, and he is able to spread his income into the years when lower earnings will result in reduced taxes. One Chrysler executive, for example, recently signed a contract yielding him $300,000 a year for the next five years, then $75,000 a year for the rest of his life. A recently retired Chairman of U.S. Steel's Board, who was receiving a $211,000 salary, now gets $14,000 a year as his pension, plus $55,000 a year in 'deferred pay.'

The classic case of deferred payment is perhaps the one worked out for a famous entertainer, who was in a position to demand $500,000 a year for 3 years. 'Instead, he arranged to take $50,000 a year for the next 30 years. No one seriously expects him to be active in show business when he is approaching 80, but by spreading out his income and keeping it in lower tax brackets he was able to cut the total income tax he will have to pay by nearly $600,000, according to one estimate. Such fabulous arrangements are not limited to the world of show business, even though there they may be more publicized: Even the most respected and staid companies are now in many instances taking care of their key people by such means.

Executives are given restricted options to buy stock at or below current market value. This keeps the executive with the company; for he is able to pick up the option only after a specified period of time such as a year, or he may only be able to use it to buy limited quantities of stock over a longer period of time—say five years. To the executive as riskless entrepreneur, at the time he picks up his option, there comes an immediate profit (the difference between the option price previously set and the market value of the stock at the time when he buys it). Most of the profit he makes if he later sells the stock is not considered taxable income by an obliging government: it is taxed at the lower capital gains rate. Nothing prevents him from borrowing money to pick up his option, and then selling the stock in six months at the higher market value. For example, in 1954, the president of an aircraft company was given—in salary, bonus, and pension credits—about $150,000, but after taxes he took home only about $75,000. However, if he wished to sell the 10,000 shares of stock he had bought on his company's option plan several months before, he could, after paying all taxes due, have also taken home $594,375. About one out of six companies listed on the New York Stock Exchange gave stock options to executives within a year or so after the 1950 tax law made them attractive as capital gains. Since then, the practice has spread.

3

The corporate rich are a propertied rich, but big property is not all that they possess; the corporate rich are able to accumulate and to retain high incomes, but high incomes are not all they accumulate for keeps. In addition to big property and high income, they enjoy the corporate privileges that are part of the newer status system of the incorporated economy of the United States. These status privileges of the corporate rich are now standard practices, essential, even though shifting, features of business-as-usual, part of the going pay-off for success. Criticism of them does not arouse indignation on the part of anyone in a position voluntarily to do anything about them, and much less about the corporate system in which they are firmly anchored.

None of these privileges are revealed by examination of the yearly income or the property holding. They are, one might say, fringe benefits of the higher circles. The 'fringe benefits' which lower salaried and wage earners have been given—primarily private pension and welfare plans, social security and unemployment insurance—have risen from 1.1 per cent of the national payroll in 1929 to 5.9 per cent in 1953. It is not possible to calculate with suitable precision the 'fringe benefits' taken by the riskless entrepreneurs of the big corporations, but it is now certain that they have become quite central to the higher emoluments. It is because of them that the corporate rich may be considered, in a decisive way, to be members of a directly privileged class. The corporations from which their property and incomes derive are also the seats of the privileges and prerogatives. The great variety of these privileges substantially increases their standard of consumption, buttresses their financial position against the ups and downs of the economic system, lends shape to their whole style of living, and lifts them into a security as great as that of the corporate economy itself. Designed to increase the wealth and the security of the rich in a manner that avoids the payment of taxes, they also strengthen their loyalties to the corporations.

Among the accoutrements that often go with the big executive job but are never reported to tax collectors are such fringe benefits as these: free medical care, payments of club fees, company lawyers and accountants available for tax, financial and legal advice, facilities for entertaining customers, private recreation areas—golf courses, swimming pools, gymnasiums—scholarship funds for children of executives, company automobiles, and dining rooms for executive use. By 1955, some 37 per cent of all the Cadillac registrations in Manhattan, and 20 per cent in Philadelphia, were in company names. 'A company dedicated to keeping its officers happy, one reliable observer recently noted, 'can with all propriety have a company airplane for business trips and a yacht and a hunting-fishing lodge in the north woods to entertain its biggest customers.'* It can also arrange to hold its conventions in Miami in midwinter. The effect, as far as company executives go, is to provide wonderful travel and vacation facilities without cost. The company officers go south in the winter and north by summer; take along enough

---

*Businessmen now fly nearly four million hours a year in private planes—more than all scheduled, commercial airlines put together.

work or enough customers to justify the trip, and proceed to have a very pleasant time of it . . . At home the executives can also ride around in company-owned and chauffeured automobiles. Naturally the company is happy to pay their dues at the best available country club, for the purposes of entertaining customers on the golf course, and at the best town club, for intimate lunches and dinners.' You name it and you can find it. And it is increasing: it is free to the executive, and deductible as an ordinary business expense by the corporation.

These higher emoluments may also extend to lavish gifts of wonderful toys for adults, like automobiles and fur coats, and conveniences like deep freezes for the purchasing agents and business contacts not directly employed by the company. All this has been widely publicized and decried in the political field,* but, as any business executive of stature well knows, such gifts of business friendship are standard practice within and especially between big firms.

Back in 1910, for example, White Sulphur Springs in the hills of West Virginia was on the same social circuit as Bar Harbor and Newport. In 1954, the Chesapeake and Ohio Railroad, which owns the Greenbrier resort hotel in White Sulphur Springs, invited as guests top level executives who are, in fact or potentially, important shippers and who feel honored to be invited. In 1948, the C & O paid for everything, but the response was so great from the business, social, and political celebrities who accepted the invitation that they now come on their own expense accounts. The resort operates year-round but the Spring Festival is the big social-business event.

In Florida, there is now being constructed an entire resort

*For example: 'Over the past two years more than 300 Congressmen have taken trips abroad at a cost to the U.S. taxpayer estimated unofficially at over $3,500,000. Many of the junkets were unquestionably useful and legitimate fact-finding tours and inspections. Others unquestionably represented some fancy free-loading. Last week the House of Representatives Rules Committee served notice that the lid was on junkets. 'The Committee, which must approve all investigating authority, said it planned to approve free foreign travel only for members of the Foreign Affairs, Armed Services, and Insular Affairs Committees. Around Congress the gag last week,' *The New York Times* concluded, 'was that it would be tough to muster the usual quorum in Paris this summer.'

town, with an average population of 3,000, which will be rented to executives and their guests on a year-round basis. The companies involved can either sublet it to their employees or write off the cost as a business-expense deduction during the times it is used for entertaining customers, holding conventions or important conferences.

The Continental Motors Corporation operates duck-hunting expeditions at Lost Island, Arkansas. Assuming that the golf, cocktail, dinner, and night club routine is 'old-hat' to any executive by the time he is big enough to be an important customer, Continental set up a 'customer relations program' which has been going some fifteen years. Such 'lodge-type' selling retreats are concentrated in the primary goods industries, where the big sales are made, president to president, rather than in consumer goods. Everyone on the hunt is 'a president or a vice-president, or maybe a general or an admiral.' In the same vicinity, at least three other corporations also operate exclusive duck-hunting clubs. Top employees as well as clients are usually among the guests at such duck, deer, and trout facilities.

More widely recognized, but still not seriously studied is the wide-ranging and far-reaching fact of the expense account. No one knows, and there is no way to find out for sure, just how much of high living and exciting entertainment is made possible for the new privileged classes solely because of the expense account. 'The vice-president of one firm,' economist Richard A. Girard recently reported, 'is assigned a flat $20,000 each year to cover any entertaining he may decide to do. His contract specifies that he does not have to account for the money. 'Tax officials play a continual game with members of the corporate rich over expense-account deductions but generally insist that each case is unique—which means there are no set rules and the revenue agent has wide responsibility.

'Theatre people estimated that thirty to forty per cent of the New York theatre audience is an expense-account audience, and that this is the percentage between life and death.' Moreover, 'in cities like New York, Washington and Chicago,' one investigator feels it 'safe to say that at any given moment well over half of all the people in the best hotels, the best nightclubs and the best restaurants are charging the bill as an expense account item to their companies, which in turn are charging it to the government in the form of tax deductions'—and goes on to assert what is well known: 'There is something about an expense account that brings out the latent rascality, rapacity and mendacity in even the otherwise most honorable man. Expense account forms have long been known affectionately by their fond possessors as "swindle sheets." Filling out an expense account itemization has been regarded as a kind of contest of wits with the company auditor, in which it is perfectly justifiable to use the most outrageous half-truths, little white lies and outright fantasies, anything at all which the auditor, regardless of how outraged he might be, cannot absolutely prove to be false.'

We have by no means reported all of the privileges of the corporate rich, confining ourselves mainly to legally and officially sanctioned types. Many of the new privileges—especially the higher emoluments—have long been known and are quite accepted by heads of state and by higher officials of public office. The governor is given 'the governor's mansion' in which to live rent free; the president, with $50,000 a year tax-free expenses, also has his White House, which contains his serviced living quarters as well as offices of administration. But what has happened, as the corporation has become the anchor point for the privileges that go with great wealth, is that such higher emoluments have become normal among the private rich as they have become transformed into the corporate rich. When, in their happier moods, corporation executives speak lovingly of their corporations as One Big Family, one can understand that in a very real sense they are asserting a sociological truth about the class structure of American society. For the powers and privileges of property, shared among the corporate rich, are now collective, and the individual has such privileges most securely only in so far as he is part of the corporate world.

4

America has *not* become a country where individual pleasures and powers are bounded by small incomes and high taxes. There are incomes high enough to remain high despite the taxes and there are many ways of escaping and minimizing taxes. There is maintained in America, and there is being created and maintained every year, a stratum of the corporate rich, many of whose members possess far more money than they can personally spend with any convenience. For many of them, the prices of things are simply irrelevant. They never have to look at the right hand column of a menu; they never have to take orders from anybody, they never have to do really disagreeable things except as a self-imposed task; they never have to face alternatives hedged in by considerations of cost. They never *have* to do anything. They are, according to all appearances, free.

But are they really free?

The answer is Yes, within the terms of their society, they are really free.

But does not the possession of money somehow limit them?

The answer is No, it does not.

But are not those just the hurried answers, are there not more considered, deeper-going answers?

What kind of deeper-going answers? And what does freedom mean? Whatever else it may mean, freedom means that you have the power to do what you want to do, when you want to do it, and how you want to do it. And in American society the power to do what you want, when you want, how you want, requires money. Money provides power and power provides freedom.

But are there no limits on all this?

Of course there are limits to the power of money, and the freedoms based on that power. And there are also psychological traps for the rich, as among misers and spendthrifts on all levels, which distort their capacity for freedom.

The miser enjoys the possession of money as such. The spendthrift enjoys the spending of money as such. Neither—in the pure type—can look upon money as a means to free and various ends of life, whatever they may be. The miser's pleasure is in the potentiality of his spending power, so he draws back from the actual spending. He is a tense man, afriad of losing the potentiality and so never realizing it. His security and his power are embodied in his hoard, and in fearing to lose it, he fears loss of his very self. He is not merely a stingy man, nor necessarily a merely avaricious man. He is an impotent voyeur of the economic system, one for whom the possession of money for its own sake, and not as a means to any further end, has become the end of life. He cannot complete the economic act. And money, which to most economic men is a means, becomes to the miser a despotic end.

The spendthrift, on the other hand, is a man for whom the act of spending is itself a source of pleasure. He does not feel happy on a spending spree because of his expected ease or pleasure from the goods acquired. The act of senseless spending is in itself his pleasure and reward. And in this act the spendthrift advertises his unconcern with mere money. He consumes conspicuously to show that he is above pecuniary considerations, thus revealing how highly he values them.

No doubt both of these oddities of the money system are available among the American rich today, but they are not typical. For most members of the corporate rich money remains a gratifying medium of exchange—a pure and unadulterated means to an enormous variety of concrete ends. For most of them, money is valued for what it will purchase in comfort and fun, status and alcoholism, security and power and experience, freedom and boredom.

On the bottom level of the money system one never has enough money, which is the key link in the hand-to-mouth way of existence. One is, in a sense, below the money system—never having enough money to be firmly a part of it.

On the middle levels, the money system often seems an endless treadmill. One never gets enough; $8,000 this year seems to place one in no better straits than did $6,000 the last. There are suspicions among people on such levels, that were they to make $15,000, they would still be on the treadmill, trapped in the money system.

But above a certain point in the scale of wealth, there is a qualitative break: the rich come to know that they have so much that they simply do not have to think about money at all: it is only they who have truly won the money game; they are above the struggle. It is not too much to say that in a pecuniary society, only then are men in a position to be free. Acquisition as a form of experience and all that it demands no longer need to be a chain. They can be above the money system, above the scramble on the treadmill: for them it is no longer true that the more they have, the harder it seems to make ends meet. That is the way we define the rich as personal consumers.

For the very poor, the ends of necessity never meet. For the middle classes there are always new ends, if not of necessity, of status. For the very rich, the ends have never been separated, and within the limits of the common human species, they are today as free as any Americans.

The idea that the millionaire finds nothing but a sad, empty place at the top of this society; the idea that the rich do not know what to do with their money; the idea that the successful become filled up with futility, and that those born successful are poor and little as well as rich—the idea, in short, of the disconsolateness of the rich—is, in the main, merely a way by which those who are not rich reconcile themselves to the fact. Wealth in America is directly gratifying and directly leads to many further gratifications.

To be truly rich is to possess the means of realizing in big ways one's little whims and fantasies and sicknesses. 'Wealth has great privileges,' Balzac once remarked, 'and the most enviable of them all is the power of carrying out thoughts and feelings to the uttermost; of quickening sensibility by fulfilling its myriad caprices.' The rich, like other men, are perhaps more simply human than otherwise. But their toys are bigger; they have more of them; they have more of them all at once.*

*One of the propositions with which Howard Hughes has been associated was the purchase of RKO from Floyd Odlum for almost nine million dollars. 'I needed it like I needed small pox!' When asked to account for this move, Hughes seriously answers, '. . . the only reason I bought RKO from Floyd Odlum was because I enjoyed the many flights down to his ranch in Indio [California] while we discussed the details of the purchase.'

As for the happiness of the rich, that is a matter that can be neither proved nor disproved. Still, we must remember that the American rich are the winners within a society in which money and money-values are the supreme stakes. If the rich are not happy it is because none of us are happy. Moreover, to believe that they are unhappy would probably be un-American. For if they are not happy, then the very terms of success in America, the very aspirations of all sound men, lead to ashes rather than fruit.

Even if everyone in America, being human, were miserable, that would be not reason to believe that the rich were *more* miserable. And if everyone is happy, surely that is no reason to believe that the rich are excluded from the general American bliss. If those who win the game for which the entire society seems designed are not 'happy,' are then those who lose the happy ones? Must we believe that only those who live within, but not of, the American society can be happy? Were it calamitous to lose, and horrible to win, then the game of success would indeed be a sad game, doubly so in that it is a game everyone in and of the American culture cannot avoid playing. For to withdraw is of course objectively to lose, and to lose objectively, although subjectively to believe one has not lost— that borders on insanity. We simply must believe that the American rich are happy, else our confidence in the whole endeavor might be shaken. For of all the possible values of human society, one and one only is truly sovereign, truly universal, truly sound, truly and completely acceptable goal of man in America. That goal is money, and let there be no sour grapes about it from the losers.

'He is king . . .' one of Balzac's characters proclaims, 'he can do what he chooses; he is above everything, as all rich men are. To him, henceforth, the expression: "All Frenchmen are equal before the law," is the lie inscribed at the head of a charter. He will not obey the laws, the laws will obey him. There is no scaffold, no headsman, for millionaires!'

'Yes, there is,' replied Raphael, 'they are their own headsmen!'

'Another prejudice,' cried the banker.

5

The newer privileges of the corporate rich have to do with the power of money in the sphere of consumption and personal experience. But the power of money, the prerogatives of economic position, the social and political weight of corporate property, is by no means limited to the sphere of accumulation and consumption, corporate or personal. In fact, from the standpoint of the American elite, of which the corporate rich are only one segment, the power over consumer goods is not nearly so important as the institutional powers of wealth.

I. The Constitution is the sovereign political contract of the United States. By its fourteenth amendment it gives due legal sanction to the corporations, now the seat of the corporate rich, managed by the executives among them. Within the political framework of the nation, this corporate elite constitutes a set of governing groups, a hierarchy developed and run from the economic top down. The chief executives are now at the head of the corporate world, which in turn is a world of economic sovereignty within the nation's politically sovereign area. In them is vested the economic initiative, and they know it and they feel it to be their prerogative. As chiefs of the industrial manorialism, they have looked reluctantly to the federal government's social responsibility for the welfare of the underlying population. They view workers and distributors and suppliers of their corporate systems as subordinate members of their world, and they view themselves as individuals of the American individualistic sort who have reached the top.

They run the privately incorporated economy. It cannot be said that the government has interfered much during the last decade, for in virtually every case of regulation that we examine the regulating agency has tended to become a corporate outpost. To control the productive facilities is to control not only things but the men who, not owning property, are drawn to it in order to work. It is to constrain and to manage their life at work in the factory, on the railroad, in the office. It is to determine the shape of the labor market, or to fight over that shape with union or government. It is to make decisions in the name of the enterprise as to how much to produce of what and when and how to produce it and how much to charge for it.

II. Money allows the economic power of its possessor to be translated directly into political party causes. In the eighteen-nineties, Mark Hanna raised money from among the rich for political use out of the fright caused by William Jennings Bryan and the Populist 'nightmare'; and many of the very rich have been unofficial advisers to politicians. Mellons, Pews, and du Ponts have long been campaign contributors of note, and, in the post-World War II period, the Texas millionaires have contributed sizable amounts of money in campaigns across the nation. They have helped McCarthy in Wisconsin, Jenner in Indiana, Butler and Beall in Maryland. In 1952, for example, one oil tycoon (Hugh Roy Cullen) made thirty-one contributions of from $500 to $5,000 each (totaling at least $53,000), and his two sons-in-law helped out (at least $19,750 more) ten Congressional candidates. It is said that the Texas multimillionaires now use their money in the politics of at least thirty states. Murchison has contributed to political candidates outside Texas since 1938, although he got no publicity until 1950, when he and his wife, at Joseph McCarthy's request, contributed $10,000 to defeat Senator Tydings of Maryland, and in 1952 sent money to beat McCarthy's Connecticut foe, Senator William Benton.

In 1952, 'the six top Republican and Democratic political committees received 55 per cent of their total receipts [this includes only those receipts of groups that spent money in two or more states] in 2,407 contributions of $1,000 or more.'* Such figures are absolute minimums since many contributions can be made by family members of different names, not easily recognized by the reporters.

*Heading the list of contributions to the Republican party were the Rockefellers ($94,000), the du Ponts ($74,175), the Pews ($65,100), the Mellons ($54,000), the Weirs ($21,000), the Whitneys ($19,000), the Vanderbilts ($19,000), the Goelets ($16,800) the Milbanks ($16,500) and Henry R. Luce ($13,000). Heading the list of contributions to the Democratic party were the Wade Thompsons of Nashville ($22,000), the Kennedys ($20,000), Albert M. Greenfield of Philadelphia ($16,000), Matthew H. McCloskey of Pennsylvania ($10,000), and the Marshall Fields ($10,000).

III. But it is not so much by direct campaign contributions that the wealthy exert political power. And it is not so much the very rich as the corporate executives—the corporate reorganizers of the big propertied class—who have translated the power of property into political use. As the corporate world has become more intricately involved in the political order, these executives have become intimately associated with the politicians, and especially with the key 'politicians' who form the political directorate of the United States government.

The nineteenth-century economic man, we are accustomed to believe, was a shrewd 'specialist' in bargaining and haggling. But the growth of the great corporation and the increased intervention of government into the economic realm have selected and formed and privileged economic men who are less hagglers and bargainers on any market than professional executives and adroit economic politicians. For today the successful economic man, either as propertied manager or manager of property, must influence or control those positions in the state in which decisions of consequence to his corporate activities are made. This trend in economic men is, of course, facilitated by war, which thus creates the need to continue corporate activities with political as well as the economic means. War is of course the health of the corporate economy; during war the political economy tends to become more unified, and moreover, political legitimations of the most unquestionable sort—national security itself—are gained for corporate economic activities.

'Before World War I, businessmen fought each other; after the war they combined to present a united front against consumers.' During World War II they served on innumerable advisory committees in the prosecution of the war. They were also brought into the military apparatus more permanently by the awarding to many businessmen of commissions in the reserve officer corps.* All this has been going on for a long time and

*A survey of the backgrounds of dollar-a-year men in Washington during World War II shows that what industry loaned the government was, except for a very few men, its financial experts, not men experienced in production: '. . . the salesmen and purchasing agents in WPB are under Ferdinand Eberstadt, former Wall Street investment banker. The alibi that these men have special qualifications for their jobs took a terrific beating when WPB within the past month

is rather well known, but in the Eisenhower administration the corporate executives publicly assumed the key posts of the executive branch of the government. Where before the more silent power and the ample contract was there, now there was also the loud voice.

Is there need for very subtle analysis of such matters when the Secretary of the Interior, Douglas McKay, blurted out to his friends in the Chamber of Commerce, on 29 April 1953, 'We're here in the saddle as an Administration representing business and industry? 'Or when Secretary of Defense Wilson asserted the identity of interests between the United States of America and the General Motors Corporation? Such incidents may be political blunders—or would be, were there an opposition party—but are they not as well revelations of deeply held convictions and intentions?

There are executives who are as afraid of such political identification as 'non-partisan' labor leaders are of third parties. For a long time the corporate rich had been in training as an opposition group; the brighter ones then came to feel vaguely that they might be on the spot. Before Eisenhower, such power as they wielded could more easily be politically irresponsible. After Eisenhower that is not so easy. If things go wrong, will not they—and with them business—be blamed?

But John Knox Jessup, chairman of the editorial board of *Fortune,* feels that the corporation can supplant the archaic system of states as a framework for self-government—and thus fill the vacuum of the middle levels of power. For, as chief of the corporate commonwealth, the manager has the political job of keeping all his constituents reasonably happy. Mr. Jessup argues that the balances of economic and political domains

---

found it necessary to put . . . through a special training course to teach them the fundamentals of industrial production . . . And that brings us to the dollar-a-year men who padded WPB's payrolls with their companies' salesmen and purchasing agents. The dollar-a-year boys were supposed to be industry's loan of its top-management experts and financial experts to the government to help run a winning war. Now top management in industry is made up of two types of men . . . production experts and financial experts . . . Its production experts industry kept for its own business.'

have already broken down: 'Any President who wants to run a prosperous country depends on the corporation at least as much as—probably more than—the corporation depends on him. His dependence is not unlike that of King John on the landed barons of Runnymede, where Magna Carta was born.'

In general, however, the ideology of the executives, as members of the corporate rich, is conservatism without any ideology. They are conservative, if for no other reason than that they feel themselves to be a sort of fraternity of the successful. They are without ideology because they feel themselves to be 'practical' men. They do not think up problems; they respond to alternatives presented to them, and such ideology as they have must be inferred from such responses as they make.

During the last three decades, since the First World War in fact, the distinction between the political and the economic man has been diminishing; although the corporation managers have, in the past, distrusted one of their own who stays too long in the political arena. They like to come and go, for then they are not responsible. Yet more and more of the corporate executives have entered government directly; and the result has been a virtually new political economy at the apex of which we find those who represent the corporate rich.

REFERENCES

Baran, Paul, and Sweezy, Paul. *Monopoly Capital.* New York: Monthly Review Press, 1966.

Beard, Charles A. *The Economic Basis of Politics.* New York: Random House, 1957.

Beard, Charles A. *An Economic Interpretation of the Constitution of the United States.* New York: Macmillan, 1935.

Domhoff, G. William. *Who Rules America?* Englewood Cliffs, N.J.: Prentice-Hall, 1968.

Domhoff, G. William. *The Higher Circles: The Governing Class in America.* New York: Random House, 1970.

Domhoff, G. William, and Ballard, Hoyt. *The Power Elite and Its Critics.* Boston: Beacon Press, 1968.

Dowd, Douglas. *Thorstein Veblen.* New York: Washington Square Press, 1966.

Josephson, Mathew. *The Robber Barons.* New York: Harcourt Brace, 1962.

Lange, Oskar. *Political Economy.* Vol. 1. New York: Pergamon Press, 1965.

Lundberg, Ferdinand. *America's Sixty Families.* New York: The Vanguard Press, 1938.

Lundberg, Ferdinand. *The Rich and the Super-Rich.* New York: Lyle Stuart, 1969; New York: Bantam Books, 1970.

Lynd, Staughton. *Class Conflict, Slavery, and the U.S. Constitution.* Indianapolis: Bobbs-Merrill, 1967.

Mandel, Ernest. *Marxist Economic Theory.* 2 vols. New York: Monthly Review Press, 1969.

Miliband, Ralph. *The State in Capitalist Society.* New York: Basic Books, 1969.

Myers, Gustavus. *History of the Great American Fortunes.* New York: Modern Library.

Zeitlin, Irving. *Marxism: A Re-Examination.* New York: Van Nostrand Reinhold, 1967.

2/Society
and Empire

"Imperialism" according to Webster, is "the policy, practice or advocacy of extending the power and domination of a nation especially by direct territorial acquisitions or by gaining indirect control over the political or economic life of other areas." It seems like a simple enough concept, and a glance at today's papers will show its central role in contemporary economic social and political developments. Yet academic sociology (indeed, academic social science generally) refuses to recognize the existence, let alone the central importance, of imperialist systems in the present era of world history. Broom and Selznick's widely used introductory textbook, Sociology, for example, doesn't have a single reference to imperialism. This omission, is hardly accidental. It stems both from the domination of organized knowledge by the ruling class and its agencies (which have no interest in promoting such knowledge), and from the bias of the existing academic methodologies in the social sciences which have their origins in conservative attempts to rationalize the status quo and to provide a theoretical alternative to the subversive theories of Karl Marx.*

Within the theoretical framework developed in the previous section of this text, however, it is a straightforward task to assimilate the phenomenon of imperialism and to subject it to

*Cf. Alvin W. Gouldner, The Coming Crisis of Western Sociology, Basic Books, 1970.

analysis. The state, it will be recalled, is the creation of the propertied interests of society, and it has the primary function of protecting those interests and providing an environment in which they can expand. When, as a result of the dynamic character of the capitalist economy, these propertied interests expand beyond national borders, it is only natural that they should enlist their respective nation-states in the expansionist effort, and in particular that they should secure the protection of their interests globally. The mechanisms by which this is accomplished are increasingly complex and in many ways less transparent than they were in the past, but the substance of the relationships is the same.

In brief, imperialism is the phenomenon of capitalist competition reproduced on an international scale, with the struggle for domination between nations, replacing, overlapping, and intersecting the struggle between economic interests and classes. Capitalist corporations strive domestically for expansion and domination, for control of markets; because markets are international, their struggle crosses the boundaries of nations as well. Corporate capital not only seeks to enter markets; it seeks to conquer them. It does not have a choice. For in the competitive struggle their are only victors and vanquished. The competitive quest leads to monopoly as its goal. But in order that monopoly may be complete, as Lenin wrote, "competitors must be eliminated not only from the home market, but also from the foreign market, from the whole world . . . ." This is the motor that drives the imperial engine(even though it may not have started the engine in the first place). Woodrow Wilson, who represents the "idealist" tendency in American foreign policy, put the whole phenomenon in a nutshell when he declared, "Since trade ignores national boundaries, and the manufacturer insists on having the world as a market, the flag of his nation must follow him, and the doors of the nations which are closed must be battered down."

* * *

"The fate of a nation lies not in words but in deeds," writes Charles A. Beard in approaching the problem of American foreign policy. "The nation lives by work not by rhetoric." To divine the fate of a nation, therefore, one "must ponder deeply its activity" in particular its "prime activities," which "are connected with the production and sale of goods." Beard's essay was written in 1922, when America was still in the early stages of staking out an overseas empire. Already Beard recognized that Asia was the hub of the empire that American leaders contemplated. "As President Harding has said, . . . we want markets in China in which to sell goods . . . that means intense and active rivalry with England, France and Japan in the Far East." Thirteen years later, in February, 1935, he analyzed President Roosevelt's dilemma in Scribner's Magazine: "Confronted by the difficulties of a deepening domestic crisis and by the comparative ease of a foreign war, what will President Roosevelt do? Judging by the past history of American politicians, he will choose the latter, or, perhaps it would be more accurate to say, amid powerful conflicting emotions he will 'stumble into' the latter. The [Democratic party] gave the nation the War of 1812, the Mexican War, and its participation in the World War. The Pacific War awaits."

Six years later, after a secret understanding with the British, President Roosevelt issued an ultimatum to Japan, which responded with an attack on Pearl Harbor. The combined effect of the European and Pacific Wars which ended in 1945 was to eliminate Japan, England, and France as significant powers in the Pacific and to open the door to American hegemony. But this hegemony was immediately faced with a new challenge in the form of revolution in China and Vietnam.

Within the perspective articulated by Beard, Washington's vast rearmament following World War II and its establishment of a global network of military bases and alliances is perfectly intelligible. An empire, i.e., an international system of domination, requires violent means to maintain it. Pax Britannica was enforced by the British Navy; the cold war Pax Americana is maintained by the American system of overseas bases and "free world" alliances. But since "imperialism" is a concept that is taboo in the American university system, academic social scientists have difficulty understanding the phenomenal growth of the American military. They tend to see the military as the maker of policy and of all that they find uncomfortable in its implementation, whereas the military, as Gabriel Kolko shows, is merely the instrument of a policy articulated and directed by American businessmen. The fantastic growth of the military has been programmed by the financiers and industrialists who reap the benefits of the Free World Empire. It is they who created the Pentagon in the first place, and they who have guided its development ever since.

Vietnam, Carl Oglesby has written, is the crucible in which America confronts herself, the meaning of her expansionist past, and the contours of her imperial fate. If the Free World is the American Empire, as Oglesby argues, then the struggle for the Vietnamese outpost must reveal an imperial logic. Such a "logic" need not reduce itself to a mere dollars-and-cents accounting of U.S. investments in Vietnam, as facile critics often suggest. The effort to understand the international politics of capitalist states as one aspect of an imperialist system does not require the reduction of all the complexities involved to a single-factor explanation. It requires rather an effort to see the inner order of these complex factors and forces and, without simplifying them or reducing them to mere reflections of each other, to understand the nature of their fit.

The essay by Jean-Paul Sartre examines one aspect of the imperial pattern: how the development of military technologies, in the context of an expanding global empire and growing global revolutionary opposition, produces a program of genocide. Commanding a world empire, unable to localize the threat posed by the refusal of the Vietnamese to be dominated or defeated, Washington is impelled by imperial logic and technological imperatives to conduct "an admonitory war in order to use genocide as a challenge and a threat to all the peoples of the world."

Just as foreign policy is the extension of domestic politics, so America's imperial expansion abroad is the extension of her colonization of the North American continent and her pursuit of Manifest Destiny. The white American republic was founded upon the extermination of the indigenous Indian nations and

*the subjection of black Africans in slavery. Until recently the
black internal colony has been submerged under the relatively
stable framework of Pax Americana, but with the upsurge of
revolutionary forces in the underdeveloped world, this black
nation has begun to define and liberate itself. Stokeley Carmichael and Charles V. Hamilton examine the parallel structures
of external and internal colonialism, and the common premises
of self-liberation.*

WORLD POWER

"In the beginning was the deed," wrote the wise poet. Activity yet remains the essential thing in the life of mankind. Political speeches, addresses on foreign policies, and Fourth of July orations exert little influence on the course of human affairs, save occasionally in time of a crisis when the spoken word indicates a line of action to be followed. The fate of a nation—its destiny—lies not in words but in deeds. The nation lives by work, not by rhetoric. It is no detraction from the high honor rightly ascribed to the Fathers of this Republic to say that, well as they built, they alone did not make America. Our America was made by the pioneers, men and women, who leveled the forests, laid out the roads, tilled the fields, and carried American life to the Pacific, and by the capitalists and laborers who constructed and operated the steel mills with their roaring furnaces and the spinning mills with their flying spindles. I do not mean to say that concepts of life and duty do not underlie this fabric of human endeavor, but merely that the majestic signs of power are the outcome of activity.

So, whoever fain would divine the fate of a nation must ponder deeply its activity. It is not what we say about the sea that counts; it is what our sailors do upon the seas. It is not our academic theories about finance that carry weight in the councils of nations; it is our dollars and our cents that imperatively command the attention and wholesome respect of those engaged in the counting houses of the earth's great cities. It is not what President Harding thinks about China or what John Hay has written about China that will shape the coming fateful

From *The Economic Basis of Politics* by Charles A. Beard. © 1922, 1934, 1945 by Alfred A. Knopf and renewed 1950, 1962 by William Beard and Miriam B. Vagts. Reprinted by permission of the publisher.

years in the Pacific; it is what our merchants, our capitalists, our railway builders, and our moneylenders do in China that will set the problem for the rising generation.

Now America is primarily an industrial and a trading nation. Its prime activities are connected with the production and sale of goods. It has no landed nobility to cultivate the graces of leisure. It has no military aristocracy devoted to the exercise of arms. Napoleon once sneered at the nation of shopkeepers, but it was the sneer of jealousy, and the Anglo-Saxon is proud of the term of contempt thus flung at him. Whether this pride is warranted or not, whether the virtues of trade—those bourgeois virtures so scorned of the emancipated—are really virtues, is a matter for the theologian and the ethical teacher. The fact remains. America is an industrial and trading nation. Our activities at home and abroad are mainly related to these essential elements in our national life. Here then is the key to our domestic history and to our future foreign policies. Our empire of trade extends to the four corners of the world. It stretches out under many flags and many governments. Those working at its periphery, under the pressure of economic laws, make the conditions with which American foreign policy must deal. They create the stern and solemn facts with which statesmen and politicians must reckon.

Moreover, recent circumstances have given a new turn to the significance of business. Many nations of antiquity in the course of their history came to rely upon the food supplies brought from distant lands. Rome in her imperial days was fed by wheat carried from her uttermost provinces; when this supply was cut off and the fields of Italy failed to make good the shortage, the staff of life failed. The new nations and new states that rose upon the foundations of Rome were almost self-sufficing. At all events they could feed their population by food grown within their own borders. With the advent of the machine age, this fortunate condition was lost by the leaders in invention and manufacture. In 1914 neither England nor Germany could maintain a standard of living for the laboring population without drawing heavily upon the granaries of America and Russia. The huge populations, called into being by the opportunities of industry, constituted a growing pressure upon the agencies of business and of government, compelling them to extend and maintain foreign markets. This naturally drove the seekers for markets into the backward places of the earth where industry had not penetrated or had made little advance. For nearly a century England had no formidable rival in this imperial enterprise, then one after another competitors appeared upon the world stage—Germany, Japan, Italy, France, and the United States. Even in China and India the whir of the spindle and the clank of the loom were heard ringing out the fate of Lancashire cotton mills. Here were the roots of imperialism, armaments, and warfare. Those who asked where this all would finally lead and what would be the outcome when every nation became industrial were silenced by the inexorable demands of current business. After us the deluge!

In this swiftly drifting world economy, the United States occupies a peculiar position. From one point of view it is very fortunate. It can feed its immense population with almost every kind of product from oranges and sugar to wheat and bacon. It can clothe its people with the cotton of the South and, did exigencies again demand, with wool from the sheep ranges. Considered abstractly it could be a self-sufficing nation. But considered practically, it is, as things now stand, dependent upon foreign trade, if not for a livelihood, at least for what is called "prosperity." It is the city populations of England and Germany that must have markets abroad and import food supplies. In the United States, the wheat and corn grower of the West, the cotton grower of the South, as well as the maker of silks in Paterson, or the manufacturer of steel in Pittsburgh, all depend upon foreign business for that margin of trade which spells prosperity. In short, having an endowment of agricultural resources beyond the strength of our domestic markets for the produce, we must perforce sell the foreigner foodstuffs as well as boots and clothes. Here is a paradox which seems to have received small attention from professional economists.

In every respect, the World War [1] has increased the dependence of the United States upon world markets even for the profitable disposal of its surplus capital. It has discharged a very large portion of its indebtedness abroad and has become an insistent moneylender itself. In 1915, European capitalists held $2,704,000,000 worth of American railway stocks and securities; two years later more than half of these holdings had been transferred to America; and the stream still continues to flow westward. In 1914 more than one-fourth of the stocks of the United States Steel Corporation were held in Europe; today less than one-tenth are in foreign hands. The crisis induced in London, long the money center of the world, by the exigencies of the war, led to the phenomenal rise of New York. To sustain their credit here for huge borrowings, England and France opened their strongboxes and sent across the sea the very finest of their gilt-edge securities. As a keen French economist puts it: "One fact dominates all others: the rise of the United States to world hegemony. Lord Robert Cecil has compared the position of the United States after the Great War with that of Great Britain after the Napoleonic wars. That comparison is not quite exact; because the British hegemony was then essentially European while that of the United States today is universal. An immense reservoir of raw materials, of manufactured products, and of capital, the United States has become an economic centre and financial centre in connection with which all the world must work and trade." Fact, stern and tremendous, as Carlyle might say, indubitable and fateful. Beside it all rhetoric fails. The loom on which is woven the texture of world politics has been brought across the sea and the picks of its flashing shuttle can be counted in the financial columns of any great New York daily.

The United States has, therefore, entered upon the role long played by England and France as an international banker and money lender. The visible signs of these activities are the numerous American banking houses which are to be found in the principal streets and squares of European cities. The Morgan House and the Bankers Trust Company look upon the monument erected to Napoleon's glories in Place Vendome. If you will turn to the financial section of such a metropolitan paper as *The New York Times,* you will see the statistical record of American operations in foreign finance. Only recently the transactions in foreign government bonds upon the Stock Exchange have become so great as to require a separate section of the daily statement. Often such transactions occupy one-fourth of the space given to the day's record. The list of bonds bought and sold on a single day is both interesting and full of meaning. The list includes Argentine (Government), Chinese Railway, City of Berne, Bordeaux, Christiania, Copenhagen, Lyons, Marseilles, Rio de Janeiro, Tokyo, Zurich, Danish Municipalities, Department of the Seine, Dominican Republic, Dominion of Canada, Dutch East Indies, French Government, Japanese Government, Belgium, Denmark, Italy, Sweden, Chile, Cuba, Uruguay, San Paulo, Queensland, Rio Grande do Sul, Swiss Confederation, United Kingdom of Great Britain and Ireland, Brazil, and Haiti, not to mention the defaulted securities of Russia and Mexico. When to the sales of these government bonds are added the transactions in the currency and bonds of Central and Eastern European powers and the transactions in the stocks and obligations of foreign industrial corporations, it becomes apparent that American investors are deeply involved in the fate of governments and enterprises in all parts of the world. Almost every week records the floating of a new loan to some foreign city or country or railway already staggering under a burden of debt. The rates are high, the commissions enormous, and the risks correspondingly great.

In accordance with a custom, consecrated by time, the bondholders, whenever a disturbance is threatened or a default is at hand, look eagerly to the government at Washington to support their interests diplomatically if not more vigorously. The genial American public, that takes up millions of oil stocks every year, seizes eagerly at the opportunity to get seven and eight per cent on the bonds of foreign countries, and so every new loan is received with enthusiasm. Let this process go on for fifty years, and the people of the United States will have reconditioned Europe and Asia, and at the same time created an interest obligation that will either flood our markets with European goods by way of repayment, or raise the dollar to a ruinous height in the exchanges of the world. They will also have incurred a gigantic financial risk which a new war or a social revolution in Europe would transform into widespread ruin with its corresponding effects on our political issues. In short, the United States, through the investment of capital, has become a silent partner in the fate of every established order in the world. Unless we are to assume on the basis of the experience of the past three hundred years that there will be no more World Wars or social cataclysms, it is safe to conjecture that days of greater trouble are ahead, whether we enter the League of Nations or stay out of it. Once a great European war merely deranged our foreign trade; in the future it will disturb every investor in every village Main Street. Entangling political alliances may be pieces of paper, as the past has shown, but the texture of the economic alliance is woven of tougher materials. Politics comes after the fact. The gilt-edged pieces of parchment handed out to American investors will speak louder than the silver tongues of professional orators.

In industry, as in finance, the upward swing of the United States after 1914 was incredible in its swiftness and majestic in its range. Our old competitors in Europe were not only paralyzed by war activities; they clamored louder and louder for the products of American mills, mines, and factories. Measured in tons of steel, pounds of copper, and bolts of cloth, the sales of the United States abroad between 1914 and 1918 were nothing short of staggering. We supplied not only belligerents in Europe but their former customers in South America, Asia, and the islands of the seas. Colossal factories sprang up on our soil. Old plants were enlarged and extended. Thousands of new workers were drawn into the cities from the countryside, especially as immigration fell off. American capital was amassed in stupendous quantities and preparations were made to seize the empire of world trade. Having an immense home market with the corresponding advantages of large-scale production, American businessmen prepared to lead the world in industry and finance. They were even able to induce a Democratic Congress, in spite of its inveterate suspicion, to enact the Webb law authorizing the formation of gigantic combinations to develop and exploit foreign markets.

In the normal course of things, if the history of England and Germany is our guide, a merchant marine and sea power follow the growth of foreign business. In this sphere also the trend of American economic development is true to form. On the eve of the World War [I], the American merchant marine was an almost negligible factor upon the high seas. It is true that long ago our wooden ships were upon every ocean and our sailors rivaled in skill and daring the best upon the wave; but the glory of our enterprise upon the waters vanished during the Civil War. After 1865 the record of nearly every year showed a decline. In 1861 American ships brought to our shores more than one-half, in values, of all the goods imported; in 1913 they carried only about eleven per cent of the values. Meanwhile the tonnage of ships for oceanic trade fell from 2,547,000 to 1,928,999, reducing the United States to a position below that of England, Germany, and Norway. During the same period the proportion of exports carried from our shores in American ships dropped from seventy-two percent in values to nine per cent. Americans, busy with the development of their continent, and content with their lake and coastwise trade, let foreign ships carry their exports and imports. The planters and farmers of the country rejected every proposal to build a merchant marine by national subsidies—the only device which American capitalists could offer as a means of bringing the ocean carrying trade into American hands.

So things stood in 1914 when the war drove the German merchant marine from the seas and compelled the other belligerents to commandeer ships for military purposes. Then the United States found itself in the presence of a crisis similar to that induced by the Napoleonic wars. One hundred years before, cotton, tobacco, corn, and bacon from American plantations and farms lay wasting at the docks for want of ships to carry them abroad. In 1914 the owners of vast masses of manufactured goods as well as the owners of farm produce clamored for ships. Thus it happened that the Democratic party, which many years before had withdrawn subsidies from the American marine, found itself confronted by a trying situation. The cry for ships went up on every hand. It was no longer the steelmakers and the owners of shipyards alone that were heard in the lobbies of Congress. The munition-makers needed ships. The farmers and planters needed them. So the Democratic party, the party of the less government the better, like all parties, laid aside theories in the presence of compelling facts and set about creating an American marine. Without utterly repudiating the teachings of half a century, it could not openly resort to the subsidies and bounties it had so long and so passionately denounced. But the ships had to be built. There was another alternative. The government itself could go into shipbuilding. In 1916, the Shipping Board was created for that purpose. Soon the war came to America. Then with lavish grants from the public treasury ships were built with a speed that astonished the world.

Thanks to what appears to be a historical accident, the United States has now become one of the great oceanic carrying powers. In 1914 our shipyards turned out 200,000 tons of shipping while those of Great Britain turned out 1,683,000 tons. In 1918, our yards launched 3,000,000 tons while the English yards set afloat 1,348,000 tons. All around our long coast-lines American ingenuity was applied with astounding zeal and marvelous results. The experiment was costly, for money was spent like water, but "the goods were delivered." Within the course of five years the American flag was restored to its old pre-eminence on the high seas. In the Atlantic and the Pacific new steamship lines made their appearance bidding for freight and passenger business. New shipping offices were opened in all the chief ports of the world. An ever increasing proportion of our exports and imports was carried in American bottoms. The steamship companies of Europe found themselves face to face with a new and formidable competitor. In 1920 the total number of American vessels, registered as engaged in foreign trade and whale fishing showed a tonnage of 9,928,595, to say nothing of the 6,395,429 tons engaged in coastwise and internal trade. In 1918 the entire merchant marine of the United Kingdom amounted to 10,000,000 tons in round numbers. Thus it happened when the war stopped that the world was overstocked with merchant vessels and in every harbor steamers and sailing ships lay rusting and rotting. Then the great cry went up that the government which by lavish expenditures had built the ships should subsidize those into whose hands they passed at a nominal cost.

With the economics of this great transaction, we are not concerned. The striking fact is established that the United States has become within six years one of the first oceanic carriers of the world, a formidable competitor of all the maritime nations.

Coincident with this growth in the merchant marine was a tremendous stride forward in battleship construction. Until the Spanish War, America was not reckoned among the great sea powers, although her sailors had given a good account of themselves in many contests upon the ocean. After Manila Bay and Santiago, however, increasing attention was given to the navy, and in 1914 the United States ranked third in naval strength. Then began a period of feverish activity marked by constantly increasing acceleration. In 1920 the Navy General Board reported its grand designs: "A navy second to none recommended by the General Board in 1915 is still required today. But in addition the great war has shown the importance of unimpeded ocean transportation for commerce. If either belligerent loses the control of the sea, the national fighting power and endurance are greatly affected. In time of peace a great and developing country needs a proportionately great merchant fleet of its own to insure its markets and preserve its commerce from subservience to rival nations and their business." That report struck home and its spirit was reflected in the new building program. So rapid was American progress that experts were able to calculate that by 1926 the fighting power of the United States on the sea would surpass that of Great Britain. The long supremacy inaugurated in the defeat of the *Armada* was on the verge of passing to America when the Washington conference called a halt in competitive armaments.

So out of the World War [I] emerged a new America, first among the investing, industrial, commercial, maritime, and naval powers of the earth—a country endowed with an immense productive equipment and ready to penetrate the most inaccessible markets of the most distant lands. At the same time, a paralysis of Europe cut down the demand for American agricultural produce and manufactured goods, and the destruction of the Russian and German empires gave a new and startling turn to events in the Orient, leaving Japan without the support of any great power save England. It was inevitable, amid these circumstances, that we should witness a burst of American activity in the Far East.

This is of course a new emphasis rather than a new factor, for Oriental trade had been an important element in American economy and politics since the maturity of the Pacific seaboard states, especially since the acquisition of the Philippines and the opening of the Panama Canal. The Pacific has become the new theater. It has been said that the drama of antiquity was played on the shores of the Mediterranean and that the drama of the modern world has been enacted on the shores of the Atlantic. The drama of the future is preparing on a more majestic stage where teeming millions stand ready to take part in it. The curtain has risen upon this new drama. The actors are in their places, but no living mind can define even the first act, to say nothing of the denouement. Asia is old, wise, fertile in ideas and rich in potential resources. It had its empires, its religions and philosophies long before the geese cackled on the banks of the Tiber. Many conquerors have tried their fortunes there. England has brought the vast southern peninsula under her imperial dominion, but her subjects stir ominously and the solid structure may in time dissolve. Japan, aroused from her lethargy by Yankee enterprise, is equipped in wealth, industrial power, and military strength to extend and defend her mighty hegemony. China, huge, amorphous, beset by a thousand ills, threatened with dissolution, and restless under the influence of western ideas, lies prostrate, but, having survived a hundred conquests and conquerors, may yet smile in her enigmatic way upon the Lilliputians who assail her. Russia, at present broken and powerless, seems out of the play, but that is an illusion except to those who reckon human affairs in terms of flags and states. The Russian people multiply with the passing years and they push out upon the Asiatic plains with the relentless force of an Alpine glacier. Those who occupy the earth and till the soil at their feet will in the long run possess it. Russia, the land of Tolstoi and Lenin and Sazonov and Nicholas Romanov, still lives and will again play a leading part in the drama that unrolls in the Pacific basin.

The first speeches of the American actors have already been delivered. The policy of "the Open Door" has been announced. It has an immense advantage. It has an ethical ring. It respects the integrity, sovereignty, and territory of the Chinese nation. It contemplates no military aggression, no forcible annexations, no political power. It merely asks that all nations have equal rights to go and come, buy and sell, invest and collect in China. In theory it corresponds to the modern ideal of free commerce, though it may mean that in practice immense monopolies may be built up, monopolies such as have arisen in Europe and the United States out of the same freedom of commerce. In theory it meets the approval of China, for China, naturally anxious to preserve her territorial unity against foreign domination, welcomes assistance. While thus corresponding to China's immediate desires and expressing an ethical doctrine, the open-door policy also satisfies the practical interests of the United States, at present. The seizure and government of Chinese territory would involve difficulties, financial and administrative; if opportunities of trade may be secured without this hazard, territorial annexations would be exercises in foolhardiness.

The belief in our own disinterestedness in the pursuit of the open-door policy is so widespread that any opposition to it on the part of other countries concerned in the Orient is viewed as a manifestation of unwarranted ill-will. Undoubtedly American policy offers a striking contrast to the policy of penetration and aggression followed by many other powers. Nevertheless, it does not appear to be entirely benevolent to the seasoned diplomats of the Old World, as the papers recently published from the Russian archives show. In these papers, the American State Department is represented as aiding vigorously in the economic penetration of China and as supporting American banks with interests hostile to those of the other powers. It is not necessary to accept these criticisms at face value or on the basis of them to entertain doubts as to the correctness of American diplomacy. That is not the point. The heart of the matter is that neither Europeans nor the Japanese look upon American imperial methods in the Orient as different in any essential respect from those of other powers. The American goal, they say, is the same, namely, opportunities for profitable trade and investment, and, as the Philippines bear witness, territorial expansion is not avoided when it becomes necessary. The spirit of cynicism and doubt as to the ultimate intentions of America in the East, though we may vigorously condemn it, must nevertheless be understood if we are to gauge correctly forces of the future. Nowhere is this spirit more accurately reflected than in an article by an eminent French publicist, in the *Mercure de France* for January, 1922. This single passage gives the heart of the matter:

"The realist, the positive, and especially the financial, mentality which is the true characteristic of the Yankee and his raison d'être has been profoundly stirred by the situation created in the United States during and after the war—a situation which he had not foreseen and which is presented under the form of a genuine paradox. Enriched in that conflict to the point of securing almost all the gold of the world, North America nevertheless is passing through a crisis of appalling proportions; unemployment, a paralysis of the export trade, and all the economic calamities, now oppressing American citizens, fell upon them at the same time as an exceptionally favorable state of exchange and an unexpected abundance of treasure. It occurred at once to the minds of these practical men that it was necessary henceforward to secure a market other than that afforded by Europe, a field of action in which their preponderant of semi-sovereign influence will permit them to sell their products and their primary materials under conditions of exchange which they will regulate themselves. Thus they will avoid as far as possible the economic laws which, in their operation, have become so dangerous for them in Europe. Since they were powerless in Europe to regulate the value of money which depends upon a number of circumstances—upon a state of affairs peculiar to the Old World and beyond their control,—it was urgent that they should have at their disposal an Asiatic country where they could act, direct, and organize at their pleasure and where their commerce would not encounter the same perils as among their old customers. China is there, immense and ready, they think, to receive all authorities, and so disorganized that she is ready to accept anything they wish to impose upon her. Hence there were, even during the war, missions of all sorts, economic, financial, religious, educational, and recreational sailing from Frisco to the Middle Kingdom.

"At that moment, Japan began to be disturbed. For other reasons than the United States, even for opposite reasons, Japan felt the need of extending her influence over the great Yellow Republic; above all for reasons connected with natural resources. Wanting in coal and iron, Japan must of necessity possess these things without depending upon any powerful nation. Moreover her seventy-seven million people are crowded into a country about as large as France and at any price it was necessary to search for an outlet for emigrants. In short, with the United States established in China, there was at her gate an enemy which had shown a tenacious hatred for her and an unchanging contempt for the yellow race, since, according to the Yankee conception of things, the yellow man, who is only a charming being when one visits him to get his money, becomes intolerable when he asks for simple reciprocity. . . . Mr. Hughes has proposed that the American republic should dominate the Pacific—twenty-eight million more inhabitants than Japan to undertake the economic conquest of China, eight super-battleships more than the Mikado possesses to curb his desires—there are the powerful trump cards, and if America succeeds in making them serve her purpose, she will have a beautiful party. Although officially disinterested for the moment in the affairs of Europe, she sees that they are being reintegrated secretly in general policy through financiers who meet in their private chambers and associate with themselves at the council table some Anglo-Saxon business men and some Germans who more than ever divide the world." Such is a view of American policy now, by an eminent French publicist. How much untruth there is in it each may decide for himself according to his knowledge. Now that we have set out upon the way it is wise to see ourselves as our critics see us, for it is our critics, not our friends, who will make trouble for us.

Whether we accept or reject the criticisms of the French observer, we cannot overlook the fact that the widely heralded

Washington conference was related mainly, even almost exclusively, to Pacific, not European, problems. Though associated in the minds of some with various world enterprises such as the League of Nations, it was in fact confined in its chief activities to the practical adjustment of Pacific matters in such a way as to facilitate the prosperity of American trade. When the conference was first called, many enthusiasts began to see visions of general disarmament and universal peace, but President Harding sharply reminded them that nothing of the sort was contemplated. He had in view reducing the cost of warlike preparations in time of peace, to the great relief of the burdened taxpayers, and settling certain specific matters likely to cause friction among the powers concerned. The two projects were closely knit in the realm of fact. As President Harding said in his address to the Senate on February 9, 1922, in submitting the results of the conference to that body: "Much as it was desirable to lift the burdens of naval armament and strike at the menace of competitive construction and consequent expenditures, the Executive branch of the Government, which must be watchful for the Nation's safety, was unwilling to covenant a reduction of armament until there could be plighted new guarantees of peace, until there could be removed probable menaces of conflict." After this plain declaration of prosaic fact, President Harding went to the heart of the matter. "We have seen the eyes of the world," he said, "turned to the Pacific. With Europe prostrate and penitent, none feared the likelihood of early conflict there. But the Pacific had its menaces and they deeply concerned us. Our territorial interests are larger there. Its waters are not strange seas to us, its farther shores are unknown to our citizens. . . . We covet the possessions of no other power in the Far East and we know for ourselves that we crave no further or greater governmental or territorial responsibilities there. Contemplating what is admittedly ours, and mindful of a long-time and reciprocal friendship with China, we do wish the opportunity to continue the development of our trade peacefully and on equality with other nations." When all the rhetoric, ceremonials, and formalities are laid aside, there is the sum and substance of the whole business. "The Pacific had its menaces and they deeply concerned us."

What were those menaces in fact and deed? Who made those menaces? No informed person is under any delusions on this matter. Russia, long the aggressor and high chief engineer of intrigues against Chinese territory, is paralyzed and powerless for the present and the indefinite future. France, though possessed of a huge Indochinese empire, offers no serious challenge. Germany is bankrupt in military power and can do no more than make commercial gestures. There remain England and Japan. They are the only powers in a position to encroach upon Chinese territorial integrity, and in 1921 these two powers were bound by an alliance. "The Pacific had its menaces." They were real; they were twofold; they were united, and the United States at the same time had no intention of surrendering any of the opportunities of American merchants, manufacturers, and financiers in China.

Thus it happened that the desires of the taxpayers for relief and the pacific aspirations of the American people, coincided with a genuine crisis in the Far Eastern relations of the American government. For eight years conditions had been abnormal. President Wilson, as the spokesman of planters, farmers, and trade unions, did not continue the aggressive policy pursued by the Secretary of State, Philander Knox, in the advancement of American trading and investing interests in the East. Moreover the war had dislocated forces, engaged the energies of England, paralyzed Russia, eliminated Germany, and given Japan a free hand. In fact, between the retirement of President Taft and the inauguration of President Harding, Japan had made immense strides in the extension of her hegemony over China. At first she operated in conjunction with Russia, with the consent of England. Then, in the midst of the war, Japan made her famous Twenty-one Demands, which in effect promised to destroy the remnants of Chinese sovereignty. Mr. Wilson, so zealous in the interest of universal peace and the League of Nations, approved the Lansing-Ishu doctrine, let Shantung go to Japan, and neglected Yap.

It is in the light of these things that the results of the Washington conference must be examined. First, there is the naval holiday and the Four Power treaty. As all conversant with naval affairs know, by 1924 or 1926 at the latest, according to the prevalent rate of construction, the United States would have been supreme at sea over Great Britain in fighting units and weight of metal. But Great Britain was united to Japan by a treaty of alliance and the two constituted a formidable power. By offering debt-burdened Britain a relief in naval construction the United States induced her to cut loose from a separate alliance with Japan. Hence the naval holiday. It is an immense gain to the taxpayers. It gives experts time to study the whole question of sea fighting in view of the great probability that dreadnoughts and super-dreadnoughts are as obsolete as wooden walls.

The accompanying Four Power treaty is likewise susceptible of many interpretations as to origin, purpose, and implications. The terms of the instrument are very general. The high contracting parties agree to respect one another's insular possessions in the Pacific and to enter into communication in case any disturbance rises in that connection. On its face that declaration appears to be a truism. President Harding informed the Senate and the country that "nothing in any of these treaties commits the United States or any other power to any kind of alliance, entanglement or envolvement." But, as if baffled by his own statement, he added: "It has been said, if this be true, these are meaningless treaties and therefore valueless. Let us accept no such doctrine of despair as that." It has been stated, but not officially, that the purpose of the Four Power treaty was to destroy the Anglo-Japanese alliance and if this is true the somewhat uncertain terms become full of meaning. At all events the way is made clear for the pursuit of the open-door trading policy in China.

More precise is the treaty laying down the principles to be pursued with regard to China. The high contracting parties once more proclaim the sovereignty, the independence, the territorial and administrative integrity of China, and free and equal opportunity for commerce and industry. They agree that they will not seek or support their nationals in seeking: (a) any arrangement which might purport to establish in favor of their interests any general superiority of right with respect to commercial or economic development in any designated regions of China;

(b) any such monopoly or preference as would deprive the nationals of any other power of the right of undertaking any legitimate trade or industry in China or of participating with the Chinese government or with any local authority in any category of public enterprise, or which by reason of its scope, duration, or geographical extent is calculated to frustrate the practical application of the principle of equal opportunity.

Two things are to be noted about this treaty. The language, though perhaps as specific as circumstances admitted, is nevertheless general in character. It is open to a variety of interpretations in the application. It is less specific and pointed than the language of the famous Algeciras compact which was supposed to put an end to friction among the powers in Morocco. It does not contain the detailed provisions, limitations, prohibitions, and specifications laid down in 1906 for the conduct of the Sultan's estate. That is the first point to be noted. The second is that it is, like the Algeciras compact, applicable to a country in disorder and revolution, to a rapidly changing situation, not to a settled society like the United States or England where commerce can be carried on without recourse to armed force. When France was reproached with having torn up the compact of Algeciras, she could with justice reply that local conditions were such that its application, according to the ordinary norms of legal procedure, was impossible. So it was.

Anyone who has given two or three years to the study of the course of affairs in Europe since 1918 will hesitate to advance with firm assurance very many "conclusions." The pages which follow should really be entitled "A Few General and Tentative Reflections." Europe is in an unstable equilibrium and serious changes may take place any moment. Generalizations are dangerous. Prophecy is more dangerous. But the human mind longs for something more positive than a glimpse at a swirling tide. Hence these last words.

The first reflection is perhaps the easiest to formulate. There are many signs of European recovery in the realm of fact. The reconstruction work in France has been truly marvelous. The basic industry, agriculture, though disturbed by agrarian changes in Eastern Europe, is being restored and a decided turn upward may be expected shortly. The quarrels among the new nationalities are being allayed by negotiations and treaties and new bonds of trade and intercourse are taking the place of those snapped by the war. In this sphere time will bring healing.

Secondly, finance and industry in Europe are in a state of chaos and conditions are growing worse rather than better. If the analysis [in another volume] . . . . is sound, it is difficult to see how business can be brought to its old course without reducing reparations and inter-allied debts, scaling down domestic debts, and restoring the currency to a gold basis. Europe must soon choose between some kind of a general economic constitution and a realignment of powers for more costly and deadly conflicts.

Thirdly, the principle of conscious and systematic support for commercial enterprise has been adopted by England, France, Germany, and Italy, and the capitalists of these countries are driving forward to the conquest of new markets with a greater zeal than in the days before the war. There is this difference: they are more effectively organized within their respective countries and more vigorously supported by their respective governments. The restoration of Europe without a constitution designed to mitigate these rivalries will mean a return to secret diplomacy and the armed peace, preparatory to a re-enactment of the great drama which we have just witnessed. What would be left of European civilization after several repetitions of this cycle may be left to the imagination. But if Europe cannot learn from experience, it is hardly probable that more pronunciamentos from Washington will have any effect upon the course of events there.

Fourthly, there seem to be only two policies open to the United States. The first is to enter into a general European council and attempt by international pressure to compel a readjustment of indemnities, debts, tariffs, and currencies; that is, to join in forcing the various nations to do what they must do before the course of business is returned to a pre-war basis. If anyone will read the European press closely, he will see what grave complications this would involve, what new hatreds, what new discords. In my opinion it would be unwise for the United

States to attempt to play the part of a general receiver or a big brother for Europe tortured by the inevitable after-war hatreds. This is not because we are wanting in the spirit of helpfulness, but because in this case intermeddling is likely to do more harm than good. The other course is that now pursued, except as far as Russia is concerned. It is the course of allowing Europe to set its own house in order under the stress of its own necessities and experiences. Its statesmen know little enough, perhaps, but they know Europe better than any agents sent out from Washington.

Fifthly, if the United States leaves Europe to its own devices in recovering its economic prosperity, then logic as well as common decency requires our government to refrain from publishing periodical homilies on the place of Russia in Europe's affairs.

Sixthly, new loans to European countries by American banking houses, though they yield high commissions and high interest rates at present, merely add to the burdens and confusion of Europe and help postpone the day of fiscal reckoning which all continental countries must face sooner or later. Indeed these very loans may involve us, in spite of ourselves, in grave problems of readjustment now facing European statesmen.

Finally, the menaces that confront the United States today are not European. As President Harding has said, they are in the Pacific. What does that mean? What does it imply in terms of American policy and of obligations for American citizens? President Harding has given us the key. He says that we do not want any more territory in the Pacific, but that we want trade. That means, in plain English, that we want markets in China in which to sell goods; we want opportunities to invest money with good commissions and high rates of interest; and we want concessions to build railways, exploit natural resources, and develop Chinese industries to our profit. Assuming that the open door is really open, that means intense and active rivalry with England, France, and Japan in the Far East. So the great question is: "Shall the government follow trade and investments?"

That is the crucial question. It is a question fraught with

momentous significance for this country. Behind all the notes, treaties, speeches and declarations, that is the one great issue in foreign affairs before the people of this country. It must be considered without bitterness or partisan rancor in the light of national interests and national destiny. There must be no sneering criticism of our manufacturers and bankers. They are following economic opportunities as other men do. Nothing short of the interest of the whole nation should come into the decisions upon policy.

At this fateful juncture in American history, there are three courses open to those who fain would mold the world to their hearts' desires. There is, first, the policy of positive imperialism, naked and unashamed. Under it, our government would give vigorous support to merchants, bankers, and manufacturers in parts of the earth in their search for trade and investment opportunities. It presupposes armies and navies adequate to all exigencies and strong enough to compel respect for all decisions taken in behalf of national economic interests. The Department of State, operating mainly in secret through a corps of consuls and diplomats, would become the adjunct to industrial and investment interests. A merchant marine would be subsidized, and government support given to the prosecution of commercial advantages. Discriminatory and preferential tariffs would be constructed with reference to the promotion of American industries.

This policy is commonly defended on two grounds. Some say that it is the natural, inevitable, and irresistible development of an imperial race—the manifest destiny of every nation to expand, conquer, and dominate. Possibly it is the decree of fate. If so, then all arguments for and against it are equally futile and irrelevant.

Others, brushing aside such philosophy, say that imperialism is necessary to American prosperity, that we must sell more and more manufactured goods every year or perish. Let us examine briefly that hypothesis in operation. More billions in trade means bringing more business to American manufacturing industries and drawing more millions of people from Europe and from our own countryside into mines, mills, and factories.

It means more billions in stocks and bonds in strongboxes, and more millions of men, women, and children in industrial cities—a vaster aristocracy of wealth and a huger proletariat. Whoever can contemplate the possibility of a hundred years of that development without thought of consequences lying beyond, deserves to wear the badge of courage. Still the policy involved in it may be pursued without regard to the long future.

Imperialism is not new. It offers no novel features to the adventurous spirit of man. The past affords ample records for the study of its processes, operations, and consequences. It cannot however be pursued today under the conditions of the past three hundred years. The experience of the British Empire is no guide to us now. The backward places of the earth are all staked out and in the possession of powers bent upon the kind of commercial and financial imperialism that is recommended to us. Imperialism of the future will involve competitive risks far more dangerous than the risks of Pitt, Disraeli, and Sir Edward Grey. Still the policy is an intelligible one and is defended by some of the ablest minds of our generation. Ample support for it is to be found in the voluminous literature of the late German Empire.

There is before us, possibly, a second policy. It is covered by that term of opprobrium hurled at it by the devotees of imperialism, namely, "Little Americanism." Its implications are likewise clear. Let us examine them. According to this philosophy, the government of the United States would not lend diplomatic or any other kind of support to investment bankers placing loans abroad, [whether] in making them, collecting the interest, or insuring the principal. It would not use the army or the navy in the collection of debts due to private citizens. The government would feel under no greater obligation to a banker who made a bad loan in Guatemala than it would to a banker who made a bad guess in lending money to a dry-goods merchant in Des Moines, Iowa. It would not seize any more territory. It would discontinue the policy of annexing spheres in the Caribbean and would invite the Latin American countries into a co-operative system for settling all disputes in this hemisphere. It would give independence to the Philippines and draw back upon the Hawaiian base. It would maintain an army and a navy adequate for the defense of our territories, by universal service if necessary, and perhaps preferably. It might possibly contemplate entering a League of Nations, provided all other countries were prepared to adopt a similar domestic policy. It would bend all national energies and all national genius upon the creation of a civilization which, in power and glory and noble living, would rise above all the achievements of the past. This policy, whatever may be said against it, has on its side at least the advantage and interest of novelty. The great power that pursued it might, indeed, sink down into dust like the empires of Tamerlane or Augustus, but at least the world's experiences would be enriched.

There is finally another alternative, that of no policy at all, save the policy of drift and muddle. It would support our capitalists and merchants abroad, but not adequately. It would encourage them to pursue their economic interests and then fail to sustain them in a crucial hour. It would create, inadvertently, situations calling for imperial military and naval forces, but would not have the forces ready on the fateful day. It would follow in the paths of Alexander and Caesar but would be content with the philosophy of Buncombe County. Yet, under Providence many things might be accomplished by this policy. It might land the nation at the gates of destruction; but that can be said of the imperial policy pursued by Rome and Germany. As in individual life we find our little plans and purposes but frail reeds in our hands, so in national life, the wisdom, understanding, and penetration of the best and most practical statesmen often prove to be in the test of time and circumstance the weirdest of delusions.

Here I take leave of the subject, saying with Bossuet, the good bishop: "All those who are engaged in the work of government are subject to a higher power. They always do more or less than they intend and their counsels have never failed to produce unforeseen effects. They are not the masters of the turn given to affairs by the ages past. Neither can they foresee the course the future will take. Far less can they force it." Still, who would not rather have the heritage of Athens than the legacy of Caesar?

MILITARY AND CIVIL AUTHORITY

GABRIEL KOLKO

In the United States the civilians, the self-styled "liberals" and "democrats," finally direct the application of American power in all its forms throughout the world. Despite the dramatic and sinister overtones in the phrase "military-industrial complex," or C. Wright Mills' vision of "the military ascendancy," the fact is that the nature of global conflict and the means of violence are so thoroughly political and economic in their essential character, so completely intricate technologically, that it is probably more correct to argue the case for the declining importance of the military in the decision-making structure. For military power is the instrument American political leaders utilize to advance their enormous and ever-growing objectives, and that they require a vast Military Establishment is the logical, necessary effect rather than the cause of the basic objectives and momentum of American foreign policy since 1943. Civilians formulated that policy, in the context of the critical postwar period, when the Military Establishment was docile and relatively starved. Belligerence requires generals and arms as tools for the advancement of permanent objectives.

The critics of America's policies in the world have focused their attacks on the visibility of the military, as if its "liberalization" would transform the reality of America's global role. The notion of an independent military dynamic and ethic occludes the real interests and purposes of American foreign policy, which is not to fight wars but to gain vital strategic and economic objectives that materially enlarge American power everywhere. That the military is a neutral instrumentality of civilian policy is inherent in the fact that increasingly the major object of strategic military policy is how to avoid using suicidal nuclear armaments while successfully advancing American economic and political goals. These ends are active, the struggle for them the potential cause of nuclear conflict that could destroy the world; only the most extreme imperatives ever led the civilians to consider this risk and option. If a distinctive military ethic, a regenerative theory of blood-letting and herosim, has ever existed, it has not caused a war in which civilian men of power did not first conceive of some more rational, material goals. This is no less true of the Cold War than of the Spanish-American War, when Washington used an essentially civilian-inspired theoretical school of heroism, which Theodore Roosevelt, Henry and Brooks Adams, and their friends led, as an ideological frosting for advancing American colonialism and global economic power.

Modern warfare is utilitarian to the furtherance of present American objectives, but only so long as it is combat between unequals and excludes great nuclear powers. This means, in brief, that in a world of revolutionary nationalist movements there are many small wars that the United States may choose to fight without confronting the U.S.S.R. or China, and that the strategic and most expensive section of the American Military Establishment will remain restrained and passive, as it has in a disciplined fashion in the past. What is left, from the numerous alternatives to anti-peasant, anti-revolutionary warfare with tiny powers, is a choice of political options for relating to the Third World, policies that civilian political leaders and their experts always determine and often call upon the military to implement. In some instances, such as Iran, Indonesia, Greece, and Cuba, the half-political, quasi-military C.I.A. has offered policy-makers more graceful-appearing means for attaining goals while skirting the more cumbersome and overt regular military. Indeed, the very existence of the C.I.A., completely removed from the military services, has increasingly strengthened the total control of the civilians over physical power and military intelligence. If the constantly changing technological escalation of the arms race has given the Military Establishment a dynamic and ever-growing appearance, we must never forget the fact that this is an effect rather than a cause of political policy, an appearance and instrumentality rather than the full nature of reality. If this were not the case, and the American military were all that the naïve element of the Left has blandly claimed, it would have destroyed the world some years ago.

So long as specialists in violence apply it only where and when higher authorities tell them to, a "garrison state" involving the disciplining of society and the politically-based unification of major economic and social institutions will be a rather different type of system than Harold D. Lasswell outlined nearly three decades ago. Indeed, a coercive elite quite willing to undermine democracy at home as well as abroad will rule the society, even in the name of "liberalism," and it will permit global necessities to define its priorities internally, but contrary to Lasswell and Mills, the elite will not base its supremacy only on skill and efficiency—the qualifications of able bureaucrats—but also on the control or servicing of the economic, business sector of power. This dual relationship—one which uses the political structure to advance the domestic and global economic interests of American capitalists—has characterized Washington leaders for the better part of this century.

The fascination with the alleged expertise of the military, as if control of technique is equivalent to real power and implies a political conflict with existing authority, was the major defect in Mills' work no less than Lasswell's. Quite apart from the fact that the labyrinthine technological and political nature of modern warfare makes the professional soldier increasingly dependent on scientists and diplomats, Mills assumed that since the military sector generated vast economic demand, it somehow gave generals and admirals equal power, or near parity, with big business in the permanent war economy, merging their identities and interests in a distinctive, new fashion. Yet how and what the government orders to attain its military goals is a much more complex process than he acknowledged, and that this created a war economy or sector should not obscure the fact that how and where—and how much—money was spent is always a decision of civilian political men as well as interested economic groups. My aim in this essay is to show that the military has always been the instrument, the effect rather than the cause of this policy. That the military intermingled with business and political leaders, and indeed shared a common social origin and outlook, is less consequential than the actual power of the various designers of American policy in the world. Quite apart from the alleged existence of what Mills called "military capitalism," the major issue is: Does this relationship serve the real interests of the military, the capitalists, or both?

BUSINESS DEFINITION OF THE MILITARY STRUCTURE

Business is both a fount and magnet for the Military Establishment. The "military-industrial complex" that exists in the United States is a lopsided phenomenon in which only businessmen maintain their full identity, interests, and commitments to their institution, while the military conforms to the needs of economic interests. Business careers are now part of the aspirations of thousands of military officers, while key businessmen and their lawyers continuously pass in and out of major bureaucratic posts in the Defense Department and national security agencies, usually remaining long enough to determine key policies and then return to business. The arms race, based on continuous technological innovations, originates as often with greedy arms firms as with generals—officers who are the instruments of the arms producers insofar as the military's strategic doctrines give the Services need for appropriate hardware. Perhaps most important, at no time has the military fully controlled or defined the budget and the vital strategic assumptions that have guided its size and allocation, for in this regard, their internal bickering over limited resources has greatly diminished their ability to dictate to the civilians.

Historically, the military has always depended on business to a great extent. The Government left the mobilization of industry for military purposes during the First World War primarily in the hands of businessmen, and the interwar mobilization plans followed the wartime precedents. Corporate executives and business school social scientists dominated and lectured to the Army Industrial College for the decade and one-half after its founding in 1924. When the Roosevelt Administration finally drew up and implemented mobilization plans for the Second World War, businessmen played the vital role in its critical economic aspects, and at no time during the war did any military leader attempt to utilize the vast procurement power to foster a distinctive ideology or collective policy in the postwar period.

One can hardly exaggerate the importance of the specific arms producers and industries in guiding the action of their respective, allied Services, both from the viewpoint of their making available new technical means for advancing Service strategies and eventually incorporating key military men into the military-based economy. Until about 1960, when missiles became the overlapping jurisdiction of all three major Services and traditional lines broke down somewhat, the industries supplying various modes of warfare—on the land, strategic airpower, and naval—all vied with each other for the largest possible slice of the limited military budgets. "The aircraft industry," Senator Barry Goldwater once remarked, "has probably done more to promote the Air Force than the Air Force has done itself." ". . . What appears to be intense interservice rivalry," General James M. Gavin has observed, ". . . in most cases . . . is fundamentally industrial rivalry." In its ultimate and always prevalent form, such business competition determines precisely which weapons systems—which often perform essentially identical functions—the government will purchase. Indeed, in the case of the B-36 bomber and TFX plane, the existence of a firm with problems and traditional Service connections may be the primary reason for the procurement of a weapons system in the first place, even at a greater cost than is necessary. In this process of competition, the officers of various Services may line up with different companies, often merely as fronts.

To survive, weapons producers, and particularly aerospace firms, must constantly devise new weapons and systems to supersede those they have already built. In 1958-59, for example, the Navy received 486 unsolicited antisubmarine-warfare proposals from the industry, and agreed to fund 155 of them. Private risk capital first developed many of the major military aircraft, even though the Services did not see their immediate relevance, only because the corporations needed the final production contracts to operate their plants and make money. In the case of the semi-official Service associations that campaign for greater expenditures for their respective branches—the Navy League, Air Force Association, and Association of the United States Army—the financing of these lobbying activities comes from corporate dues and advertising in their journals.

The ultimate discipline in making key officers subservient to the major arms firms is the hiring of retired officers, about two-thirds of whom left the military voluntarily to take up their new posts. Their ability to make favorable contacts for new careers while in the Services depends, in the last analysis, on avoiding conflicts with arms firms that can close off these lucrative posts. In 1959, the 72 largest arms suppliers alone employed 1,426 retired officers, 251 of them being of flag or general rank. Many of these former officers have special skills and background in procurement, modern weaponry, or the more technologically exotic aspects of warfare, and often meet their future employers in tax-deductible luxury. In effect, corporations are asking them to sell arms to their former military associates. "Every time I go to the Pentagon to obtain a contract for one of my constituents," one congressman complained in 1960, "I run into hundreds of retired officers." Today congressmen and military officers both work for various, if competing, corporations.

THE MILITARY ETHIC

Radical social scientists such as Mills, and conservatives such as Samuel P. Huntington, nurtured the myth that a distinctive military ethic exists, common only to men in uniform. But the concept of aristocracy and discipline allegedly defining the military system hardly appreciates the decisive value of the military's inefficiency and incompetence in creating vast markets for civilian interests. In fact, the notion of an independent military sector, with its own codes and objectives, saves critical observers the trouble of viewing the nature of American power as a much larger integrated phenomenon. The military is a most conformist and pliable aspect of the power system, quite drably bureaucratic, and it serves the purposes of capitalists and politicians without much reticence.

While it is true the technicians of violence are an intrinsic part of American leadership, these men begin with and often play many other roles as well, and as I have already argued, these roles are primary and a greater revelation of their true function. The ideologists of expansion and militarism in the United States have, with rare exceptions, been civilians in the tradition of what Huntington calls neo-Hamiltonianism, and not since Alfred T. Mahan has a professional officer penned a respectable rationale for the enlargement of American might that reflected distinctive ideological assumptions. Indeed, what is most significant about neo-Hamiltonianism is its role as a justification for the political capitalism that was the most critical outcome of American liberal reform, and its affinity for classic international expansion and adventure abroad. The failure of any significant sector of the military openly to rally to such theories of the positive and predatory state at any time reveals mainly that the American military is nonideological, even when civilians formulate a seemingly appropriate frame of reference for it.

There have been no coups, no hints of physical insubordination, no serious general political-military alliances. The one possible exception, the MacArthur controversy of 1951, was essentially a case of heading off the obvious political aims of a man whose overweening personal ambition and conceit was a quality of personality rather than a spearhead for a military alliance or a distinctive policy orientation. And it was a general, who, as President in 1961, warned of the dangers of the "military-industrial complex" *and* the "scientific-technological elite," and reaffirmed the virtue of civilian supremacy. Even MacArthur ended his days as an articulate opponent of total war, calling for nuclear disarmament.

No later than November 1947 the Army quietly informed its leading generals that they could neither write nor speak in a manner that contradicted the existing government policy toward Russia or the United Nations, an admonition that it often repeated. Publicly, in subsequent years such figures as General Omar N. Bradley, then head of the Joint Chiefs of Staff, stated that the function of the military was to assume responsibility for a military policy adequate for the implementation of the national political criteria and goals which the President and his chosen advisers defined. It was in this context during the Truman Administration that the State Department became the leading single exponent of expanded military power and the construction of an H-bomb, with the responsible military men operating within given and more stringent budgetary assumptions. "The Army respects its civilian leadership and abstains from any involvement in politics," General Maxwell D. Taylor, Army Chief of Staff, wrote to his major officers in September 1955. When General Matthew B. Ridgway published his iconoclastic memoir the following year, he only revealed an intense desire to permit his Service freedom to war with the Air Force and Navy for a larger portion of the military budget, and not to be subject to some "politico-military" party line before the civilians made their final decisions, at which point ". . . they could expect completely loyal and diligent execution of those decisions."

There are, of course, the much publicized but ultimately unrepresentative extremes in the military viewpoint. At the one pole is the view of the professional nonideological technician of death, which the then head of the Marine Corps, General David M. Shoup, expressed in a statement in 1961: "We're professional soldiers. We fight any enemy the President designates. We don't have to develop hate. We don't just keep talking communism. . . . You might build up a hate against one enemy and find yourself fighting another." The other position, even less consequential, is the jingoist reaction which so alarmed liberals in 1961 when the press revealed that John Birch and similar reactionary notions were a part of a military education program on about a score of bases, or a small minority of the total. What was truly significant about the phenomenon was that it was not more widespread, perhaps much less than in high schools and newspapers, and that it revealed how far the military had gone to censor the eccentric, idiosyncratic, and reactionary speeches of some of its generals. Such revelations were useful, for the fierce statements of a few impotent professorial geopoliticans, and the minor officers who used them, made the Kennedy Administration look relatively moderate at a time when it was advocating a vast civil defense program and a conventional military build-up, and attempting to create a first-strike nuclear strategy that, combined or individually, constituted a truly irrational new course in the arms race.

The moral of the few incidents of which we know is that the Birchite General Walker and those like him are summarily forced from the military and government service if their superiors cannot bring them into line. During the barely undercover "preventive war" discussions of August 1950, when Secretary of the Navy Francis Mathews publicly called for ". . . instituting a war to compel cooperation for peace," only the fact that he was "very contrite" when the President called him in saved Mathews his post. While Hanson Baldwin claimed Mathews really reflected the views of Secretary of Defense Louis Johnson, thus posing a military challenge to civilian authority, what was most consequential was that all the personalities involved until that time were civilians. When shortly thereafter the head of the Air War College publicly urged preventive war against Russia, the Pentagon suspended him from his command.

The military, in brief, has been docile, its alleged "ethic" nebulous and meaningless. It has dissented no more than any other group of bureaucrats serving the state, and unquestionably it has been among the most restrained of those in power. A closer look at the manner in which the Military Establishment has operated only confirms this point.

THE MILITARY AFTER
THE SECOND WORLD WAR

The central fact of the immediate postwar experience is that although the American Military Establishment was more than sufficient in regard to what Washington considered to be the major military problem—the Soviet Union—it was relatively starved not merely in contrast to the potential of the American economy, but also when measured against the actual as opposed to the perceived global challenges to American power abroad. Nearly everyone in Washington saw the question of communism and the Left as essentially a matter of the Soviet Union and Europe, and not until 1949 and thereafter did the question of Asia assume sufficiently high priority to warrant a shift toward a slightly more balanced military capacity. In reality, the American political definition of the world's main "problems" served as a usefully reinforcing underpinning to an almost universal desire to limit the military budget, for if Russia was the primary opponent, the relatively low cost of the strategic atomic theory of the Air Force made sense. The significant point is that the Air Force atomic strategy, which Congress endorsed, made it possible to place a ceiling on arms expenditures, and only the rude events of Korea, Indo-China, and the gradual shift of American priorities from Europe to Asia and Latin America inevitably forced arms expenditures ever upward.

In this process of changing concerns, lasting from 1946 to the beginning of the "New Look" under Eisenhower, Service divisions over fundamental strategic assumptions left the civilians quite free to continue to make the critical decisions regarding the extent and use of military power. It is this profound disunity that is the central fact of the potential political role of the military in the United States, and it was especially sharp during the lean years of 1946–50, when the military budget ranged from a low of $11.8 billion in 1948, or 4.5 percent of the gross national product, to a high of $14.4 billion in 1947, 6.2 percent of the GNP. In the context of opposition to Truman's two-year efforts to unify the military services into a single Department of Defense, eventually embodied in the National Security Act of July 1947, the Navy had overtly opposed any move toward reducing the future role of sea power. Less openly, the Army hoped to save its weakened position against the Air Force, which claimed total capacity to deter or win a war with Russia cheaply, by advancing a Universal Military Training bill in Congress, a politically unpopular proposal that Truman also mildly endorsed. And to relate itself to military probabilities, the Navy advanced plans for supercarriers capable of delivering bombs against the Soviet heartland.

Since all these conflicting strategic and organizational claims carried substantial price tags, and Congress was unwilling to pay for them all, the more attractive doctrine and political connections of the Air Force prevailed. Congress, with the Air Force's assistance, killed U.M.T., and the Army passively watched while the advocates of air power in Congress undercut the Navy supercarrier program. By the spring of 1949, when the Secretary of the Navy resigned in protest over the course of events, both the Air Force and Navy were engaged in a propaganda war against each other, unquestionably the most interesting and artful in the history of American strategic doctrine.

A number of officers of the tactical fighter section of the Air Force, who resented the emphasis on big bombers, aided the Navy, but the furor over the B-36 bomber—on which the Air Force pinned its hopes for lack of a better plane—was the chief factor in strengthening the Navy's position. The Air Force's own experts privately had shown little enthusiasm for the B-36, which, with the aid of memos that Navy officers and competitive air frame producers distributed, correctly looked too much like an effort to bail out the sinking fortunes of the politically well-connected Consolidated Vultee Aircraft Company, whose links reached as high as Secretary of Defense Louis Johnson. In the course of House hearings during October 1949 the Navy tendentiously advocated the value of carrier-based mobile air power and limited warfare, arguing the immorality of a city-busting atomic blitz as "morally reprehensible" and the illegal "mass killing of noncombatants." Such pleading was hollow, since the supercarrier was also useful mainly as a "city buster" against civilian populations. And as the Secretary of the Air

Force, W. Stuart Symington maintained with greater consistency, the destruction of civilians is ". . . an unavoidable result of modern total warfare," and ". . . this opinion that war is immoral is a fairly recent one for anybody in the Military Establishment, and I wondered how and why it came up."

No one in the Navy truly believed their moralistic contentions, and when eventually the Polaris submarine missile was invented, they too developed a strategic doctrine appropriate to that "city-busting" weapon. Truman was to fire at least one key Navy officer for his resistance to the official line, the Chief of Naval Operations, Admiral Louis E. Denfeld, and he disciplined others. What was at stake was not merely the independence of the various Services, but the belief, as General Bradley phrased it, that ". . . a nation's economy is its ultimate strength," and how they might obtain maximum security for the least expense remained the crucial issue. Most of the Army generals who rose to prominence in the Joint Chiefs of Staff, as well as Herbert Hoover, Eisenhower, and the main forces of the budget-minded Republican Party, reinforced this assumption at the time. Congress itself has exerted control over the military not by aligning with it but rather by working within the President's broad guidelines and budgetary allocations to make certain that the Administration cut their constituents into as large a slice of the pie as possible. Other than this pork barrel impulse, which occasionally Congress translates into specific weapons systems that hardly alter the larger contours of the Executive branch's strategy, the role of Congress has merely been passively self-interested.

If later the Army was to produce its own dissidents, the nature of the competitive struggle for limited budgetary resources in the 1950's meant that the profound divisions within the Military Establishment would always permit the civilians to play one Service bloc, consisting of the generals and their contractors, against the other. It is less significant to speculate what might have happened had the military assumed a common front, which is nearly impossible, then to realize that at no time did the political decision-makers lose control of the policy process.

America's civilian leaders applied the nation's policies within the informal and shifting committee-like structure that they organized into the National Security Council after mid-1947. United States leadership first defined those goals during the period 1896–1920, when McKinley, Roosevelt, and Wilson first scaled the objectives of American foreign policy to the capacity of American power to extend into the world. No later than the end of the Second World War those aims included a full-blown ideology of United States hegemony in the Western Hemisphere and Pacific, and primary leadership in the greater part of the areas that remained. Those goals reflected the American peace aims hammered out during the war, a process that excluded the Military Establishment on most of the key questions.

The very disunity within the military Services filled various key leaders in Washington with suspicion toward the consistency and reliability of the new Department of Defense, and they learned to depend on their own resources within the National Security Council and other committees. Although the original Council included the three Service secretaries, these men were all civilians; and while the Joint Chiefs attended meetings during the first years of the Council's existence, not until after the Korean War did they participate in the Council's vital staff functions. During 1949 Truman dropped the Service secretaries, and after the Korean War sharply cut back on the size of Council meetings, and the Defense Department has largely restricted itself to technical advice and analysis of the military implications of foreign policy decisions of the President, Secretary of State, or the advisers that the President uses informally. If Cabinet agencies set up independent planning committees from time to time, meshing foreign and military policy, the Executive ultimately considered their recommendations in a manner that lowers the relative weight of Defense and military opinion. The Government, for the most part, has not determined basic foreign policy otherwise.

Significantly, the civilians rather than the military attempted to break out of the traditional straitjacket of budgetary limitations to attain a force level equal to American political goals and ideological conceptions. During 1949 George Kennan argued for greater emphasis on mobile conventional armies. And it was with the budgetary restriction in mind that Dean Acheson, David Lilienthal, and Louis Johnson urged the President in January 1950 to authorize preliminary studies on the H-bomb, a weapon most of Washington then considered necessary in light of the Soviet discovery of the secret of making an A-bomb, to retain military superiority within a limited budget. The State Department, developing Kennan's original impulse and making it more grandiose, at the same time took the lead in a joint Defense-State committee to urge a vast increase in the military budget, which the State Department proposed to make between $35–50 billion, tying it to general ideological descriptions of the communist menace. The Joint Chiefs and Defense leaders, more modest and less ideological, and split within their own ranks due to Secretary Johnson's desire to cut the Defense budget, could propose only $17–18 billion, a modest increase over existing levels. At this juncture the Korean War began, with the conflicting positions in the policy paper now known as JCS 68 still unresolved.

By 1953 the military budget had grown to 13.8 percent of the gross national product, but in the White House a former general undertook to reduce the percentage with his "New Look" military policy of greater reliance on nuclear power. Eisenhower was concerned with the problem of how to maintain vast military power over a long period of time without overheating the nonmilitary economic sector and without assuming, as had the Democrats, that the danger of war with Russia increased with growing Soviet military and economic power. Above all, he wished to confront the extraordinarily difficult and ultimately unresolvable dilemma of how to combat or neutralize the diverse social revolutionary threats to the permanent strategic, political, and economic goals of the United States—a dilemma which has characterized American foreign policy since the fall of China. America's capacity to confront successfully the Soviet Union required a budgetary expenditure and strategic posture that was predictable. However, such a policy was inadequate to meet the challenge of the many, often yet unborn local revolutionary situations, where crude weapons made strategic nuclear weaponry inappropriate and potentially suicidal.

America's economic and political limitations could not halt a world drifting beyond its control.

Ultimately, the Eisenhower Administration chose to confront Russia and to risk its ability effectively to respond militarily to the rest of the world. The General and his government rejected a full mobilization of American manpower and economic resources into a total warfare state capable of seriously retarding revolutionary movements everywhere. The result was a doctrine of massive retaliation appropriate for warfare against highly industrialized powers, which the Government now frankly acknowledges as unlikely, and a beginning in the long-term decline in the coveted American hegemony in the world. The upshot, too, has been that in the rare instances which tempted factions of the military to use nuclear weapons, such as in Indo-China during the spring of 1954, the Army's fundamental skepticism toward this strategy made employment of it impossible. Under the New Look policy, the absolute and percentage decline in military expenditures and Army-Navy manpower continued, much to the disgust of Army generals, until Kennedy came to office. In effect, military policy and outlays were sufficient only to maintain a high level of economic activity at home, but insufficient to cope with social revolution and guerrilla warfare, against which missiles and atomic weapons were largely useless.

THE "CIVILIANIZED" MILITARY

Within the context of these internal military divisions, the Services' lack of a unified strategic doctrine, and the overriding limits of the budgetary process in defining options, it would be difficult to prove C. Wright Mills' contention that ". . . as a coherent group of men the military is probably the most competent now concerned with national policy; no other group has had the training in co-ordinated economic, political, and military affairs. . . ." On the contrary, nothing in the operational structure of the Defense Establishment nor in the changing character of military technology alters the fact that civilian, even "liberal," leadership and civilian ideology have led the United

States and the world into its present morass of global crises and interventionism.

Each successive reorganization of the Defense Establishment since 1947 has further consolidated the decisive role of civilians in military policy. In 1949 Congress deprived the Services of independent executive status and placed over it a Defense Department structure with superior powers. In one of his first and most critical acts, the stronger civilian Secretary created an independent, superior office to control all missile developments within the three Services, thereby dominating the most essential sector of future military technology. The Defense Reorganization Act of 1953 further accelerated the civilian domination of the Defense Department by increasing the number of civilian assistant secretaries from three to nine and assigning them many responsibilities hitherto left to civilian-military boards. While certain of their functions were vague, it placed larger control of functional problems in the hands of civilians who were not responsible to the Services but to the Defense Secretary. One of them, indeed, represented unified Defense policy on international affairs directly to the National Security Council. In this context, with the three services so profoundly divided on strategy and in competition for limited budgetary resources which the civilians could use to split their ranks, the Joint Chiefs of Staff were unable to stem the supremacy of the civilians in the Pentagon. The President usually selected a politically reliable officer to be the head of the Joint Chiefs, and the Air Force was more than willing to break away from the other Services at the sacrifice of a possible common front because, in the showdown, it usually could better protect its own interests against the others. When united, which meant primarily on minor questions, the civilian leaders treated the Joint Chiefs deferentially. In any event, the Defense Reorganization Act of 1958 further strengthened the role of the civilian secretaries, and in that year the Secretary, via the Advanced Research Projects Agency, took over responsibility for all important weapons systems developments.

In the context of the ever-growing dependence of the professional soldiers on the civilian Defense Secretaries, both the soldiers and civilians in the Pentagon in turn increased their reliance on the civilians in business and the universities for the major technological innovations and strategies which are the most grotesquely threatening aspect of the arms race and the condition of the world today. The fact was that the generals and admirals were incapable of managing and developing scientifically sophisticated "hardware" programs with which the United States hoped to compensate for its man-power and ideological disadvantages in a revolutionary world. Most, indeed, were near illiterates in the major critical areas, and alone were patently unable to attain the maximum military impact and resources from the budgets that Congress had allocated. Conscious of these limitations, in 1946 Eisenhower had decided for the Army that ". . . there appears little reason for duplicating within the Army an outside organization which by its experience is better qualified than we are to carry out some of our tasks," which meant the Army would ". . . find much of the talent we need for comprehensive planning in industry and universities." Thus began a vast research and development program and military dependence on industry and universities, and an even larger stake on the part of a vital sector of these institutions in an arms race. In 1948 the Air Force took over the Rand Corporation on contract to secure its advice, and from 1953 to 1948 relied for the direction of its missile program, on the Ramo-Wooldridge Corporation, whose ballistic missile staff grew from 18 to 3,269 in five years. After 1953 the Air Force left the coordination of its specific weapons systems to its prime contractors, and by 1959 drew 46 percent of its procurement personnel at the supervisory level from private business backgrounds—a figure the Navy and Army almost matched. In the field of missiles almost all of the government's key advisers have been civilians from industry and the universities. By 1955 the Pentagon's in-house Weapons System Evaluation Group was near collapse, and only a contract between M.I.T. and the Defense Department, which led to the creation of the multi-university-sponsored Institute for Defense Analysis, saved that undertaking—but in civilian, private hands. By the time the Kennedy Administration took office, civilians had so thoroughly permeated the Military

Establishment with their techniques, ideology, and objectives that it was apparent that professional officers were hardly more than docile instruments of the state, less credible to its civilian leadership than even many facile and ambitious Ivy League Ph.D.'s who, in their ability to translate American power into strategies and arms systems, saw the opportunity of becoming advisers to the men already at the top.

The final reorganization of the Defense Department, which Robert McNamara merely completed, utterly depersonalized the distinctive aspects of a military bureaucracy on the premise ". . . that the techniques used to administer these affairs of a large organization are very similar whether that organization be a business enterprise or a Government institution, or an educational institution, or any other large aggregation of human individuals working to a common end." In reality, McNamara's model and experience was the Ford Motor Company, but in the Defense Department he sought to maximize objectives at the lowest possible price rather than accumulate an annual profit. Ph.D.'s managed the resulting "package programs" and increasingly centralized procurement at the further expense of the professional soldiers, who whimpered bitterly but continued to lose vital leverage and administrative directions. Complaints from the generals still often centered on the matter of budgetary allocations for the various Services, or their deflated egos and the roles of officers in ever-narrowing areas, but they did not alter the essential reality of the further "civilianization" of the commanding sectors of the Military Establishment, mainly in the hands of political "liberals" dedicated to civil rights, social welfare, and art centers which have become the liberal's surrogates for a society based on economic foundations of justice.

The collapse of the McNamara empire did not end civilian predominance, even as these civilians chose the new generation of generals more for their technical competence than their military prowess. As a materialist *par excellence*, McNamara eventually realized that the unattainable ideological goals of American policy had outstripped physical resources, turning the war in Vietnam into a seemingly endless series of escalations, each one only further intensifying the defeats America was suffering in the hands of peasants. His elimination came not from his disagreements with the military but with the other civilians who were even more belligerent than he had been throughout his career. Indeed, this episode perhaps more than any other exposed how totally military in means and ends were the ideological premises of those who believed also in the supremacy of civilian authority over the military. It showed how fully the Military Establishment was merely the instrument of warfare liberalism in the Fair Deal-Great Society period of American history. And Vietnam, in turn, revealed how irrelevant the ingenuity and technical efficiency of American policy had been in a Third World whose fate revolutionary mass movements would determine, despite resistance, repression, and occasional setbacks.

> The commercial supremacy of the Republic means
> that this nation is to be the sovereign factor in the
> peace of the world. For the struggles of the future
> are to be conflicts of trade—struggles for markets—
> commercial wars for existence. And the golden rule
> of peace is impregnability of position and invincibil-
> ity of preparedness.
> —SENATOR ALBERT J. BEVERIDGE, 1898.

THE VIETNAM CASE

CARL OGLESBY

If cold war anticommunism is most basically an ideological mask
for Free World imperialism, then one should be able to show
somehow that the issue of the Vietnam war is not Western
freedom versus Eastern slavery but foreign versus local control
of Vietnam—to show, that is, that the war is being fought to
determine how and by whom the Vietnamese political economy
is going to be developed. And since the United States has
committed itself so unreservedly to Vietnam's Free World salvation, this line of analysis is also obliged to show that Vietnam
is somehow crucial for the security and growth of the American
commercial state.

It is precisely on this point that the imperialism theory confronts a simple, serious objection: Are American commercial
interests in that very poor, very backward part of the world
so substantial as to justify so dangerous and unlimited a war?
The war is now costing Americans upward of $20 billion a year.
How many years will it take for a "saved" Vietnam to start paying

Reprinted by permission of the Macmillan Company from *Containment and
Change* by Carl Oglesby and Richard Shaull. © 1967 by Carl Oglesby and Richard
Shaull.

dividends on that kind of military investment? The accountant will observe that saving Vietnam is costing us a great deal more than any resulting "colonial" advantage will ever be worth. This entirely common sensical observation, on its face quite persuasive, directs us to dismiss the imperialist theory (at least for *this* war) and return to a more purely "political," noncommercial explanation.

But probe the case more curiously. We shall find that America's Vietnam policy does not merely illustrate American imperialism, it is a paradigm instance of it; and that in its fusion of imperialist motive and anticommunist ideology, the war is not only exemplary, it is also climactic.

There are four important points, argued below in ascending order of importance.

First, a direct American commercial interest in Vietnam exists. For the most part it is potential. That makes it no less real.

In its issue of January 1, 1966, *Newsweek* ran an essay called "Saigon: A Boomtown for U.S. Businessmen." A similar piece by Edmund K. Faltermayer appeared in the March 1966 issue of *Fortune* under the title "The Surprising Assets of South Viet-Nam's Economy." There is the possibility that both pieces may have been a bit contrived or calculated. Perhaps they were brought forth to bolster the business community's enthusiasm for a war which creates a few domestic nuisances (e.g., inflation, labor scarcities in key-skill areas, higher taxes, tighter credit). But whatever the motive, these pieces—and Faltermayer's especially—must have convinced many that South Vietnam is a plum quite delectable enough to be saved. "A South Viet-Nam preserved from Communism," Faltermayer wrote, "has the potential to become one of the richest nations in Southeast Asia." He notes that the country could become an exporter of sugar and cotton, both of which it now imports; that it exported a record 83,000 tons of rubber in 1961, and could easily surpass that record under normal conditions; that the Mekong Delta, the "rice bowl" which now produces about four million tons of rice annually, could produce 12 to 15 million tons. It is not by magic that the rice, the rubber, the sugar, the cotton—and the promising industrial crops, jute, ramie, and kenaf—will come leaping from the ground into the holds of cargo ships. That will require capital, whether the socialist or the capitalist kind.

The capitalist pioneers are already staking their claims. Chase Manhattan and the Bank of America have opened branch offices in Saigon. The New York firm of Parsons & Whittemore holds 18 percent interest in a $5-million American-managed paper mill at Bien Hoa. Foremost Dairies of California has controlling interest in a new condensed-milk plant and half-interest in a new textile mill. Another textile mill has been partly financed by the Johnson International Corporation. The American Trading Co. and Brownell Lane Engineering Co. are selling and servicing heavy equipment—bulldozers, tractors, trucks, and railroad locomotives—and averaging 20 to 30 percent returns on their investments.

The giant is RMK-BRJ, a construction combine formed by Raymond International, Morrison-Knudsen, Brown & Root, and J. A. Jones Construction. RMK-BRJ is the major contractor for the enormous military construction program in airbases, ports, and roads (economic "infrastructure"), and its contracts may eventually reach $700 million. As of March 1966, it was already the biggest private employer in the country, with 25,000 workers on its payroll and plans for an increase up to 75,000.

"Never before," said Newsweek, "have U.S. businessmen followed their [sic!] troops to war on such a scale." Faltermayer is careful not to exaggerate the size of the present stake. He emphasizes that our total direct investment in Vietnam is at the moment no more than $6 million. But the niggardliness of that amount is itself a clear enticement: There is a new wide-open frontier's-worth of opportunity in Vietnam. The situation, he says.

> could change radically in the next few years. Esso and Caltex
> . . . are studying proposals to build a $16-million oil refinery,
> the country's first. Shell Oil and the South Vietnamese Gov-
> ernment would participate in the venture, and the refinery
> might be included in the proposed Cam Ranh Bay industrial
> complex.

(It is surprising, however, that Faltermayer represents this "venture" as something new. The same $16-million refinery plans were already "under study" as early as April 1962, according to Indochina scholar Bernard B. Fall, who adds to the story a touching note: "There is strong evidence that the American Government 'urgently invited' the oil companies to proceed with the contract in order to show American confidence in the future of Viet-Nam.")

An important aspect of the commercial picture is, of course, the donation of American dollars to finance the Vietnamese import of American goods. We have already quoted *Forbes* (which calls itself a "capitalist tool") on the Agency for International Development: It "is the principal agency through which the U.S. Government finances business abroad. . . . AID distributes about $2 billion a year. Of this, 85 percent is spent in the U.S. for American products and raw materials." In 1966, AID allocations to Vietnam were about a sixth of the $2 billion total. In 1967, this goes to a fourth: $550 million. If 85 percent of that is spent on American exports, South Vietnam will rank among our ten top buyers.

All new frontiers need their Paul Bunyans. Faltermayer offers a strong candidate in a New York entrepreneur named Herbert Fuller, head of an investor group which since 1958 has been promoting a $10-million sugar mill for the coastal city of Tuy Hoa:

> When the troops arrive to clear the area, as they sooner or later must, this American capitalist will literally be one step behind them. "I am in it for the money," Fuller says. "We could get back our investment in two years." Like all entrepreneurs, Fuller once again is pushing ahead with his plans because he assumes the U.S. is now committed to saving Viet-Nam.

But so what? Why is it so wrong for our businessmen to be right behind "their" troops? There is nothing strange about the pursuit of profit and opportunity; and that the businessmen should at once occupy, settle on, and begin to develop the ground just cleared by our troops does not mean that it is for them that the troops are there. Does it?

We encounter a problem of vision. It is hard to see these particular businessmen as being in any way crucial to the Vietnam drama. Their appearance in it seems incidental—important perhaps, but not especially significant. The war would be the same with or without them. It is being fought for freedom or to hold back the Communists. It is not being fought for this Herbert Fuller, "American capitalist."

No doubt. If Fuller decided the Tuy Hoa project was a bad bet and went back to New York, another coastal city, no one thinks the Marines would forgo the conquest of Tuy Hoa. But what do we suppose "freedom" means? And what is the real purpose of keeping the Communists back? Our functional definition of a free country is clear from our behavior. The definition says that a country is free when Americans like Fuller are free to do business in it if they have the skill and the drive to do so. It is free when there are native counterparts of Fuller. It is free when there is free enterprise. When there is *no* free enterprise, the country *is* Communist. It cannot be doubted that Vietnam's importance lies far more basically in its geographic and *historical* position than in its inherent commercial potentials, whether immediate or long-term. But, as we shall see, that is only because Vietnam is imagined to be the key to larger areas—areas whose commercial accessibility *is* important to us, and which will or will not themselves be "free," depending on the possibility of our doing business in them. Thus, when Faltermayer talks of "saving Vietnam," he is at one and the same time talking about saving both it and the region for Fuller, free enterprise, and Western-style freedom—for the last two are considered to define each other, and the first is an instance of their realization. "After the war," says Arthur Tunnell, of Investors Overseas Services' Saigon office, "there is going to be a big future for American businessmen here." Analyze to the surface the vision which that statement makes concrete, and one will approach an exhaustive ideological description of the Vietnam war.

Second, the militarized economy demands a militarized politics; a militarized politics demands a militarized economy. Vietnam, as conflict colony, helps turn this wheel.

Consider that since 1946 the federal government has laid out about 60 percent of its budget for support of the military-industrial complex, a 20-year total of better than $850 billion. This is a *political* fact.

In 1959, when Khrushchev came to Camp David and the Cold War seemed up for reappraisal, the stock market took its sharpest downturn in nearly four years. This was called "peace jitters." In 1960, when Eisenhower came back from Paris via that broken U-2 (a Lockheed novelty), *The New York Times'* financial page headlined: "Summit Failure a Market Tonic."

During the summer of 1965, as is very well known, certain informed people were again fretful about the national economy. Having cantilevered themselves out into the future on act of faith after vote of confidence, the lenders and the borrowers and their analysts began to make uneasy murmurs. News of an important inner-sanctum debate about the national metabolism drifted out in bits and pieces. The Administration seemed to favor confidence. But then the Federal Reserve Board's chairman, William McChesney Martin, Jr., began to say aloud in public places that he was not convinced things were as right as they ought to be. He even confessed that the economy was putting him in mind of 1929. No one knew quite how to react to this crack in the expert consensus. Was it deep? Was there any real danger? There was a ripple of discreet uncertainty.

In this subdued Perils-of-Pauline atmosphere, there all of a sudden appeared an unexpected hero whom no one was really surprised to see. The hero was the war: It would not get smaller, much less come to a quick end, and it became common knowledge that its direct costs would go to at least $21 billion a year. However nervous it might remain, the bull market had won its reprieve.

Those who argue that the Vietnam war *must* have been forced upon us since it is so uneconomical do not grasp the economics of state capitalism. The economic effects of the war are anything but unambiguous. The war generates very real fiscal management problems and disturbing anomalies in the pattern of foreign exchange. But over all, the war is good for the economy because the economy is addicted to federal subsidy in general and to military subsidy in particular. It appears that we *have* to spend, because what a high-employment economy produces has to be vended. Whether it goes into the sweet life or the limbo of government silos, the product has to go some place and it has to be paid for. Consider, then, a key economic fact about the defense product: *It is not produced at the expense of recognized domestic necessities.* It is not as if Americans are standing in queues to purchase automobiles, which, for the sake of tanks, are going unbuilt. The opposite comes closer to being the case: If it were not for the tanks, the planes, the submarines, the missiles—where would the economy be? Which is very much like asking: If it were not for the heroin, where would the junkies be? Obviously: in hospitals undergoing very painful therapy. Perhaps even of a revolutionary nature.

One does not claim that the Vietnam war was escalated only to cheer up an overblown, dour economy with that "external" and "expanded" market which it could not otherwise procure. But what if the Vietnam war ended and China said, Have it your way? What if the Cold War faded and faded until one day someone noticed that it had disappeared? What would become of this gargantuan Lockheed with its $500 million in research and development contracts alone? What would become of the intensively specialized scientists, engineers, technicians, administrators, and line workers it employs? Or of the tens of thousands of shopkeepers, middlemen, lenders, and suppliers their salaries keep in business? Where are the concrete plans, the great Congressional debates, the enabling legislation on the management of defense-to-civilian industrial conversion? Who is hammering out the answers?

We have a scatterfire from assorted blue-ribbon commissions of scientists, economists, and businessmen whom everyone very well knows to be nonserious. They are a step wiser than Sisyphus, for they only circle their rock, staring at it soberly, poking at it now and then. What else? Are they foolish, these men of science, economics, and businss? But it really seems not to matter. Not so deep down inside at all, quite on the surface of intuition, we are all privy to the main secret of state, which is that we are in no real danger of being abandoned by this "threat" that keeps the corporate state in its fighting trim.

Look at Europe, where there is no claim that the "threat" is increasing. The reverse is true: more trade with East Europe and the U.S.S.R., moves on both sides of the Curtain (of which de Gaulle's in the West and Ceausecu's in the East are only the most dramatic) to bring Europe toward accord and integration. Yet in this atmosphere of calm and confidence, after several years of the preaching and the apparent practice of coexistence, what is America's policy on European militarization? Over the past fifteen years we have given or sold to other countries some $35 billion worth of military equipment. Since mid-1961, military export sales have run to more than $9 billion, and the profit to American defense suppliers totals about $1 billion—nicely concentrated in the hands of three big and highly influential firms, General Dynamics, Lockheed, and McDonnell. Overseas military sales for 1965 were about $2 billion and, let the Cold War thaw as it pleases, they will run on at that high rate into the foreseeable future. Why does this happen, if the threat is diminishing? It happens because our military sales abroad represent one of our major handles on our chronic balance-of-payments deficit. These sales are actively promoted by the Pentagon, which seems to care little more about the buyers' need and ability to pay for guns than any ordinary used-car salesman: The goodness of the guns is a good enough need, and if the price seems high, never mind, another part of our government will put up an easy-term loan. The number-one salesman—the Pentagon calls him a "negotiator"—is Henry J. Kuss, Jr., Deputy Assistant Secretary of Defense for International Logistics Negotiations. In May 1965, in recognition of his section's "intensive sales effort," Kuss was awarded the Meritorious Civilian Service Medal.

Here is a prime instance: Germany earns about $675 million a year from the American troops who are stationed there. To offset these U.S. payments, Germany "has been encouraged" to purchase $1.3 billion worth of American military goods over the 1966–67 period. Very convenient, that Germany's military equipment "needs" so closely match our expenses. But Germany seems reluctant to buy what we insist she cannot do without. Foreign military sales in the first quarter of 1966 were the lowest since 1964, and the big reason was Germany's tardiness in making the agreed-upon purchases. That tardiness might have something to do with Germany's recession and budget problems. But that is small concern of ours. We have to move these goods.

It is argued that these weapons stabilize the world and make peace, as if the financial benefit which accrues to us from their sale were only a happy incidental. But the most elementary survey of what is now happening in European politics will make it clear that armaments—on both sides—are increasingly irrelevant to peace and stability, and that if they have any effect at all on the larger pattern of European reintegration, it is a negative and obstructing one. Outside Europe, realities counter the arms-for-stability thesis even more ominously. Former Ambassador to India John Kenneth Galbraith testified before the Foreign Relations Committee on April 25, 1966, that "the arms we supplied . . . caused the war between India and Pakistan. . . . If we had not supplied arms, Pakistan would not have sought a military solution [to the Kashmir dispute]."

As bad as it was—and may yet be again—the India-Pakistan encounter will be nothing compared to what may at any moment erupt in the Near and Middle East. Neither the Arabian war with Israel nor Nasser's vendetta with Saudi Arabia has anything at all to do with the Cold War; no one thinks the Russians are about to come howling down the Caspain or across the Kopet Mountains, and once upon a time it was American policy (as Rusk put it as recently as January 1966) "not to stimulate and promote the arms race in the Near East and not to encourage it by our direct participation." Little more than two months after that statement, the State Department announced an agreement to sell Jordan (which already had American tanks) "a limited number" of advanced fighter-bomber aircraft, reportedly Lockheed F-104s. Senator Eugene McCarthy commented: "It is not clear how Jordan, which has an annual per capita GNP of $233 and which has been dependent on U.S. military grants and economic aid, will pay for these planes, which cost $2,000,000 apiece. *The availability of U.S. credit for arms purchases is undoubtedly an important factor."* [Emphasis added.]

Selling arms to both Israel and the Arab world at the same time is an embarrassing business, so we do it behind the barn as much as we can—but do it nevertheless because we suppose we have to. One interesting sequence begins with our demand that Britain purchase American fighter planes. Having complied, Britain now has need of sales to "offset" *her* imbalance. Britain is therefore allowed to bid on American munitions contracts. But should she win such bids, *that would result in a market loss for American munitions-makers.* So the Pentagon arranges to find British bids not quite up to standard. American sellers are content. But Britain still has her deficit. Enter Saudi Arabia, convinced that she will be unsafe so long as she does not have a big fleet of fighters. She would like to have American ones, the best. But against the background of American policy on Israel, this is a "need" which it would be politically ticklish for us to service—at least openly. So we persuade Saudi Arabia that ours are not the only aircraft in the world worth flying and she will be just as happy with a British mark. Britain thereupon sells Saudi Arabia what she wants—$400 million worth of supersonic fighters. And we, having lost no market which we might gracefully have entered, *count this British aircraft sale to Saudi Arabia as the quid-pro-quo balancer of our original aircraft sales to Britain.*

So it goes. Apparently we are not really proud of this sort of thing, but what can we do? There stand the bright weapons in a row. Behind them stand their engineers. Behind the engineers, the executives, who serve on presidential committees and travel often to the capital. Behind the executives, the booming system for which they work, for which they speak, in which they have their being. The system must boom, the executives must have their being, the military engineers must design, the riveters must rivet, and the shining bright weapons must therefore be *marketed.* And that marketing is easier if there is a certain uneasiness in the world, a little tension and anxiety. Who could market aspirin if there were no headaches? Yet what is more antiheadache than aspirin? Preventive aspirin, these sleek fighter aircraft. But the world should not forget what a headache is. So to go with that conceptual beauty called "preventive war," we have preventive *threats,* just big enough to put an edge on things and keep the system from coming unstuck.

Harvard economist Sumner Slichter explained the system very movingly in a 1949 address to a group of bankers. The Cold War, he said, "increases the demand for goods, helps sustain a high level of employment, accelerates technological progress and thus helps the country to raise its standard of living. . . . So we may thank the Russians for helping make capitalism in the United States work better than ever."

Sad to say, we have had to watch Russia's glory fade, her power to inspire our capitalism decline. Besides, when we have put 7000 long-range nuclear rockets in West Europe alone, we have perhaps begun to saturate a good market. But we are in luck, for new Russians keep entering the Cold War market. Today we have China—and therefore Vietnam. And in the wings, to-morrow's starlets—Guatemala? the Philippines? Iran?—are even now trying on their black-pajama *campesino* costumes and rehearsing their most splenetic Marxist curses. And the Third World is crawling with CIA and Special Forces talent scouts.

Third, the strategic heart of the matter.

Increasingly from the turn of the century, American policy has been preoccupied with the problem of pacifying the global commercial environment. As early as the mid-1890s we had already become the world's leading manufacturer and therefore internationalist in spite of ourselves. It had become critical to us that our foreign markets should not be disturbed. How were the required stability and freedom of access to be won? A distinctly minority opinion was that they could not be: The old nations were too bent on conquering one another. America should therefore be neutral and trade with all who would trade on proper terms. (This is one of the so-called isolationist posi-tions. It is not isolationist, it is neutralist. Neutralism *might* be isolationist, but it need not be and usually is not. Neutralist Switzerland, for example, is anything but isolationist. For an example closer home, there is the prewar period of the New Deal, during which time we were internationalist, politically partisan, and economically neutralist all at once: our trade with Germany, Italy, and Japan remained basically solid in the years 1933–40.)

But what came to be the dominant belief was that the problems of advanced-power aggression and backward-state revolution *had* to be solved, *could* be solved, and *would* be solved through some combination of the advanced powers. The world needed a concert of industrial giants whose collective strength, will, and prestige would restrain aggressions and suppress revolutions. The question for statesmanship was which powers should make up the club. The question for diplomacy was how to get them into it.

Before World War I, the general belief was that the proper combination would consist of the United States, Britain, and France. After that war, Wilson explicitly revised this outlook, holding that Germany and Japan would now have to be integrated into the Atlantic concert. In this way, revolutionary Russia could be isolated and the Big Powers acting coordinately could protect the security of the world's increasingly integrated political economy. So in the 1920s the United States underwrote the reconstruction of Germany's prewar industrial structure, and in 1922 (the Nine-Power Treaty) brought Japan by the ears into a modern open-doorist agreement on hapless China. When trouble began to brew in the 1930s, Chamberlain struggled with all the considerable anxiety at his command to establish Four-Power hegemony in Europe (i.e., Britain, France, Germany, and Italy). The New Deal, not much more instructed by Japan's invasion of Manchuria than was Britain by Germany's Rhineland remilitarization, maneuvered with carrots and sticks through most of that period to secure a China accommodation with Japan.

We were steadily trying, that is, with a really remarkable constancy, to establish that political integration of the Big Powers which finally *was* established—at least temporarily—as one of the chief results of World War II. De Gaulle's France portends change today, and perhaps (it is debatable) Gaullism represents genuinely different ideas about how European power should be arranged and what its fundamental goals should be. But at least well into the mid-sixties, the postwar world was dominated by explicit or implicit alliances that linked the United States, Britain, France, Germany, and Japan into one another's economies, all our partners sharing our belief in a demo-cratic-liberal political philosophy, and all of them more or less willing to accept and support our views on the Communist threat.

This system has two separate but integrated domains, the At-lantic and the Pacific. As Germany is the pivotal state of the Atlantic domain, Japan is the pivot of the Pacific. It is the situation of this Japan which we shall now examine more closely.

The first point is that Japan is a traditionally vigorous trader, one which has long been important to the commerce of the United States. From 1929 through 1940, our total volume of trade with Japan was surpassed only by our trade with Canada and Britain. The much-lusted-after China trade was not even half as heavy (over that period, about $3.5 billion total volume with Japan as opposed to about $1.5 billion with China). Our view of Japan's distinction is reflected in the fact that besides the quite special cases of Vietnam, Korea, and Formosa, no country outside Europe has received as much assistance from the United States (some $4 billion over the 1945–63 period). Her comeback in the postwar period was rapid and strong. Her 1965 volume of trade was close to $17 billion (more than double her 1960 volume), placing her ahead of Italy among the world's busi-ness-doers behind the United States, West Germany, England, France, and Canada. By 1961, she had taken over second place among our trade partners, with only Canada ahead. In 1965 she sold us $2.5 billion and bought from us $2.4 billion, achieving for the first time a favorable balance of trade both with the United States and the world ($8.5 billion exports vs. $8.3 billion imports).

The second point is that a healthy, westward-looking Japan is just as crucial to the containing of China as containing China is to the health and Western-orientation of Japan. To understand the essentials of this dynamic, we have to unpack the meaning of this concept "containment."

It can, of course, mean several things. For a pathetically brief period, Czechoslovakia's Benes "contained" Hitler by answering the German troop concentration at his border with a military mobilization of his own. Thus, there is a type of containment that is distinctively military. The United States "contained" the growth of domestic communism by a program of systematic legislative, judicial, and propaganda harassment. Containment, then, can be political and legalistic. We could go through a set of such differing situations and define for each a differing form of containment. The common characteristic would be that in each case a perception of an active threat elicits a counter-measure that is specifically pitched to the threat's nature, and that does not commit itself to the direct and final liquidation of the threat.

What is the nature of the Chinese Communist threat? As should be perfectly clear, the threat is not basically military. No real threat ever is. China's power to aggress against her neighbors is not to be doubted. But two other things are also not to be doubted. One is that she would be all but defenseless against the kind of strategic nuclear attack which a clear act of aggression would surely provoke. The other is that she has never attacked for spoils, nor without provocation. (The Korean "invasion" came only after repeated U.S. bombings of Man-churia, the Tibetan "invasion" only after a clear mutiny of the theocracy, the Indian "invasion" as a result of a very plain border dispute in which she had by no means the worst of the argument.)

The threat is political. And as with any political threat, the guts of it are economic. It has long been a statesmanly wisdom in the West that any China which could organize herself would be a China indeed. Only recall Napoleon's words about the slumbering giant who will awaken to shake the world, Lenin's observation that "for world communism the road to Paris lies through Peking and Calcutta." She has the people, the resources, the energy, and the ingenuity to be—what? Given equity in what time can purchase, what time will inevitably bring, China could become the peer of America, Europe, and the U.S.S.R. What she lacked for centuries was order, a sense of national unity, and positive control over her inherent resources. The people—industrious—and the land—rich—have been there all along, waiting for some iron-minded Johnny Appleseed.

China's rate of growth in the first ten years following Chiang's flight to Formosa was anywhere from 15 to 30 percent, depending on which of several experts one believes. Apart from the problem of insufficient data, none seems to be really sure how to measure the performance of an immature planned economy. But there is general agreement that growth was strong, even allowing for the very abysmal state of the initial conditions. Assessments of the Great Leap experience vary even more widely, some scholars arguing a "catastrophe" interpretation, others claiming that the failure, now mostly recouped, was chiefly agricultural and that basic industrial growth remained healthy. To dare to say anything conclusive about China's economy one would have to base it on a lengthy analysis, and a major reason for its lengthiness would be the need to explain why nothing exactly conclusive could be said. But we need not be so technical here. What is important is that no one denies that for the first time in centuries there *is* such a thing as a Chinese nation, that is *has* an economy, and that this economy has established contact with the intrinsic potential of the land and the people. That potential, plagued as it is with natural and political difficulties, is as great as it needs to be. Reflect then, as our statesmen surely must, on the China of a hundred or even fifty years from now. Imagine a world in which creative action—economic, political, cultural—is no longer so densely and disproportionately concentrated in the North Atlantic global core—a world, that is, in which an independent and dynamic Asia *exists*.

Our response to the mammoth fact of Chinese revolution—something which has nothing at all to do with communism, but rather with the independent organization of China and her acquisition of modern fire—has not been exactly pragmatic. First we chose to believe that it was not happening. We exhausted ourselves in mirthful tales of the new China's blunders, sorrows, and epidemic pain, and poised ourselves for the next news dispatch, for it would tell us of the end of this extravagant mistake. The news was different. Then we adopted the view that its own inner evil would in time surely destroy this most total of totalitarianisms. Merely to give its self-destruction a little nudge, a little momentum, we set up an embargo. And it did not die. But then surely the Chinese people would rise against the "yellow peril" internalized, demanding capitalism and Chiang Kai-shek. Merely to give them pluck, we ostentatiously armed their real and true hero, that leashed whirling dervish of Formosa. And the people did not rise up. Strange ways of the Orient! Our recriminations meanwhile were endless. Clearly, this was all the work of Joe Stalin and certain State Department infidels. Reputations were garroted. China was still there, however, coming on like a freight train.

And there sits Japan in the very beam of the Manchurian industrial headlamp, *quite powerless to move.* (A roughly comparable situation would be one in which England found herself politically misallied against a Europe united to the Urals, a battering ram.) What are Japan's options? Isolationism vis-à-vis China was never even thinkable. Whether coerced by future political apprehensions or lured by present commercial opportunities, Japan is already China's foremost trade partner,* surpassing even the Soviet Union (with which, adroitly enough, Japan's businessmen are also arranging increased commerce). It is not as if Japan could pretend that China is just not there. It would be strange economics, politics, and history if she tried to. The only questions that are at all open are how much, when, and on what terms. Most specifically: Will Japan contrive to maintain her present pro-American political bias? Will she submit to world history's commonest law that the Higher Economics determines the Lower Politics and so cast in with Peking? Or will she try instead the Greek way of golden-meansmanship and make of herself

---

*Japan's sales to China, $245 million in 1965, are rising annually at a rate matched only by her purchases from China. Exports (and imports) in her China trade from 1960 through 1965 are as follows (in millions of U.S. dollars): 2.7 (20.7; 16.0 (30.9); 38.5 (46.0); 82.4 (74.6); 152.8 (157.8); 245.3 (224.7).

a bridge between the two supergiants, well knowing (as one Japanese has remarked) that bridges get walked on?

It will be clear what the United States expects Japan to do. But how much pressure do we ask that nation to bear in our name whose principal cities we atomized? Japan understands that she bombed Pearl Harbor with no very great moral finesse. Japan understands that her new economy was built by us. But there is something especially memorable about that Bomb, callous about our ·nuclear appearances at her ports of call, humiliating about the 1960 Mutual Security Treaty for which the Kishi government had to pay with its life, infuriating about our overt colonization of Okinawa and the Ryukyu chain, frightening about our Vietnam war, which three quarters of her people oppose: the elements of Japanese anti-Americanism subsist. Japan, the keystone of our Asian containment perimeter, may do what she can to remain our long-haul affiliate. She will not do what she cannot do. If America has certain expectations, it is up to America to make their possibility concrete.

We now ask: Does Vietnam bear materially on this drama? The key facts would seem to be the following: (1) Two of China's principal import needs are rubber and rice, improved access to which will in some measure accelerate her rate of development and thus her over-all power. (2) The two principal export commodities of a normalized South Vietnam will be rubber and rice. (3) Japan's unemployment figure is an irreducible one percent. Increased industrialization will draw more workers from the farm to the factory. Urbanization of labor will reduce yield of unmechanized farms at the same time that the resultant higher purchasing power will raise demand. (4) Japan is traditionally a food importer, and she is becoming a greater one, her food imports being on the rise both proportionately and absolutely. Of 1962's total $5.6 billion imports, $700 million (12 percent) went for food; of 1963's $6.7 billion total, $1 billion (16 percent) went for food; of 1964's $7.9 billion total, $1.3 billion (17 percent) went for food. (5) Japanese are the world's foremost shipbuilders and among its strongest steelmakers and textilers. They need markets. China needs ships, steel, and textiles. A developing Vietnam will want steel certainly and probably ships, but may be inclined to protect her textile industry.

Let us join a final fact with a professional observation. The fact is reported by the Indochina scholar Bernard B. Fall:

> DRVN [North Vietnamese] trade with Japan, after a period of coolness when Japan decided to pay war reparations to South Viet-Nam only, has reached important proportions that might well provoke concern in the United States. Trade rose from about $10 million in 1959 to more than $40 million in 1961-62 and involves such items as chemicals, machinery of all kinds, and four seagoing 5,000-ton cargo ships and one 2,000 tons; for these, North Viet-Nam pays in raw materials, notably coal.

The observation was made by President Eisenhower at his press conference of April 7, 1954, almost exactly one month before the French collapse at Dien Bien Phu and the opening of the Geneva Conference on Indochina. The stenographic report reads:

> In its economic aspects, the President added, [loss of Indochina] would take away that region that Japan must have as a trading area, or it would force Japan to turn toward China and Manchuria, or toward the Communist areas in order to live. The possible consequences of the loss [of Japan] to the free world are just incalculable, Mr. Eisenhower said.

All the foregoing would appear to support the following propositions:

1. Japan's economic strength is the crucial element in America's policy of containing China and maintaining the peace in Asia. Japan is the bastion.

2. Behind only Canada among our trade partners, Japan is of major commercial importance to us. In fact, a primary direct purpose of containing China is the safeguarding of our commercial interest in Japan. Japan is thus both the bastion of the containment-expansion struggle and the prize of victory.

3. South Vietnam is an important prospective trade area for both Japanese sellers and Chinese buyers.

4. But China is also an important Japanese trade partner and cannot fail to become increasingly magnetic. The authoritative *Finance* (June 1966) said: "Some trade experts in Washington expect the Communist Bloc to supersede the U.S. as Japan's biggest trading partner during the next decade." (West Germany's sale of a steel plant to China further disarms the ideological argument against mainland trade and can only sharpen the commercial appetite of the Japanese businessman.)

5. If Japan and China develop economic interdependency—and as things now stand only shattering disturbances can even postpone that—then the brute mathematics of the relationship will doom Japan to juniority (much as Britain would be junior to an economically integrated European continent). If Japan has no long-term alternative to massive China trade, she will be left without an alternative to a progressively more pro-Chinese orientation. The bastion and the prize, one and the same, hear the same clock ticking.

6. Japan's only remote chance (it *is* remote) for a long-term alternative to the developing market of China lies with the more slowly developing and less organizable markets of the South Pacific, South Asia, and Southeast Asia. In the first, America's position is traditionally privileged, especially in the crucial Philippines (where economic nationalism is growing) and in Australia (where direct U.S. investments, at about $1.5 billion, are greater than in all other countries but Canada, Britain, Venezuela, and Germany). In the second, India proves all but inert under the most exasperated Western proddings. In the third, South Vietnam's position is central owing to her coasts, harbors, resources wealth, and the fact that the war has *made* it central. South Vietnam's now buried treasures mean that her markets, once developed, will exert a great pull on Japan the Trader *regardless of who develops them.*

What the West faces in the Pacific is the formation of a regional economic system *(a)* whose potential and power are inherent in the Pacific situation itself, *(b)* which must include Japan, and *(c)* which would quite naturally be dominated by China. This is the "threat." America feels it most keenly because among the Western powers she now enjoys the dominant economic position there in the Pacific, because her postwar Asian investment in blood and treasure is steep, and because she is by any measure the most international of the international states. Our purpose, then, is to frustrate the drawing together of this geoeconomic system by imposing political and military barricades between its elements and by holding out the alternative of other economic configurations. Thus, the struggle to hold South Vietnam. Thus, the United States-promoted Northeast Asia Treaty Organization (NEATO), which died a-borning. And thus, for more recent and more sensible approaches, the Asian Bank and the new, tentatively titled Asian and Pacific Cooperation Council (so it can be called ASPAC—"an attractive name with a masculine sound," said Thailand's Foreign Minister Thanat Khoman). *New York Times* reporter Robert Trumbull, reporting the manly ASPAC's birth at Seoul in June 1966, quoted the chief of one delegation as saying that "although the organization initially will be purely for economic cooperation [e.g., a regional bank to handle development of rice and other commodities, and an international technician pool], it cannot avoid strengthening the policies of these non-Communist and anti-Communist countries." The nine members are South Korea, Thailand, Malaysia, the Philippines, Australia, New Zealand, Nationalist China, South Vietnam, and Japan.

We lead from this into a final reduction:

The aim of the North Atlantic political economy is to frustrate the independent organization of the Pacific political economy.

Such has been Europe's traditional policy in Africa. Such has been the United States' traditional policy in Latin America. Such has been the traditional Asian policy of the Atlantic powers together. Nor does it very much matter that such a policy may or may not have been made explicit and consciously acted upon. An eloquent two and a half centuries of Western mucking about in Asia tell the story quite clearly enough. Everywhere in the poor world, in fact, the inveterate habit of the Western powers has been to absorb and integrate what they could command and to scatter and harass what they could not.

The most elemental meaning of the hit-and-miss, chaotic, and in many respects chronically malformed poor-world revolution is that to the traditional alternatives of subservient integration and harassment there shall now be added a third course: a South American South America, an African Africa, an Asian Asia—the very straightforward argument of it being that there can be no equable integration of the several global spheres (that's where peace is) until there is an approximate economic and political equity among them. Whether we happen to like it or not, and however we conceal the roots of our antagonism to it with panegyrics on democracy and equally irrelevant diatribes against Communism, this is the testament of revolution and this is what we are struggling to resist with our isolation of China, quarantining of Cuba, and pacifying in Vietnam.

The *fourth* point—for its powers of commentary on our culture, it seems to me, much the most important—is coiled up in a not very puzzling puzzle.

Saving Vietnam at the price of deploying some 600 Special Forces guerrilla experts, or even 16,000 Marine "advisers," whatever one thinks of the political motive, seems at least to be a proportionate act, cost-conditional and controllable. But half a million men? Who will apparently have to become a million? And a hundred billion dollars? Moreover, this "military solution" has long since proved to be no solution at all. Everyone can see that the air raids on North Vietnam, officially described as the best way to stop infiltration, have led only to stepped-up infiltration. In the south, the B-52s kill more monkeys, tigers, and civilians than Vietcong. The napalm destroys more villages than fighting forces. Sophisticated reports on our ground war argue most persuasively (if sometimes unintentionally) that it is fought without relevant pattern and without significant effect, our mechanized forces being unable to engage in any sustained and decisive way the guerrillas, whose mobility is not of the machine but of the culture itself.* And besides being militarily

*See, for example, Special Forces veteran Donald Duncan's "I Quit!" in the February 1966 *Ramparts*. Or a piece from the hand of a protagonist of the war, S. L. A. Marshall's "The Death of a Platoon" in the September 1966 *Harper's*, an essay of disaster whose between-the-lines message is distinct and harrowing. Or one of the few really powerful psychological studies of the ground war,

ineffectual, this destruction exacts a steadily higher toll in that political good will in which Johnson's America is in such miserably short supply. It means decades, if not centuries, of recrudescent anti-Americanism in Vietnam, the rest of Indochina, all of Asia; even West Europe begins to gag. One might suppose that a rational imperialist could invent other, more sensible ways to shore up the quivering dominoes of the Pacific—indeed, that he could see problems there that make Vietnam's "salvation" seem a small item. Without a wholly new order of concentrated Western will and wisdom, India will be communist within two decades. Every day, South Korea slips further behind North Korea in economic development and political independence. The political economy of the Philippines is stagnant and the Huks are again on the rise. Thailand's northeast remains as vulnerable as ever to those "outside agitators" whose main crime is pointing out the emperor's nakedness. Above all, there is what Stillman and Pfaff have strikingly called "the furious material energy and the eerie political passivity of contemporary Japan," an energy which we have seen to be in fact freighted with political meanings of the most momentous sort.

In sum: The military solution to the problem of Vietnam is not working; the attempt to achieve such a solution worsens and may begin to cripple our political position in Asia; and the really important and defensible eastern salients of the Western world—India, Thailand, the Philippines, Korea, Japan—drift every day a bit closer to that distinctively Oriental future which our policy-makers can hardly fail to see.

The government's computers have been no guard against a loss of control which may very well be unparalleled. Why does this happen?

This happens because the ideology that demanded and vindicated this "necessary" act of war continues to demand and vindicate the act even after it has overreached its necessity and

John Sack's "M, An Account of One Company of American Soldiers in Fort Dix, New Jersey, Who Trained for War and Who Found It in South Viet-Nam Fifty Days Later" in the October 1966 *Esquire*. Or Marshall Sahlins' close-in study of Special Forces operations, "The Destruction of Conscience in Viet-Nam," *Dissent*, Jan.-Feb. 1966.

become, on its own terms, *irrational*. What Western power opposes is the anti-imperialist social revolution of the poor. But in a time in which Western liberals have oversold themselves on their own slick humanism-*cum*-realpolitics, that position is not easy to sloganize. We have ourselves lately cursed imperialism—the more primitive imperialism of others; have ourselves once glorified revolution—our own. Perhaps because of this, America's leaders seem to have doubted that their subjects had the stomach for a repressive counterrevolutionary and imperialist war. Such a war, since it had to be fought, would have to be sweetened with a different name. Imperialism is thus rechristened as anticommunism, and our foe is instantly transformed from a human being into a pawn, a dupe, or an outright hardcore agent of that International Communist Conspiracy whose ultimate objective (so we are guaranteed) is the conquest of America.

This theory of the International Communist Conspiracy is not the hysterical old maid that many leftists seem to think it is. It has had an intimate affair with reality and it has some history on its mind when it speaks. There *is* a revolution which *is* international—one only has to count the perturbations and look at a map to see as much. In some less than technical sense, this revolution *is* "communistic," if by that we mean that it will probably not produce capitalist economies, that it will probably create autarkic and controlled economies, authoritarian central governments, programs of forced-march wealth accumulation, and the forcible dismantling of rich elites. And if not by any means melodramatically conspiratorial, the several liberation movements in their early stages, do make an effort to coordinate themselves; they do so, pathetically unadept, because they consider their enemy to be internationally coordinated himself—a view which is entirely correct. And to the extent to which this revolution aims at terminating the masterdom of the rich, an aim which automatically implicates America, the revolution *does* aim itself at America—it aims itself, rather, at an America which most Americans have forgotten about: Rockefeller, Englehard, U.S.A. There is just no use being deluded about that. But what is added on for pure political effect is that ugly edge of clandestinity, pointless and merciless ambition, that cloud of diabolism which has nothing to do with the sustaining force of the revolution itself. And what is *subtracted* from the reality—much more important—is the *source* of the ferment, the *cause* of the anger, the supreme question of the *justice* of rebellion. What this theory gives us is a portrait whose outlines are not unreal, but whose colors have been changed from human blacks and browns and yellows into devil's red, and whose background has been entirely erased. Thus, the theory wildly disorganizes and mismanages the very real history that allows it to survive. And if it lies within the power of an idea to pervert a nation's generosity and curse its children, then the widespread American acceptance of this view of revolution may forecast a bitter future for us all.

It is through the ideology of Cold War anticommunism (a cynic might abbreviate it to CWAC and call it "cwackery") that the masters of American power have rationalized, and quite successfully dissembled their opposition to the Third World's diffuse and uneven movement for independence. This ideology is the root-and-branch descendant of that ideology by which the fathers of these same masters once sought to break the American labor movement. It has the sort of truth in it now, and the same sort of lies, that it had in the long bitter period between the Civil War and World War II. After years of perfection, and applied now to a remote world familiar to Americans only as the well-controlled mass media see fit to make it so, one has to say of this ideology that it is more effective now than ever. It entirely rearranges the moral terms of the encounter between the rich and the poor, and in one stroke deprives the revolutionary of the very right to name and explain himself. He stands already named—a criminal; already explained—an enemy. He is *not* the revolutionary which he pretends to be. The *real* social revolutionaries, it seems, are ourselves. This other one is a fraud, whether willfully so or not; and, whether or not *he* knows it, *we* happen to know that he is an imposter, an intruder on the scene of social change whose real hope, real demand—is the destruction of our country. Whatever he may think, we know that he will never be satisfied with Moscow or Peking, Havana or Algiers, Caracas or Saigon. He is out to get *us* — Kansas City, Birmingham, Washington, D.C. So it follows that the inner, central, driving theme of the drama being acted out in Vietnam's jungles is nothing less than the question of our own national survival. This is the theory by which the war has been explained to us.

If it is a good theory, then it is good *absolutely*. If it is correct to say that our national well-being requires the defeat of the NLF, then the NLF will have to be defeated. The explanation will remain correct regardless of how hard it might be to carry out its implicit commands. Preserving the well-being of the nation is an overriding and transcendent objective. It is not possible to imagine that such an objective can be qualified or repealed *even for one moment* by any other objective. It is an imperative. The awesome consequence of this is that *any struggle that is rationalized in its name is one from which we cannot withdraw.*

Everyone knows that some people in this country, some of them strong, consistently demand that we use all needed force to bring this war to a "speedy and favorable conclusion." If their view of history is not backward, then their moral system is; but to characterize them as ultraconservatives, to try to erase their argument by calling them names like warmonger, is to miss entirely the good, clear point which they make. The main thing wrong with this "ultraconservative warhawk" may in fact have nothing at all to do with conservatism or bellicosity, but rather with his unreserved acceptance of a theory which liberal American administrations have been drumming into his head for at least a quarter of a century—namely, the theory that there is an International Communist Conspiracy that threatens to capture the world, including *us;* that plans to impose upon that imprisoned world, including *us,* the bleakest tyranny that history ever saw; and that aims to achieve all this through the piecemeal conquest of increasingly less marginal states.

Let it be remembered that the government speaks to its people with a measure of authority. People do not expect it to lie, distort, or deceive. People trust it. When this self-same trustworthy government informs the people that the war takes place because agents of the world-hungry tyranny came to a happy land from outside and proceeded to agitate, propagandize, subvert, terrorize, and spread chaos, hatred, and ammunition, then the people have every right to demand, Why not go after such a threat *at its source?* When our trusted government explains to us that the Red takeover of Vietnam (Laos, Cuba, Hispaniola, the Congo) is merely secondary, nothing but a conquistadorial way station on the road to this Xanadu of ours, then the people have every right to demand, *Why not act now?* Looked at *in itself,* as a problem of national survival, it does not seem to me that this has anything very much to do with conservatism. There is a murder going on out there in the street: A man with a knife is killing Kitty Genovese; after he finishes her off, he aims to invade the apartment house itself and kill one by one the empty-headed, empty-hearted cowards who gape at the atrocity from their windows. So *of course* the right thing to do is to leap now to her defense. First, because she is an innocent victim and not to defend her is dishonorable. Second, because her murder will not appease but only whet the killer's appetite, and we have before us an official American fact that unless someone stops him he will soon be putting his fangs into us. What is "conservative" about wanting to fight in that situation? What kind of whimpering lunatic thinks it is "warmongering" to intervene under such circumstances? The bravest case to be made against these reactionaries of ours is that they are so overeager to believe what the liberals have been feeding them. On terms of that belief, what nonsense it is to talk about a "limited" war with "limited" objectives.

"We are at total war right now," say the right-wingers—only making more succinct what Truman told them, what Eisenhower and Kennedy allowed them to believe, what Johnson's homilies have convinced them of all over again.

An ideology which originates in a distortion of history acquires an intrinsic power to sustain and add to historical distortions. It achieves an independent authority in the explanation of events and therefore in the forcing of national policy. We go to Vietnam to maintain a segment of the Western, North Atlantic community's sphere of influence—an objective which on its own terms is practical, concrete, definite, and perhaps not at all without limits; one which is subject to a cost accounting and for which there may be an excessive price to pay. But because they have rationalized this venture in terms of the ideology of anticommunism, our leaders are obliged to insist that we are in Vietnam to protect our vital organs of national increase—an objective that is not practical and cost-conditional but absolute and sacred. To ask what is the value of holding Vietnam becomes, in the grip of this ideology, as pointless as asking the value of the king in a game of chess. The war escapes the political relativity to become transcendent and sublime.

This is an affliction of the people. We might assume (although Johnson, Rusk, and Rostow make us shaky about it) that the political technicians of the State and Defense Departments only purvey, but themselves do not use, the quasi-religious doctrine of the Great Conspiracy. That will not help those whom they have made true-believer addicts to it. A big minority of Americans is one day going to be *betrayed*. The ideological bridgework between the fact and the fancy is coming unstuck today as perhaps never before for America. And when it crumbles, a great many good, strong people are going to find themselves marooned in the unreal. Their anger will shake the nation. To them, the conduct of the war already seems an act of madness if not perfidy. Here we are in a death duel with a most relentless foe, and look at us pulling our punches! The two basic criticisms of the war, which correlate with the leftist and the rightist dissents, aim at resolving the tension that exists between the war's most common political and military descriptions. The rightist accepts the political description and therefore wants the war to be more fiercely waged. The leftist repudiates that political description and therefore wants the war to be broken off. Both aim at a more rational position. Both have a much more solid line of argument than the center, which is only confused and trapped by its own dissembling gobbledygook. In a way, this warhawk is even more humane than the slow-death advocates, for he may at least lay claim to the stark compassion of Macbeth: "If it were done when 'tis done, then 'twere well it were done quickly." If we must destroy Vietnam, then let us have the mercy to do it with dispatch and put those poor people, broken-legged horses, out of their misery.

And the very sad fact is that when the time comes to pay the piper, it will not be to these "moderates" of ours that the deepest, most spirit-tearing agony will come. The example of the French experience in Algeria is all too instructive.

France fought to maintain her colonial control of Algeria for many of the same reasons that mobilize America in Vietnam today. Like America, France rationalized the colonial war in terms of transcendent national imperatives. When it became clear to the leaders of France that disengagement was required, important elements in the French army were outraged. The Secret Army Organization (OAS) was formed to resist what its members felt was the betrayal of the nation. The OAS aimed at nothing less than a *coup d'état,* and its existence created for France the most punishing internal torment. How did this happen in France, the heartland of European humanism? Western liberals have a theory about that which restores their confidence: The OAS happened because there were fascists in the Frency army who wanted it to happen. The OAS was only the last gasp of the old Nazi collaborationists. There is nothing like that in America.

But look again—not at America to find fascists, but beyond the fascist label itself, which has merely substituted a curse where an explanation is required.

On the first of August 1962, Captain Estoup, a lawyer of the First Foreign Legion Paratroop Regiment, arguing before a high French military tribunal, summed up his defense of one of the OAS conspirators: "How can it happen," he asked, "that a brilliant young St.-Cyr cadet, one of the outstanding young men . . . at the military academy . . . today stands accused [of treason] before a military court . . . ?"

Let us fix our eye on the American counterpart of this "brilliant young cadet" before we go on. Let us imagine a good blond and upright young man, square-shouldered with a heart full of bravery, a West Point graduate from some very American place like Colorado Springs or Trenton or Seattle—in E. E. Cummings' phrase, "a yearning nation's blue-eyed pride." We must imagine the ballgames he has played, the cotton candy and the sweet spring nights and the sweetheart he has left behind him; the strong old clapboard houses, the gracious elms, the broad green lawns of the quiet streets from which he came. All that. He is not monocled or mustached. There is no *Mein Kampf* hidden in his footlocker. His voice is well modulated, his demeanor perhaps a bit retiring. He is proud but not arrogant about his Green Beret. He is not happy to be in Vietnam. He would prefer to be home. There is, however, a job to be done. Such is the villain of the peace: the traitor.

Estoup proceeds to explain that it was to the members of the elite forces—men like our young St.-Cyr cadet from Wyoming—that the most odious and dangerous of assignments fell. It was the cadet's duty to procure vital information about the enemy—"by all means available." That is, he was instructed to use torture. "I do not know," says Estoup,

> what sort of mental turmoil someone who gives an order like this must go through; but I do know the sense of shock and revulsion suffered by those who have to carry it out. All the fine ideas and the illusions of the young St.-Cyr cadet crumble. . . . But you will say, "Then why did not the young St.-Cyr cadet refuse to carry out the order?" Because the ultimate end had been so described to him that it appeared to justify the means. It had been proved to him that the outcome of the battle depended on the information he obtained, that the victory of France was at stake. . . . If the means are justified only by the end, there is no justification at all unless the end is achieved. If it is not, nothing is left but a senseless pattern of dirty indelible stains. . . . It is my testimony that for the most part the true motive for [the actions of the conspirators] was a secret, silent, inward gnawing determination not to have committed crimes that achieved no object. In the final analysis, these are the actions of the damned souls making their last desperate effort to wreak vengeance on the devil who has lured them into hell. The people of France, in whose name justice is now being done, should know that it was in their name and for their

sake that the accused were pushed, by those in authority,
over the edge of this pit of destruction.

No one knows better than the torturer himself what torture means. No one understands bombing better than the bomber, guns than the gunner, death than he who kills. You need not inform this Wyoming lad that his hands are bloody. He is the expert about that. But the blood will wash away, will it not? The dirty indelible stains will one day be removed? The cleansing water is victory. The sacrifice is redeemed by the rebirth for which it prepares the conquered land. But if the water is not brought, that deferred innocence in whose name the present guilt is borne vanishes from the future. And what becomes of this strange savage blood? It fuses permanently with the skin of the hands that shed it.

We ought to be able to understand a very simple thing: From now on in America it shall be with such hands that children are soothed, office memoranda signed, cocktails stirred, friends greeted, poems written, love made, the Host laid on the tongue and wreaths on graves, the nose pinched in meditation. In the forthcoming gestures of these hands—this is really very simple— we shall behold an aspect of Vietnam's revenge.

ON GENOCIDE

JEAN-PAUL SARTRE

The word "genocide" is relatively new. It was coined by the jurist Raphael Lemkin between the two world wars. But the fact of genocide is as old as humanity. To this day there has been no society protected by its structure from committing that crime. Every case of genocide is a product of history and bears the stamp of the society which has given birth to it. The one we have before us for judgment is the act of the greatest capitalist power in the world today. It is as such that we must try to analyze it—in other words, as the simultaneous expression of the economic infrastructure of that power, its political objectives and the contradictions of its present situation.

In particular, we must try to understand the genocidal intent in the war which the American government is waging against Vietnam, for Article 2 of the 1948 Geneva Convention defines genocide on the basis of intent; the Convention was tacitly referring to memories which were still fresh. Hitler had proclaimed it his deliberate intent to exterminate the Jews. He made genocide a political means and did not hide it. A Jew had to be put to death, whoever he was, not for having been caught carrying a weapon or for having joined a resistance movement, but simply *because he was a Jew*. The American government has avoided making such clear statements. It has even claimed that it was answering the call of its allies, the South Vietnamese, who had been attacked by the communists. Is it possible for us, by studying the facts objectively, to discover implicit in them such a genocidal intention? And after such an investigation, can we say that the armed forces of the United States are killing

Vietnamese in Vietnam for the simple reason that they are Vietnamese?

This is something which can only be established after an historical examination: the structure of war changes right along with the infrastructures of society. Between 1860 and the present day, the meaning and the objectives of military conflicts have changed profoundly, the final stage of this metamorphosis being precisely the "war of example" which the United States is waging in Vietnam.

In 1856, there was a convention for the protection of the property of neutrals; 1864, Geneva: protection for the wounded; 1899, 1970, The Hague: two conferences which attempted to make rules for war. It is no accident that jurists and governments were multiplying their efforts to "humanize war" on the every eye of the two most frightful massacres that mankind has ever known. Vladimir Dedijer has shown very effectively in his study "On Military Conventions" that the capitalist societies during this same period were giving birth to the monster of total war in which they express their true nature. He attributes this phenomenon to the following:

1. The competition between industrial nations fighting for new markets produces a permanent antagonism which is expressed in ideology and in practice by what is known as "bourgeois nationalism."

2. The development of industry, which is the source of this hostility, provides the means of resolving it to the advantage of one of the competitors, through the production of more and more *massively* destructive weapons. The consequence of this development is that it becomes increasingly difficult to make any distinction between the front and behind the lines, between the civilian population and the soldiers.

3. At the same time, new military objectives—the factories—arise near the towns. And even when they are not producing materiel directly for the armies, they maintain, at least to some extent, the economic strength of the country. It is precisely this strength that the enemy aims to destroy: this is at once the aim of war and the means to that end.

4. The consequence of this is that everyone is mobilized: the

peasant fights at the front, the worker fights behind the lines, the peasant women take over for their husbands in the fields. This *total* struggle of nation against nation tends to make the worker a soldier too, since in the last analysis the power which is economically stronger is more likely to win.

5. The democratic facade of the bourgeois nations and the emancipation of the working class have led to the participation of the masses in politics. The masses have no control at all over government decisions, but the middle classes imagine that by voting they exercise some kind of remote control. Except in cases of defensive wars, the working classes are torn between their desire for peace and the nationalism which has been instilled in them. Thus war, seen in a new light and distorted by propaganda, becomes the ethical decision of the whole community. All the citizens of each warring nation (or almost all, after they have been manipulated) are the enemies of all those of the other country. War has become absolutely total.

6. These same societies, as they continue their technological expansion, continue to extend the scope of their competition by increasing communications. The famous "One World" of the Americans was already in existence by the end of the 19th century when Argentine wheat dealt a final blow to English agriculture. Total war is no longer only between all members of one national community and all those of another: it is also total because it will very likely set the whole world up in flames.

Thus, war between the bourgeois nations—of which the 1914 war was the first example but which had threatened Europe since 1900—is not the "invention" of one man or one government, but simply a necessity for those who, since the beginning of the century, have sought to "extend politics by other means." The option is clear: either *no* war or *that* kind of total war. Our fathers fought that kind of war. And the governments who saw it coming, with neither the intelligence nor the courage to stop it, were wasting their time and the time of the jurists when they stupidly tried to "humanize" it.

Nevertheless, during the First World War a genocidal intent appeared only sporadically. As in previous centuries, the essential aim was to crush the military power of the enemy and only secondarily to ruin his economy. But even though there was no longer any clear distinction between civilians and soldiers, it was still only rarely (except for a few terrorist raids) that the civilian population was expressly made a target. Moreover, the belligerent nations (or at least those who were doing the fighting) were industrial powers. This made for a certain initial balance: against the possibility of any real extermination each side had its own deterrent force—namely the power of applying the law of "an eye for an eye." This explains why, in the midst of the carnage, a kind of prudence was maintained.

However, since 1830, throughout the last century and continuing to this very day, there have been countless acts of genocide whose causes are likewise to be found in the structure of capitalist societies. To export their products and their capital, the great powers, particularly England and France, set up colonial empires. The name "overseas possessions" given by the French to their conquests indicates clearly that they had been able to acquire them only by wars of aggression. The adversary was sought out in his own territory, in Africa and Asia, in the underdeveloped countries, and far from waging "total war" (which would have required an initial balance of forces), the colonial powers, because of their overwhelming superiority of firepower, found it necessary to commit only an expeditionary force. Victory was easy, at least in conventional military terms. But since this blatant aggression kindled the hatred of the civilian population, and since civilians were potentially rebels and soldiers, the colonial troops maintained their authority by terror—by perpetual massacre. These massacres were genocidal in character: they aimed at the destruction of "a part of an ethnic, national, or religious group" in order to terrorize the remainder and to wrench apart the indigenous society.

After the bloodbath of conquest in Algeria during the last century, the French imposed the *Code Civil*, with its middle-class conceptions of property and inheritance, on a tribal society where each community held land in common. Thus they systematically destroyed the economic infrastructure of the country, and tribes of peasants soon saw their lands fall into the hands of French speculators. Indeed, colonization is not a matter of mere conquest as was the German annexation of Alsace-Lorraine; it is by its very nature an act of cultural genocide. Colonization cannot take place without systematically liquidating all the characteristics of the native society—and simultaneously refusing to integrate the natives into the mother country and denying them access to its advantages. Colonialism is, after all, an economic system: the colony sells its raw materials and agricultural products at a reduced price to the colonizing power. The latter, in return, sells its manufactured goods to the colony at world market prices. This curious system of trade is only possible if there is a colonial subproletariat which can be forced to work for starvation wages. For the subject people this inevitably means the extinction of their national character, culture, customs, sometimes even language. They live in their underworld of misery like dark phantoms ceaselessly reminded of their subhumanity.

However, their value as an almost unpaid labor force protects them, to a certain extent, against physical genocide. The Nuremberg Tribunal was still fresh in people's minds when the French massacred 45,000 Algerians at Setif, as an "example." But this sort of thing was so commonplace that no one even thought to condemn the French government in the same terms as they did the Nazis.

But this "deliberate destruction of a part of a national group" could not be carried out any more extensively without harming the interests of the French settlers. By exterminating the subproletariat, they would have exterminated themselves as settlers. This explains the contradictory attitude of these *pieds-noirs* during the Algerian war: they urged the Army to commit massacres, and more than one of them dreamed of total genocide. At the same time they attempted to compel the Algerians to "fraternize" with them. It is because France could neither liquidate the Algerian people nor integrate them with the French that it lost the Algerian war.

These observations enable us to understand how the structure of colonial wars underwent a transformation after the end of the Second World War. For it was at about this time that the colonial peoples, enlightened by that conflict and its impact on the "empires," and later by the victory of Mao Tse-tung, resolved to regain their national independence. The characteristics of the struggle were determined from the beginning: the colonialists had the superiority in weapons, the indigenous population the advantage of numbers. Even in Algeria—a colony where there was settlement as much as there was exploitation— the proportion of *colons* to natives was one to nine. During the two world wars, many of the colonial peoples had been trained as soldiers and had become experienced fighters. However, the short supply and poor quality of their arms—at least in the beginning—kept the number of fighting units low. These objective conditions dictated their strategy, too: terrorism, ambushes, harassing the enemy, extreme mobility of the combat groups which had to strike unexpectedly and disappear at once. This was made possible only by the support of the entire population. Hence the famous symbiosis between the liberation forces and the masses of people: the former everywhere organizing agrarian reforms, political organs and education; the latter supporting, feeding and hiding the soldiers of the army of liberation, and replenishing its ranks with their sons.

It is no accident that people's war, with its principles, its strategy, its tactics and its theoreticians, appeared at the very moment that the industrial powers pushed total war to the ultimate by the industrial production of atomic fission. Nor is it any accident that it brought about the destruction of colonialism. The contradiction which led to the victory of the FLN in Algeria was characteristic of that time; people's war sounded the death-knell of conventional warfare at exactly the same moment as the hydrogen bomb. Against partisans supported by the entire population, the colonial armies were helpless. They had only one way of escaping this demoralizing harassment which threatened to culminate in a Dien Bien Phu, and that was to "empty the sea of its water"—i.e. the civilian population. And, in fact, the colonial soldiers soon learned that their most redoubtable foes were the silent, stubborn peasants who, just one kilometer from the scene of the ambush which had wiped out a regiment, knew nothing, had seen nothing. And since it was the unity of an entire people which held the conventional army at bay, the only anti-guerrilla strategy which could work was the destruction of this people, in other words, of civilians, of women and children.

Torture and genocide: that was the answer of the colonial powers to the revolt of the subject peoples. And that answer, as we know, was worthless unless it was thorough and total. The populace—resolute, united by the politicized and fierce partisan army—was no longer to be cowed as in the good old days of colonialism, by an "admonitory" massacre which was supposed to serve "as an example." On the contrary, this only augmented the people's hate. Thus it was no longer a question of intimidating the populace, but rather of physically liquidating it. And since that was not possible without concurrently liquidating the colonial economy and the whole colonial system, the settlers panicked, the colonial powers got tired of pouring men and money into an interminable conflict, the mass of the people in the mother country opposed the continuation of an inhuman war, and the colonies became sovereign states.

There have been cases, however, in which the genocidal response to people's war is not checked by infrastructural contradictions. Then total genocide emerges as the absolute basis of an anti-guerrilla strategy. And under certain conditions it even emerges as the explicit objective—sought either immediately or by degrees. This is precisely what is happening in the Vietnam war. We are dealing here with a new stage in the development of imperialism, a stage usually called neo-colonialism because it is characterized by aggression against a former colony which has already gained its independence, with the aim of subjugating it anew to colonial rule. With the beginning of independence, the neo-colonialists take care to finance a *putsch* or *coup d'état* so that the new heads of state do not represent the interests of the masses but those of a narrow privileged strata, and, consequently, of foreign capital.

Ngo Dinh Diem appeared—hand-picked, maintained and armed by the United States. He proclaimed his decision to reject the Geneva Agreements and to constitute the Vietnamese territory to the south of the 17th parallel as an independent state. What followed was the necessary consequence of these premises: a police force and an army were created to hunt down people who had fought against the French, and who now felt thwarted of their victory, a sentiment which automatically marked them as enemies of the new regime. In short, it was the reign of terror which provoked a new uprising in the South and rekindled the people's war.

Did the United States ever imagine that Diem could nip the revolt in the bud? In any event, they lost no time in sending in experts and then troops, and then they were involved in the conflict up to their necks. And we find once again almost the same pattern of war as the one that Ho Chi Minh fought against the French, except that at first the American government declared that it was only sending its troops out of generosity, to fulfill its obligations to an ally.

That is the outward appearance. But looking deeper, these two successive wars are essentially different in character: the United States, unlike France, has no economic interests in Vietnam. American firms have made some investments, but not so much that they couldn't be sacrificed, if necessary, without troubling the American nation as a whole or really hurting the monopolies. Moreover, since the U.S. government is not waging the war for reasons of a *directly* economic nature, there is nothing to stop it from ending the war by the ultimate tactic—in other words, by genocide. This is not to say that there is proof that the U.S. does in fact envision genocide, but simply that nothing prevents the U.S. from envisaging it.

In fact, according to the Americans themselves, the conflict has two objectives. Just recently, Dean Rusk stated: "We are defending ourselves." It is no longer Diem, the ally whom the Americans are generously helping out: it is the United States itself which is in danger in Saigon. Obviously, this means that the first objective is a military one: to encircle Communist China. Therefore, the United States will not let Southeast Asia escape. It has put its men in power in Thailand, it controls two-thirds of Laos and threatens to invade Cambodia. But these conquests will be hollow if it finds itself confronted by a free and unified Vietnam with 32 million inhabitants. That is why the military leaders like to talk in terms of "key positions." That is why Dean

Rusk says, with unintentional humor, that the armed forces of the United States are fighting in Vietnam "in order to avoid a third world war." Either this phrase is meaningless, or else it must be taken to mean: "in order to *win* this third conflict." In short, the first objective is dictated by the necessity of establishing a Pacific line of defense, something which is necessary only in the context of the general policies of imperialism.

The second objective is an economic one. In October 1966, General Westmoreland defined it as follows: "We are fighting the war in Vietnam to show that guerrilla warfare does not pay." To show whom? The Vietnamese? That would be very surprising. Must so many human lives and so much money be wasted merely to teach a lesson to a nation of poor peasants thousands of miles from San Francisco? And, in particular, what need was there to attack them, provoke them into fighting and subsequently to go about crushing them, when the big American companies have only negligible interests in Vietnam? Westmoreland's statement, like Rusk's, has to be filled in. The Americans want to show others that guerrilla war does not pay: they want to show all the oppressed and exploited nations that might be tempted to shake off the American yoke by launching a people's war, at first against their own pseudo-governments, the compradors and the army, then against the U.S. "Special Forces," and finally against the GIs. In short, they want to show Latin America first of all, and more generally, all of the Third World. To Che Guevara who said, "We need several Vietnams," the American government answers, "They will all be crushed the way we are crushing the first."

In other words, this war has above all an admonitory value, as an example for three and perhaps four continents. (After all, Greece is a peasant nation too. A dictatorship has just been set up there; it is good to give the Greeks a warning: submit or face extermination.) This genocidal example is addressed to the whole of humanity. By means of this warning, six per cent of mankind hopes to succeed in controlling the other 94 per cent at a reasonably low cost in money and effort. Of course it would be preferable, for propaganda purposes, if the Vietnamese would submit before being exterminated. But it is not certain that the situation wouldn't be clearer if Vietnam *were* wiped off the map. Otherwise someone might think that Vietnam's submission had been attributable to some *avoidable* weakness. But if these peasants do not weaken for an instant, and if the price they pay for their heroism is *inevitable death,* the guerrillas of the future will be all the more discouraged.

At this point in our demonstration, three facts are established: (1) What the U.S. government wants is to have a base against China and to set an example. (2) The first objective *can* be achieved, without any difficulty (except, of course, for the resistance of the Vietnamese), by wiping out a whole people and imposing the Pax Americana on an uninhabited Vietnam. (3) To achieve the second, the U.S. *must carry out,* at least in part, this extermination.

The declarations of American statesmen are not as candid as Hitler's were in his day. But candor is not essential to us here. It is enough that the facts speak; the speeches which come with them are believed only by the American people. The rest of the world understands well enough: governments which are the friends of the United States keep silent; the others denounce this genocide. The Americans try to reply that these unproved accusations only show these governments' partiality. "In fact," the American government says, "all we have ever done is to offer the Vietnamese, North and South, the option of ceasing their aggression or being crushed." It is scarcely necessary to mention that this offer is absurd, since it is the Americans who commit the aggression and consequently they are the only ones who can put an end to it. But this absurdity is not undeliberate: the Americans are ingeniously formulating, without appearing to do so, a demand which the Vietnamese cannot satisfy. They do offer an alternative: Declare you are beaten or we will bomb you back to the stone age. But the fact remains that the second term of this alternative is genocide. They have said: "genocide, yes, but *conditional* genocide." Is this juridically valid? Is it even conceivable?

If the proposition made any juridical sense at all, the U.S. government might narrowly escape the accusation of genocide. But the 1948 Convention leaves no such loopholes: an act of genocide, especially if it is carried out over a period of several years, is no less genocide for being blackmail. The perpetrator may declare he will stop if the victim gives in; this is still—without any juridical doubt whatsoever—a genocide. And this is all the more true when, as is the case here, a good part of the group has been annihilated to force the rest to give in.

But let us look at this more closely and examine the nature of the two terms of the alternative. In the South, the choice is the following: villages burned, the populace subjected to massive bombing, livestock shot, vegetation destroyed by defoliants, crops ruined by toxic aerosols, and everywhere indiscriminate shooting, murder, rape and looting. This is genocide in the strictest sense: massive extermination. The other option: what is *it?* What are the Vietnamese people supposed to do to escape this horrible death? Join the armed forces of Saigon or be enclosed in strategic or today's "New Life" hamlets, two names for the same concentration camps?

We know about these camps from numerous witnesses. They are fenced in by barbed wire. Even the most elementary needs are denied: there is malnutrition and a total lack of hygiene. The prisoners are heaped together in small tents or sheds. The social structure is destroyed. Husbands are separated from their wives, mothers from their children; family life, so important to the Vietnamese, no longer exists. As families are split up, the birth rate falls; any possibility of religious or cultural life is suppressed; even work—the work which might permit people to maintain themselves and their families—is refused them. These unfortunate people are not even slaves (slavery did not prevent the Negroes in the United States from developing a rich culture); they are reduced to a living heap of vegetable existence. When, sometimes, a fragmented family group is freed—children with an elder sister or a young mother—it goes to swell the ranks of the subproletariat in the big cities; the elder sister or the mother, with no job and mouths to feed reaches the last stage of her degradation in prostituting herself to the GIs.

The camps I describe are but another kind of genocide, equally condemned by the 1948 Convention:

"Causing serious bodily or mental harm to members of the group.

"Deliberately inflicting on the group conditions of life calculated to bring about its physical destruction in whole or in part.

"Imposing measures intended to prevent births within the group.

"Forcibly transferring children of the group to another group."

In other words, it is not true that the choice is between death or submission. For submission, in those circumstances, is submission to genocide. Let us say that a choice must be made between a violent and immediate death and a slow death from mental and physical degradation. Or, if you prefer, *there is no choice at all.*

Is it any different for the North?

One choice is *extermination.* Not just the daily risk of death, but the systematic destruction of the economic base of the country: from the dikes to the factories, nothing will be left standing. Deliberate attacks against civilians and, in particular, the rural population. Systematic destruction of hospitals, schools and places of worship. An all-out campaign to destroy the achievements of 20 years of socialism. The purpose may be only to intimidate the populace. But this can only be achieved by the daily extermination of an ever larger part of the group. So this intimidation itself in its psycho-social consequence is a genocide. Among the children in particular it must be engendering psychological disorders which will for years, if not permanently, "cause serious . . . mental harm."

The other choice is *capitulation.* This means that the North Vietnamese must declare themselves ready to stand by and watch while their country is divided and the Americans impose a direct or indirect dictatorship on their compatriots, in fact on members of their own families from whom the war has separated them. And would this intolerable humiliation bring an end to the war? This is far from certain. The National Liberation Front and the Democratic Republic of Vietnam, although fraternally united, have different strategies and tactics because their war situations are different. If the NLF continued the struggle, American bombs would go on blasting the DRV whether it capitulated or not.

If the war were to cease, the United States—according to official statements—would feel very generously inclined to help in the reconstruction of the DRV, and we know exactly what this means. It means that the United States would destroy, through private investments and conditional loans, the whole economic base of socialism. And this too is genocide. They would be splitting a sovereign country in half, occupying one of the halves by a reign of terror and keeping the other half under control by economic pressure. The "national group" Vietnam would not be physically eliminated, yet it would no longer exist. Economically, politically and culturally it would be suppressed.

In the North as in the South, the choice is only between two types of liquidation: collective death or dismemberment. The American government has had ample opportunity to test the resistance of the NLF and the DRV: by now it knows that only total destruction will be effective. The Front is stronger than ever; North Vietnam is unshakable. For this very reason, the calculated extermination of the Vietnamese people cannot really be intended to make them capitulate. The Americans offer them a *paix des braves* knowing full well that they will not accept it. And this phony alternative hides the true goal of imperialism, which is to reach, step by step, the highest stage of escalation—total genocide.

Of course, the United States government *could* have tried to reach this stage in one jump and wipe out Vietnam in a *Blitzkrieg* against the whole country. But this extermination first required setting up complicated installations—for instance, creating and maintaining air bases in Thailand which would shorten the bombing runs by 3000 miles.

Meanwhile, the major *purpose* of "escalation" was, and still is, to prepare international opinion for genocide. From this point of view, Americans have succeeded only too well. The repeated and systematic bombings of populated areas of Haiphong and Hanoi, which two years ago would have raised violent protests in Europe, occur today in a climate of general indifference resulting perhaps more from catatonia than from apathy. The tactic has borne its fruit: public opinion now sees escalation as a slowly and continuously increasing pressure to bargain, while in reality it is the preparation of minds for the final genocide. Is such a genocide possible? No. But that is due to the Vietnamese and the Vietnamese alone; to their courage, and to the remarkable efficiency of their organization. As for the United States government, it cannot be absolved of its crime just because its victim has enough intelligence and enough heroism to limit its effects.

We may conclude that in the face of a people's war (the characteristic product of our times, the answer to imperialism and the demand for sovereignty of a people conscious of its unity) there are two possible responses: either the aggressor withdraws, he acknowledges that a whole nation confronts him, and he makes peace; or else he recognizes the inefficacy of conventional strategy, and, if he can do so without jeopardizing his interests, he resorts to extermination pure and simple. There is no third alternative, but making peace is still at least *possible*.

But as the armed forces of the U.S.A. entrench themselves firmly in Vietnam, as they intensify the bombing and the massacres, as they try to bring Laos under their control, as they plan the invasion of Cambodia, there is less and less doubt that the government of the United States, despite its hypocritical denials, has chosen genocide.

The genocidal intent is implicit in the facts. It is necessarily premeditated. Perhaps in bygone times, in the midst of tribal wars, acts of genocide were perpetrated on the spur of the moment in fits of passion. But the anti-guerrilla genocide which our times have produced requires organization, military bases, a structure of accomplices, budget appropriations. Therefore, its authors must meditate and plan out their act. Does this mean that they are thoroughly conscious of their intentions? It is impossible to decide. We would have to plumb the depths of their consciences—and the Puritan bad faith of American works wonders.

There are probably people in the State Department who have

become so used to fooling themselves that they still think they are working for the good of the Vietnamese people. However, we may only surmise that there are fewer and fewer of these hypocritical innocents after the recent statements of their spokesmen: "We are defending ourselves; even if the Saigon government begged us, we would not leave Vietnam, etc., etc." At any rate, we don't have to concern ourselves with this psychological hide-and-seek. The truth is apparent *on the battlefield* in the racism of the American soldiers.

This racism—anti-black, anti-Asiatic, anti-Mexican—is a basic American attitude with deep historical roots and which existed, latently and overtly, well before the Vietnamese conflict. One proof of this is that the United States government refused to ratify the Genocide Convention. This doesn't mean that in 1948 the U.S. intended to exterminate a people; what it does mean— according to the statements of the U.S. Senate—is that the Convention would conflict with the laws of several states; in other words, the current policymakers enjoy a free hand in Vietnam because their predecessors catered to the anti-black racism of Southern whites. In any case, since 1966, the racism of Yankee soldiers, from Saigon to the 17th parallel, has become more and more marked. Young American men use torture (even including the "field telephone treatment"*), they shoot unarmed women for nothing more than target practice, they kick wounded Vietnamese in the genitals, they cut ears off dead men to take home for trophies. Officers are the worst: a general boasted of hunting "VCs" from his helicopter and gunning them down in the rice paddies. Obviously, these were not NLF soldiers who knew how to defend themselves; they were peasants tending their rice. In the confused minds of the American soldiers, "Viet Cong" and "Vietnamese" tend increasingly to blend into one another. They often say themselves, "The only good Vietnamese is a dead Vietnamese," or what amounts to the same thing, "A dead Vietnamese is a Viet Cong."

*The portable generator for a field telephone is used as an instrument for interrogation by hitching the two lead wires to the victim's genitals and turning the handle (editor's note).

For example: south of the 17th parallel, peasants prepare to harvest their rice. American soldiers arrive on the scene, set fire to their houses and want to transfer them to a strategic hamlet. The peasants protest. What else can they do, bare-handed against these Martians? They say: "The quality of the rice is good; we want to stay to eat our rice." Nothing more. But this is enough to irritate the young Yankees: "It's the Viet Cong who put that into your head; they are the ones who have taught you to resist." These soldiers are so misled that they take the feeble protests which their own violence has aroused for "subversive" resistance. At the outset, they were probably disappointed: they came to save Vietnam from "communist aggressors." But they soon had to realize that the Vietnamese did not want them. Their attractive role as liberators changed to that of occupation troops. For the soldiers it was the first glimmering of consciousness: "We are unwanted, we have no business here." But they go no further. They simply tell themselves that a Vietnamese is by definition suspect.

And from the neo-colonialists' point of view, this is true. They vaguely understand that in a people's war, civilians are the only visible enemies. Their frustration turns to hatred of the Vietnamese; racism takes it from there. The soldiers discover with a savage joy that they are there to kill the Vietnamese they had been pretending to save. All of them are potential communists, as proved by the fact that they hate Americans.

Now we can recognize in those dark and misled souls the truth of the Vietnam war: it meets all of Hitler's specifications. Hitler killed the Jews because they were Jews. The armed forces of the United States torture and kill men, women and children in Vietnam merely *because they are Vietnamese*. Whatever lies or euphemisms the government may think up, the spirit of genocide is in the minds of the soldiers. This is their way of living out the genocidal situation into which their government has thrown them. As Peter Martinson, a 23-year-old student who had "interrogated" prisoners for ten months and could scarcely live with his memories, said: "I am a middle-class American. I look like any other student, yet somehow I am a war criminal."

And he was right when he added: "Anyone in my place would have acted as I did." His only mistake was to attribute his degrading crimes to the influence of war *in general*.

No, it is not war in the abstract: it is the greatest power on earth against a poor peasant people. Those who fight it are *living out* the only possible relationship between an over-industrialized country and an underdeveloped country, that is to say, a genocidal relationship implemented through racism—the only relationship, short of picking up and pulling out.

Total war presupposes a certain balance of forces, a certain reciprocity. Colonial wars were not reciprocal, but the interests of the colonialists limited the scope of genocide. The present genocide, the end result of the unequal development of societies, is total war waged to the limit by one side, without the slightest reciprocity.

The American government is not guilty of inventing modern genocide, or even of having chosen it from other possible and effective measures against guerrilla warfare. It is not guilty, for example, of having preferred genocide for strategic and economic reasons. Indeed, genocide presents itself as the *only possible reaction* to the rising of a whole people against its oppressors.

The American government is guilty of having preferred, and of still preferring, a policy of war and aggression aimed at total genocide to a policy of peace, the only policy which can really replace the former. A policy of peace would necessarily have required a reconsideration of the objectives imposed on that government by the large imperialist companies through the intermediary of their pressure groups. America is guilty of continuing and intensifying the war despite the fact that every day its leaders realize more acutely, from the reports of the military commanders, that the only way to win is "to free Vietnam of all the Vietnamese." The government is guilty—despite the lessons it has been taught by this unique, unbearable experience—of proceeding at every moment a little further along a path which leads it to the point of no return. And it is guilty—according to its own admissions—of consciously carrying out this admonitory war in order to use genocide as a challenge and a threat to all peoples of the world.

We have seen that one of the features of total war has been the growing scope and efficiency of communication. As early as 1914, war could no longer be "localized." It had to spread throughout the whole world. In 1967, this process is being intensified. The ties of the "One World," on which the United States wants to impose its hegemony, have grown tighter and tighter. For this reason, as the American government very well knows, the current genocide is conceived as an answer to people's war and perpetrated in Vietnam not against the Vietnamese alone, but against humanity.

When a peasant falls in his rice paddy, mowed down by a machine gun, every one of us is hit. The Vietnamese fight for all men and the American forces against all. Neither figuratively nor abstractly. And not only because genocide would be a crime universally condemned by international law, but because little by little the whole human race is being subjected to this genocidal blackmail piled on top of atomic blackmail, that is, to absolute, total war. This crime, carried out every day before the eyes of the world, renders all who do not denounce it accomplices of those who commit it, so that we are being degraded today for our future enslavement.

In this sense imperialist genocide can only become more complete. The group which the United States wants to intimidate and terrorize by way of the Vietnamese nation is the human group in its entirety.

The dark ghettos are social, political, educational and—above all—economic colonies. Their inhabitants are subject peoples, victims of the greed, cruelty, insensitivity, guilt, and fear of their masters.

DR. KENNETH B. CLARK

In an age of decolonization, it may be fruitful to regard the problem of the American Negro as a unique case of colonialism, an instance of internal imperialism, an underdeveloped people in our very midst.

I. F. STONE

WHITE POWER:
The Colonial Situation

STOKELY CARMICHAEL and
CHARLES V. HAMILTON

What is racism? The word has represented daily reality to millions of black people for centuries, yet it is rarely defined—perhaps just because that reality has been such a commonplace. By "racism" we mean the predication of decisions and policies on considerations of race for the purpose of *subordinating* a racial group and maintaining control over that group. That has been the practice of this country toward the black man; we shall see why and how.

Racism is both overt and covert. It takes two, closely related forms: individual whites acting against individual blacks, and acts by the total white community against the black community. We call these individual racism and institutional racism. The first consists of overt acts by individuals, which cause death, injury or the violent destruction of property. This type can be recorded by television cameras; it can frequently be observed in the process of commission. The second type is less overt, far more subtle, less identifiable in terms of *specific* individuals committing the acts. But it is no less destructive of human life. The second type originates in the operation of established and respected forces in the society, and thus receives far less public condemnation than the first type.

When white terrorists bomb a black church and kill five black children, that is an act of individual racism, widely deplored by most segments of the society. But when in that same city— Birmingham, Alabama—five hundred black babies die each year because of the lack of proper food, shelter and medical facilities, and thousands more are destroyed and maimed physically, emotionally and intellectually because of conditions of poverty and discrimination in the black community, that is a function of institutional racism. When a black family moves into a home in a white neighborhood and is stoned, burned or routed out, they are victims of an overt act of individual racism which many people will condemn—at least in words. But it is institutional racism that keeps black people locked in dilapidated slum tenements, subject to the daily prey of exploitative slumlords, merchants, loan sharks and discriminatory real estate agents. The society either pretends it does not know of this latter situation, or is in fact incapable of doing anything meaningful about it. We shall examine the reasons for this in a moment.

Institutional racism relies on the active and pervasive operation of anti-black attitudes and practices. A sense of superior group position prevails: whites are "better" than blacks; therefore blacks should be subordinated to whites. This is a racist attitude and it permeates the society, on both the individual and institutional level, covertly and overtly.

"Respectable" individuals can absolve themselves from individual blame: *they* would never plant a bomb in a church; *they* would never stone a black family. But they continue to support political officials and institutions that would and do perpetuate institutionally racist policies. Thus *acts* of overt, individual racism may not typify the society, but institutional racism does—with the support of covert, individual *attitudes* of racism. As Charles Silberman wrote, in *Crisis in Black and White,*

> What we are discovering, in short, is that the United States —all of it, North as well as South, West as well as East—is a racist society in a sense and to a degree that we have refused so far to admit, much less face. . . . The tragedy of race relations in the United States is that there is no American Dilemma. White Americans are not torn and tortured by the conflict between their devotion to the American creed and their actual behavior. They are upset by the current state of race relations, to be sure. But what troubles them is not that justice is being denied but that their peace is being shattered and their business interrupted [pp. 9-10].

To put it another way, there is no "American dilemma" because black people in this country form a colony, and it is not in the interest of the colonial power to liberate them. Black people are legal citizens of the United States with, for the most part, the same *legal* rights as other citizens. Yet they stand as colonial subjects in relation to the white society. Thus institutional racism has another name: colonialism.

Obviously, the analogy is not perfect. One normally associates a colony with a land and people subjected to, and physically separated from, the "Mother Country." This is not always the case, however; in South Africa and Rhodesia, black and white inhabit the same land—with blacks subordinated to whites just as in the English, French, Italian, Portuguese and Spanish colonies. It is the objective relationship which counts, not rhetoric (such as constitutions *articulating* equal rights) or geography.

The analogy is not perfect in another respect. Under classic colonialism, the colony is a source of cheaply produced raw materials (usually agricultural or mineral) which the "Mother Country" then processes into finished goods and sells at high profit—sometimes back to the colony itself. The black communities of the United States do not export anything except human labor. But is the differentiation more than a technicality? Essentially, the African colony is selling its labor; the product itself does not belong to the "subjects" because the land is not theirs. At the same time, let us look at the black people of the South: Cultivating cotton at $3.00 for a ten-hour day and from that buying cotton dresses (and food and other goods) from white manufacturers. Economists might wish to argue this point endlessly; the objective relationship stands. Black people in the United States have a colonial relationship to the larger society, a relationship characterized by institutional racism. That colonial status operates in three areas—political, economic, social—which we shall discuss one by one.

Colonial subjects have their political decisions made for them by the colonial masters, and those decisions are handed down directly or through a process of "indirect rule." Politically, decisions which affect black lives have always been made by white people—the "white power structure." Thre is some dislike for this phrase because it tends to ignore or oversimplify the fact that there are many centers of power, many different forces making decisions. Those who raise that objection point to the pluralistic character of the body politic. They frequently overlook the fact that American pluralism quickly becomes a monolithic structure on issues of race. When faced with demands from black people, the multi-faction whites unite and present a common front. This is especially true when the black group increases in number: ". . . a large Negro population is politically both an asset and a liability. A large Negro populace may not only expect to influence the commitments and behavior of a governor, but it also may expect to arouse the fears of many whites. The larger the Negro population, the greater the perceived threat (in the eyes of whites) and thus the greater the resistance to broad civil rights laws."[*]
Again, the white groups tend to view their interests in a particularly united, solidified way when confronted with blacks

[*]James Q. Wilson, "The Negro in American Politics: The Present," *The American Negro Reference Book* (ed. by John P. Davis), Englewood Cliffs, New Jersey: Prentice-Hall, 1966, p 453.

making demands which are seen as threatening to vested interests. The whites react in a united group to protect interests they perceive to be theirs—interests possessed to the exclusion of those who, for varying reasons, are outside the group. Professor Robin M. Williams, Jr. has summed up the situation:

> In a very basic sense, "race relations" are the direct outgrowth of the long wave of European expansion, beginning with the discovery of America. Because of their more highly developed technology and economic and political organization, the Europeans were able by military force or by economic and political penetration to secure control over colonies, territories, protectorates and other possessions and spheres of influence around the world. In a way, the resulting so-called race relations had very little to do with "race"—initially it was an historical accident that the peoples encountered in the European expansion differed in shared physical characteristics of an obvious kind. But once the racial ideologies had been formed and widely disseminated, they constituted a powerful means of justifying political hegemony and economic control.
>
> In much the same way, present-day vested political, economic and social privileges and rights tend to be rationalized and defended by persons and groups who hold such prerogatives.
>
> . . . Whenever a number of persons within a society have enjoyed for a considerable period of time certain opportunities for getting wealth, for exercising power and authority, and for successfully claiming prestige and social deference, there is a strong tendency for these people to feel that these benefits are theirs "by right." The advantages come to be thought of as normal, proper, customary, as sanctioned by time, precedent and social consensus. Proposals to change the existing situation arouse reactions of "moral indignation." Elaborate doctrines are developed to show the inevitability and rightness of the existing scheme of things.
>
> An established system of vested interests is a powerful thing, perhaps especially when differences in power, wealth

> *and prestige coincide with relatively indelible symbols of*
> *collective membership, such as shared hereditary physical*
> *traits, a distinctive religion, or a persistently held culture.* The
> holders of an advantaged position see themselves as a group
> and reinforce one another in their attitudes; any qualms about
> *the justice of the status quo seem to be diminished by the*
> *group character of the arrangements.**

But what about the official "separation of powers"—the system
of "checks and balances"? We are well aware that political
power is supposedly divided at the national level between the
President, the Congress and the courts. But somehow, the war
in Vietnam has proceeded without Congressional approval. We
are aware that Constitutional niceties (really, they quickly become irrelevancies) divide power between the Federal Government and the states. but somehow the Supreme Court has found
no difficulty in expanding the power of Congress over interstate
commerce. At the same time, we are told that the Federal
Government is very limited in what it can do to stop whites
from attacking and murdering civil rights workers. A group
interest does exist and it crosses all the supposed lines when
necessary, thereby rendering them irrelevant. Furthermore,
whites frequently see *themselves* as a monolithic group on racial
issues and act accordingly.

The black community perceives the "white power structure"
in very concrete terms. The man in the ghetto sees his white
landlord come only to collect exorbitant rents and fail to make
necessary repairs, while both know that the white-dominated
city building inspection department will wink at violations or
impose only slight fines. The man in the ghetto sees the white
policeman on the corner brutally manhandle a black drunkard
in a doorway, and at the same time accept a pay-off from
one of the agents of the white controlled rackets. He sees the
streets in the ghetto lined with uncollected garbage, and he
knows that the powers which could send trucks in to collect

*Robin M. Williams, Jr., "Prejudice and Society," *The American Negro Reference
Book* (ed. by John P. Davis), Englewood Cliffs, New Jersey: Prentice-Hall, 1966,
pp. 727-29.

that garbage are white. When they don't, he knows the reason: the low political esteem in which the black community is held. He looks at the absence of a meaningful curriculum in the ghetto schools—for example, the history books that woefully overlook the historical achievements of black people—and he knows that the school board is controlled by whites.* He is not about to listen to intellectual discourses on the pluralistic and fragmented nature of political power. He is faced with a "white power structure" as monolithic as Europe's colonial offices have been to African and Asian colonies.

There is another aspect of colonial politics frequently found in colonial Africa and in the United States: the process of indirect rule. Martin Kilson describes it in *Political Change in a West African State, A Study of the Modernization Process in Sierra Leone:* "Indirect rule is the method of local colonial administration through the agency of Chiefs who exercise executive authority. It was applied in one form or other throughout British colonial Africa and was, from the standpoint of the metropolitan power's budget, a form of colonialism-on-the-cheap" (p. 24). In other words, the white power structure rules the black community through local blacks who are responsive to the white leaders, the downtown, white machine, not to the black populace. These black politicians do not exercise effective power. They cannot be relied upon to make forceful demands in behalf of their black constituents, and they become no more than puppets. They put loyalty to a political party before loyalty to their constituents and thus nullify any bargaining power the black community might develop. Colonial politics causes the subject to muffle his voice while participating in the councils of the white power structure. The black man forfeits his opportunity to speak forcefully and clearly for his race, and he justifies this in terms of expediency. Thus, when one talks of a "Negro

*Studies have shown the heavy preponderance of business and professional men on school boards throughout the country. One survey showed that such people, although only fifteen percent of the population, constituted seventy-six percent of school board members in a national sample. The percentage of laborers on the boards was only three percent. William C. Mitchell, *The American Polity: A Social and Cultural Interpretation,* Glencoe, Illinois: Free Press, 1962.

Establishment" in most places in this country, one is talking of an Establishment resting on a white power base; of hand-picked blacks whom that base projects as showpieces out front. These black "leaders" are, then, only as powerful as their white kingmakers will permit them to be. This is no less true of the North than the South.

Describing the political situaton in Chicago, Wilson wrote in Negro Politics:

> Particularly annoying to the Negro politicians has been the partial loss of their ability to influence the appointment of Negroes to important or prestigious jobs on public boards and agencies. Negroes selected for membership on such bodies as the Board of Education, the Land Clearance Commission, the Community Conservation Board, the Chicago Plan Commission, and other groups are the "token leaders" . . . and control over their appointment has in part passed out of the Negro machine [p. 84].

Before Congressman William O. Dawson (black Congressman from the predominantly black First Congressional District of Southside Chicago) was co-opted by the white machine, he was an outspoken champion of the race. Afterward, he became a tool of the downtown white Democratic power structure; the black community no longer had an effective representative who would articulate and fight to relieve their grievances. Mr. Dawson became assimilated. The white political bosses could rule the black community in the same fashion that Britain ruled the African colonies—by indirect rule. Note the result, as described in Silberman's Crisis in Black and White:

> Chicago provides an excellent example of how Negroes can be co-opted into inactivity. . . . Dawson surrendered far more than he has obtained for the Negro community. What Dawson obtained were the traditional benefits of the big city political machine: low-paying jobs for a lot of followers; political intervention with the police and with bail bondsmen, social workers, housing officials, and other bureaucrats whose decisions can affect a poor constituent's life; and a slice of the

"melon" in the form of public housing projects, welfare payments, and the like.

What Dawson surrendered was the pride and dignity of his community; he threw away the opportunity to force Chicago's political and civic leaders to identify and deal with the fundamental problems of segregation and oppression [p. 206].

Dawson, and countless others like him, have an answer to this criticism: this is the proper way to operate; you must "play ball" with the party in order to exact maximum benefits. We reject this notion. It may well result in particular benefits—in terms of status or material gains—for individuals, but it does not speak to the alleviation of a multitude of social problems shared by the masses. They may also say: if I spoke up, I would no longer be permitted to take part in the party councils. I would be ousted, and then the black people would have neither voice nor access. Utlimately, this is, at best, a spurious argument, which does more to enhance the security of the individual person than it does to gain substantial benefits for the group.

In time, one notes that a gap develops between the leadership and the followers. The masses, correctly, no longer view the leaders as their legitimate representatives. They come to see them more for what they are, emissaries sent by the white society. Identity between the two is lost. This frequently occurred in Africa, and the analogy, again, is relevent. Former President of Ghana, Kwame Nkrumah, described the colonial situation in pre-independent Africa in his book *Africa Must Unite:*

The principle of indirect rule adopted in West Africa, and also in other parts of the continent, allowed a certain amount of local self-government in that chiefs could rule their districts provided they did nothing contrary to the laws of the colonial power, and on condition they accepted certain orders from the colonial government. The system of indirect rule was notably successful for a time in Northern Nigeria, where the Emirs governed much as they had done before the colonial period. But the system had obvious dangers. In some cases,

> autocratic chiefs, propped up by the colonial government,
> became inefficient and unpopular, as the riots against the
> chiefs in Eastern Nigeria in 1929, and in Sierra Leone in 1936,
> showed.
>
> In wide areas of East Africa, where there was no developed
> system of local government which could be used, headmen
> or "warrant" chiefs were appointed, usually from noble fami-
> lies. They were so closely tied up with the colonial power
> that many Africans thought chiefs were an invention of the
> British [p. 18].

This process of co-optation and a subsequent widening of
the gap between the black elites and the masses is common
under colonial rule. There has developed in this country an
entire class of "captive leaders" in the black communities. These
are black people with certain technical and administrative skills
who could provide useful leadership roles in the black communities but do not because they have become beholden to the
white power structure. These are black school teachers, county
agents, junior executives in management positions with companies, etc. In a study of New Orleans contained in Professor
Daniel C. Thompson's *The Negro Leadership Class,* public school
teachers emerge as the largest professional group in the black
community of that city: there were 1,600 of them in 1961. These
people are college-trained, articulate, and in daily contact with
the young minds of the black South. For the most part (fortunate-
ly there are a few exceptions), they are not sources of positive
or aggressive community leadership. Thompson concluded:

> Depending as they do upon white officials, public school
> teachers have been greatly restricted in their leadership role
> . . . several laws passed by the Louisiana State Legislature,
> as well as rules and regulations adopted by the state and
> local school boards in recent years, have made it almost
> impossible for Negro teachers to identify with racial uplift
> organizations, or even to participate actively in the civil rights
> movement. This is definitely an important reason why some
> teachers have remained inactive and silent during heated
> controversies over civil rights [p. 46].

It is crystal clear that most of these people have accommodated themselves to the racist system. They have capitulated to colonial subjugation in exchange for the security of a few dollars and dubious status. They are effectively lost to the struggle for an improved black position which would fundamentally challenge that racist system. John A. Williams tells in *This is My Country Too* of how he went to Alabama State College (the state college for black people) in 1963 to interview a black professor, who brusquely told him: "Governor Wallace pays my salary; I have nothing to say to you. Excuse me, I have a class to get to" (pg. 62).

When black people play colonial politics, they also mislead the white community into thinking that it has the sanction of the blacks. A professor of political science who made a study of black people in Detroit politics from 1956–1960 has concluded:

> The fact that the Negro participates in the system by voting and participating in the party politics in the North should not lead us to conclude that he has accepted the popular consensus of the society about the polity. His support and work for the Democratic party is more a strategic compromise in most cases than a wholehearted endorsement of the party. My own work in Detroit led me to conclude that Negro party officers are not "loyal" to the Democratic party in the way that the ethnic groups or other organized groups such as labor have been. Although the Democratic Party-UAW coalition in Detroit has given the Negro a number of positions in the party hierarchy, it has not included him in the decision-making process.
>
> . . . As in the colonial situation, the Negro has developed a submission-aggression syndrome. When he attends campaign strategy meetings he appears to be submissive, willingly accepting the strategies suggested by the white leaders. Despite their seeming acceptance of this condescending treatment, after these meetings the Negro precinct workers will tell you that they had to "go along with all that talk" in order to make sure that they were represented. They openly express

> *their resentment of the party hierarchy and reveal themselves*
> *as much more militant about the Negro cause then was*
> *apparent during the meeting.**

This stance is not an uncommon one. More than a handful of black people will admit privately their contempt for insincere whites with whom they must work and deal. (In all likelihood, the contempt is mutual.) They feel secure in articulating their true feelings only when out of hearing range of "the man."

Those who would assume the responsibility of representing black people in this country must be able to throw off the notion that they can effectively do so and still maintain a maximum amount of security. Jobs will have to be sacrificed, positions of prestige and status given up, favors forfeited. It may well be—and we think it is—that leadership and security are basically incompatible. When one forcefully challenges the racist system, one cannot, at the same time, expect that system to reward him or even treat him comfortably. Political leadership which pacifies and stifles its voice and then rationalizes this on grounds of gaining "something for my people" is, at bottom, gaining only meaningless, token rewards that an affluent society is perfectly willing to give.

A final aspect of political colonialism is the manipulation of political boundaries and the devising of restrictive electoral systems. The point is frequently made that black people are only ten percent of the population—no less a personage than President Johnson has seen fit to remind us of this ratio. It is seldom pointed out that this minority is geographically located so as to create potential majority blocs—that strategic location being an ironic side-effect of segregation. But black people have never been able to utilize fully their numerical voting strength. Where we could vote, the white political machines have gerrymandered black neighborhoods so that the true voting strength is not reflected in political representation. Would anyone looking at the distribution of political power and representation in Manhattan even think that black people represent

*A. W. Singham, "The Political Socialization of Marginal Groups." Paper presented at the 1966 annual meeting of the American Political Science Association, New York City.

sixty percent of the population? On the local level, election to City Councils by the at-large system, rather than by district, reduces the number of representatives coming out of the black community. In Detroit, which uses the at-large system, there was not a black man on the City Council until 1957 despite a vast black population, especially during World War II. Also, the larger the electoral district, the greater the likelihood of there not being a Negro elected because he has to appeal to whites for their votes too. Los Angeles, with very large City Council electoral districts, saw the first black Councilman only in 1963.

The decision-makers are most adept at devising ways or utilizing existing factors to maintain their monopoly of political power.

The economic relationship of America's black communities to the larger society also reflects their colonial status. The political power exercised over those communities goes hand in glove with the economic deprivation experienced by the black citizens.

Historically, colonies have existed for the sole purpose of enriching, in one form or another, the "colonizer"; the consequence is to maintain the economic dependency of the "colonized." All too frequently we hear of the missionary motive behind colonization: to "civilize," to "Christianize" the underdeveloped, backward peoples, But read these words of a French Colonial Secretary of State in 1923:

> What is the use of painting the truth? At the start, colonization was not an act of civilization, nor was it a desire to civilize. It was an act of force motivated by interests. An episode in the vital competition which, from man to man, from group to group, has gone on ever increasing; the people who set out to seize colonies in the distant lands were thinking primarily of themselves, and were working for their own profits, and conquering for their own power.*

One is immediately reminded of the bitter maxim voiced by

*Albert Sarraut, French Colonial Secretary of State, speaking at the Eĉolé Colonialé in Paris. As quoted in Kwame Nkrumah's *Africa Must Unite*, London: Heinemann Educational Books, Ltd., 1963, p. 40.

many black Africans today: the missionaries came for our goods, not for our good. Indeed, the missionaries turned the Africans' eyes toward heaven, and then robbed them blind in the process. The colonies were sources from which raw materials were taken and markets to which finished products were sold. Manufacture and production were prohibited if this meant—as it usually did—competition with the "mother country." Rich in natural resources, Africa did not reap the benefit of these resources herself. In the Gold Coast (now Ghana), where the cocoa crop was the largest in the world, there was not one chocolate factory.

This same economic status has been perpetrated on the black community in this country. Exploiters come into the ghetto from outside, bleed it dry, and leave it economically dependent on the larger society. As with the missionaries, these exploiters frequently come as the "friend of the Negro," pretending to offer worthwhile goods and services, when their basic motivation is personal profit and their basic impact is the maintenance of racism. Many of the social welfare agencies—public and private—frequently pretend to offer "uplift" services; in reality, they end up creating a system which dehumanizes the individual and perpetuates his dependency. Conscious or unconscious, the paternalistic attitude of many of these agencies is no different from that of many missionaries going into Africa.

Professor Kenneth Clark described the economic colonization of the *Dark Ghetto* as follows:

> The ghetto feeds upon itself; it does not produce goods or contribute to the prosperity of the city. It has few large businesses. . . . Even though the white community has tried to keep the Negro confined in ghetto pockets, the white businessman has not stayed out of the ghetto. A ghetto, too, offers opportunities for profit, and in a competitive society profit is to be made where it can.
>
> In Harlem there is only one large department store and that is owned by whites. Negroes own a savings and loan association; and one Negro-owned bank has recently been organized. The other banks are branches of white-owned downtown banks. Property—apartment houses, stores, busi-

nesses, bars, concessions, and theaters—are for the most part
owned by persons who live outside the community and take
their profits home. . . .

When tumult arose in ghetto streets in the summer of 1964,
most of the stores broken into and looted belonged to white
men. Many of these owners responded to the destruction
with bewilderment and anger, for they felt that they had been
serving a community that needed them. They did not realize
that the residents were not grateful for this service but bitter,
as natives often feel toward the functionaries of a colonial
power who in the very act of service, keep the hated structure
of oppression intact [pp. 27–28].

It is a stark reality that the black communities are becoming
more and more economically depressed. In June, 1966, the
Bureau of Labor Statistics reported on the deteriorating condition of black people in this country. In 1948, the jobless rate
of non-white* males between the ages of fourteen and nineteen
was 7.6 percent. In 1965, the percentage of unemployment in
this age group was 22.6 percent. The corresponding figures for
unemployed white male teen-agers were 8.3 percent in 1948,
and 11.8 percent in 1965.

In the ten-year period from 1955 to 1965, total employment
for youth between the ages of fourteen and nineteen increased
from 2,642,000 to 3,612,000. Non-white youth got only 36,000
of those 970,000 new jobs. As for adults, the ratio of non-white
to white adult unemployment has remained double: in June,
1966, 4.1 percent for whites and 8.3 percent for non-whites.†

Lest someone talk about educational preparation, let it quickly
be added here that *unemployment rates in 1965 were higher*
for non-white high school graduates than for white high school
drop-outs. Furthermore, the median income of a non-white male
college graduate in 1960 was $5,020—actually $110 less than the
earnings of white males with only one to three years of high

---

*Non-whites in this and subsequent statistics includes Puerto Ricans, but the
vast majority of non-whites are black people.
†William A. Price, "Economics of the Negro Ghetto," *The National Guardian*
(September 3, 1966), p. 4.

school. Dr. Andrew F. Brimmer, the Negro former Assistant Secretary for Economic Affairs in the Department of Commerce, further highlights this situation in speaking of expected lifetime earnings:

> Perhaps the most striking feature . . . is the fact that a non-white man must have between one and three years of college before he can expect to earn as much as a white man with less than eight years of schooling, over the course of their respective working lives. Moreover, even after completing college and spending at least one year in graduate school, a non-white man can expect to do about as well as a white person who only completed high school.*

A white man with four years of high school education can expect to earn about $253,000 in his lifetime. A black man with five years or more of college can expect to earn $246,000 in his lifetime. Dr. Brimmer is presently a member of the Federal Reserve Board, and many people will point to his new position as an indication of "the progress of Negroes." In Chapter II, we shall discuss the absurdity of such conclusions.

Again, as in the African colonies, the black community is sapped senseless of what economic resources it does have. Through the exploitative system of credit, people pay "a dollar down, a dollar a week" literally for years. Interest rates are astronomical, and the merchandise—of relatively poor quality in the first place—is long since worn out before the final payment. Professor David Caplovitz of Columbia University has commented in his book, *The Poor Pay More*, "The high markup on low-quality goods is thus a major device used by merchants to protect themselves against the risks of their credit business" (p. 18). Many of the ghetto citizens, because of unsteady employment and low incomes, cannot obtain credit from more legitimate businesses; thus they must do without important items or end up being exploited. They are lured into the stores by attractive advertising displays hawking, for example, three

---

*Andrew F. Brimmer, "The Negro in the National Economy," *The American Negro Reference Book* (ed. by John P. Davis), Englewood Cliffs, New Jersey: Prentice-Hall, 1966, p. 260.

rooms of furniture for "only $199." Once inside, the unsuspecting customer is persuaded to buy lesser furniture at a more expensive price, or he is told that the advertised items are temporarily out of stock and is shown other goods. More frequently than not, of course, all the items are over-priced.

The exploitative merchant relies as much on threats as he does on legal action to guarantee payment. Garnishment of wages is not particularly beneficial to the merchant—although certainly used—because the employer will frequently fire an employee rather than be subjected to the bother of extra bookkeeping. And once the buyer is fired, all payments stop. But the merchant can hold the threat of garnishment over the customer's head. Repossession is another threat; again, not particularly beneficial to the merchant. He knows the poor quality of his goods in the first place, and there is little resale value in such goods which have probably already received substantial use. In addition, both the methods of garnishment and repossession give the merchant a bad business image in the community. It is better business practice to raise the prices two to three hundred percent, get what he can—dogging the customer for that weekly payment—and still realize a sizeable profit. At the same time the merchant can protect his image as a "considerate, understanding fellow."

The merchant has special ways of victimizing public welfare recipients. They are not supposed to buy on credit; installment payments are not provided for in the budget. Thus a merchant can threaten to tell the caseworker if a recipient who isn't meeting his payments does not "come in and put down something, if only a couple of dollars." Another example: in November, 1966, M.E.N.D. (Massive Economic Neighborhood Development), a community action, anti-poverty agency in New York City, documented the fact that some merchants raise their prices on the days that welfare recipients receive their checks. Canned goods and other items were priced as much as ten cents more on those specific days.

Out of a substandard income, the black man pays exorbitant prices for cheap goods; he must then pay more for his housing than whites. Whitney Young, Jr. of the Urban League writes in his book, *To Be Equal:* "most of Chicago's 838,000 Negroes live in a ghetto and pay about $20 more per month for housing than their white counterparts in the city" (pp. 144–45). Black people also have a much more difficult time securing a mortgage. They must resort to real estate speculators who charge interest rates up to ten percent, whereas a FHA loan would carry only a six percent interest rate. As for loans to go into business, we find the same pattern as among Africans, who were prohibited or discouraged from starting commercial enterprises. "The white power structure," says Dr. Clark in *Dark Ghetto,* "has collaborated in the economic serfdom of Negroes by its reluctance to give loans and insurance to Negro business" (pp. 27–28). The Small Business Administration, for example, in the ten-year period prior to 1964, made only *seven* loans to black people.

This is why the society does nothing meaningful about institutional racism: because the black community has been the creation of, and dominated by, a combination of oppressive forces and special interests in the white community. The groups which have access to the necessary resources and the ability to effect change benefit politically and economically from the continued subordinate status of the black community. This is not to say that every single white American consciously oppresses black people. He does not need to. Institutional racism has been maintained deliberately by the power structure and through indifference, inertia and lack of courage on the part of white masses as well as petty officials. Whenever black demands for change become loud and strong, indifference is replaced by active opposition based on fear and self-interest. The line between purposeful suppression and indifference blurs. One way or another, most whites participate in economic colonialism.

Indeed, the colonial white power structure has been a most formidable foe. It has perpetuated a vicious circle—the poverty cycle—in which the black communities are denied good jobs, and therefore stuck with a low income and therefore unable to obtain a good education with which to obtain good jobs. They cannot qualify for credit at most reputable places; they then resort to unethical merchants who take advantage of them by charging higher prices for inferior goods. They end up having less funds to buy in bulk, thus unable to reduce overall costs. They remain trapped.

In the face of such realities, it becomes ludicrous to condemn black people for "not showing more initiative." Black people are not in a depressed condition because of some defect in their character. The colonial power structure clamped a boot of oppression on the neck of the black people and then, ironically, said "they are not ready for freedom." Left solely to the good will of the oppressor, the oppressed would never be ready.

And no one accepts blame. And there is no "white power structure" doing it to them. And they are in that condition "because they are lazy and don't want to work." And this is not colonialism. And this is the land of opportunity, and the home of the free. And people should not become alienated.

But people *do* become alienated.

The operation of political and economic colonialism in this country has had social repercussions which date back to slavery but did not by any means end with the Emancipation Proclamation. Perhaps the most vicious result of colonialism—in Africa and this country—was that it purposefully, maliciously and with reckless abandon relegated the black man to a subordinated, inferior status in the society. The individual was considered and treated as a lowly animal, not to be housed properly, or given adequate medical services and by no means a decent education. We shall concentrate on the human and psychological results of social colonialism, first as it affected white attitudes towards blacks and then the attitude of black people toward themselves.

As we have already noted, slaves were brought to this land for the good of white masters, not for the purpose of saving or "civilizing" the blacks. In *From Slavery to Freedom*, Professor John Hope Franklin writes:

> When the countries of Europe undertook to develop the New World, they were interested primarily in the exploitation of America's natural resources. Labor was, obviously, necessary, and the cheaper the better [p. 47].

Indians would have been a natural solution, but they were too susceptible to diseases carried by Europeans, and they would not conform to the rigid discipline of the plantation system. Poor whites of Europe were tried but proved unsatisfactory. They were only indentured servants, brought over to serve for a limited time; many refused to complete their contract and ran away. With their white skins, they assimilated easily enough into the society. But black Africans were different. They proved to be the white man's economic salvation. Franklin concludes:

> Because of their color, Negroes could be easily apprehended. Negroes could be purchased outright and a master's labor supply would not be in a state of constant fluctuation. Negroes, from a pagan land and without exposure to the ethical ideals of Christianity, could be handled with more rigid methods of discipline and could be morally and spiritually degraded for the sake of stability on the plantation. In the long run, Negro slaves were actually cheaper. In a period when economic considerations were so vital, this was especially important. Negro slavery, then, became a fixed institution, a solution to one of the most difficult problems that arose in the New World. With the supply of Negroes apparently inexhaustible, there would be no more worries about labor. European countries could look back with gratitude to the first of their nationals who explored the coasts of Africa, and brought back gold to Europe. It was the key to the solution of one of America's most pressing problems [p. 49].

The fact of slavery had to have profound impact on the subsequent attitudes of the larger society toward the black man. The fact of slavery helped to fix the sense of superior group position. Chief Justice Taney, in the Dred Scott decision of 1857, stated ". . . that they (black people) had no rights which the white man was bound to respect; and that the negro might justly and lawfully be reduced to slavery for his benefit." The emancipation of the slaves by legal act could certainly not erase such notions from the minds of racists. They believed in their superior status, not in paper documents. And that belief has persisted. When some people compare the black American to "other immigrant" groups in this country, they overlook the fact that slavery was peculiar to the blacks. No other minority group in this country was ever treated as legal property.

Even when the black man has participated in wars to defend this country, even when the black man has repeatedly demonstrated loyalty to this country, the embedded colonial mentality has continued to deny him equal status in the social order. Participation of black men in the white man's wars is a characteristic of colonialism. The colonial ruler readily calls upon and expects the subjects to fight and die in defense of the colonial empire, without the ruler feeling any particular compulsion to grant the subjects equal status. In fact, the war is frequently one to defend the socio-political status quo established between the ruler and subject. Whatever else may be changed by wars, the fundamental relation between colonial master and subordinates remains substantially unaltered.

Woodrow Wilson proclaimed that this country entered World War I "to make the world safe for democracy." This was the very same President who issued executive orders segregating most of the eating and rest-room facilities for federal employees. This was the same man who had written in 1901:

> An extraordinary and very perilous state of affairs had been created in the South by the sudden and absolute emancipation of the Negroes, and it was not strange that the Southern legislatures should deem it necessary to take extraordinary steps to guard against the manifest and pressing dangers which it entailed. Here was a vast "laboring, landless, homeless class," once slaves; now free; unpracticed in liberty, unschooled in self-control; never sobered by the discipline of self-support; never established in any habit of prudence; excited by a freedom they did not understand, exalted by false hopes, bewildered and without leaders, and yet insolent and aggressive; sick of work, covetous of pleasure—a host of dusky children untimely put out of school.*

". . . dusky children untimely put out of school," freed too

*Woodrow Wilson, "Reconstruction in the Southern States," Atlantic Monthly (January, 1901).

soon—it is absolutely inconceivable that a man who spoke in such a manner could have black people in mind when he talked of saving the world (i.e., the United States) for democracy. Obviously, black people were not included in Woodrow Wilson's defense perimeter. Whatever the life of blacks might have been under German rule, this country clearly did not fight Germany for the improvement of the status of black people—under the saved democracy—in *this* land.

Even during the war, while black soldiers were dying in Europe, Representative Frank Park of Georgia introduced a bill to make it unlawful to appoint blacks to the rank of either noncommissioned or commissioned officers. Following the war, black veterans returned to face a struggle no less fierce than the one overseas. More than seventy black people were lynched during the first year after armistice. Ten black soldiers, some still in uniform, were lynched. And few who are knowledgeable of twentieth-century American history will fail to remember "the Red summer" of 1919. Twenty-five race riots were recorded between June and December of that year. The Ku Klux Klan flourished during this period, making more than two hundred public appearances in twenty-seven states. The Klan cells were not all located in the South; units were organized in New York, Indiana, Illinois, Michigan and other northern cities.

World War II was basically little different. The increased need for manpower in defense industries slowly opened up more jobs for black people as a result of the war effort, but as Professor Garfinkel has pointed out in *When Negroes March*, "When defense jobs were finally opened up to Negroes, they tended to be on the lowest rungs of the success ladder." Garfinkel also tells of how the President of the North American Aviation Company, for example, issued this statement on May 7, 1941:

> *While we are in complete sympathy with the Negroes, it is against company policy to employ them as aircraft workers or mechanics . . . regardless of their training. . . . There will be some jobs as janitors for Negroes* [p. 17].

This country also saw fit to treat German prisoners of war more humanely than it treated its own black soldiers. On one occasion, a group of black soldiers was transporting German prisoners by train through the South to a prisoner-of-war camp. The railroad diner required the black American soldiers to eat in segregated facilities on the train—only four at a time and with considerable delay—while the German prisoners (white, of course) ate without delay and with other passengers in the main section of the diner!

Thus does white man regard the black, an attitude rooted in slavery. Clearly it would be and has been very difficult for subsequent generations of whites to overcome—even if they wanted to—the concept of a subordinate caste assigned to blacks, of black inferiority. They had to continue thinking this way and developing elaborate doctrines to justify what Professor Williams had called "the inevitability and rightness of the existing scheme of things." Herbert Blumer draws the following conclusion:

> . . . The sense of group position is a norm and impera-tive—indeed, a very powerful one. It guides, incites, cows, and coerces . . . this kind of sense of group position stands for and involves a fundamental kind of group affiliation for the members of the dominant racial group. To the extent that they recognize themselves as belonging to that group they will automatically come under the influence of the sense of position held by that group.*

Blumer allows for the exception: those who do not recognize themselves as belonging to the group. Inside and outside the civil rights movement, there have been whites who rejected their own whiteness as a group symbol and who even tried sometimes "to be black." These dissidents have endured os-tracism, poverty, physical pain and death itself in demonstrating their non-recognition of belonging to the group because of its racism. But how fully can white people free themselves from the tug of the group position—free themselves not so much from overt racist attitudes in themselves as from a more subtle paternalism bred into them by the society and, perhaps more

* Herbert Blumer, "Race Prejudice as a Sense of Group Position," *Pacific Sociolog-ical Review* (Spring, 1958).

important, from the conditioned reaction of black people to their whiteness? For most whites, that freedom is unattainable. White civil rights workers themselves have often noted this:

> Too often we have found our relationships with the local community leaders disturbingly like the traditional white-black relationship of the deep South: the white organizer finds the decision-making left up to him, while the local leader finds himself instinctively assuming a subservient role. . . . Since the organizer's purpose is not to lead but to get the people to lead themselves, being white is an unsurmountable handicap.*

The social and psychological effects on black people of all their degrading experiences are also very clear. From the time black people were introduced into this country, their condition has fostered human indignity and the denial of respect. Born into this society today, black people begin to doubt themselves, their worth as human beings. Self-respect becomes almost impossible. Kenneth Clark describes the process in *Dark Ghetto*:

> Human beings who are forced to live under ghetto conditions and whose daily experience tells them that almost nowhere in society are they respected and granted the ordinary dignity and courtesy accorded to others will, as a matter of course, begin to doubt their own worth. Since every human being depends upon his cumulative experiences with others for clues as to how he should view and value himself, children who are consistently rejected understandably begin to question and doubt whether they, their family, and their group really deserve no more respect from the larger society than they receive. These doubts become the seeds of a pernicious self- and group-hatred, the Negro's complex and debilitating prejudice against himself.
>
> The preoccupation of many Negroes with hair straighteners, skin bleachers, and the like illustrates this tragic aspect of American racial prejudice—Negroes have come to believe in their own inferiority [pp. 63–64].

*Bruce Detwiler, "A Time to be Black," *The New Republic* (September 17, 1966).

There was the same result in Africa. And some European colonial powers—notably France and Portugal—provided the black man "a way out" of the degrading status: to become "white," or assimilated. France pursued a colonial policy aimed at producing a black French elite class, a group exposed and acculturated to French "civilization." In its African colonies of Mozambique and Angola, Portugal has attempted a colonial policy of assimilation which goes even further. There is no pretense—as in the British colonies and in American rhetoric—of black people moving toward self-government and freedom. All Independence groups have been suppressed. There prevails in these Portuguese colonies a legal process whereby an African may become, in effect, a "white" man if he measures up to certain Western standards. The *assimilado* is one who has adopted Portuguese customs, dress, language, and has achieved at least a high school education. He is, of course, favored with special jobs and better housing. This status likewise qualifies him to receive a passport to travel abroad, mainly to Portugal and Brazil. Otherwise, such freedom of movement is denied. The *assimilado* is accepted socially by the whites in the restaurants and night clubs. In fact, the Portuguese officials will even import a white Portuguese woman to Mozambique to marry an *assimilado* man. (American colonialism has not gone this far.) But to submit to all of this, the *assimilado* must reject as intrinsically inferior his entire African heritage and association.

In a manner similar to that of the colonial powers in Africa, American society indicates avenues of escape from the ghetto for those individuals who adapt to the "mainstream." This adaptation means to disassociate oneself from the black race, its culture, community and heritage, and become immersed (dispersed is another term) in the white world. What actually happens, as Professor E. Franklin Frazier pointed out in his book, *Black Bourgeoisie,* is that the black person ceases to identify himself with black people yet is obviously unable to assimilate with whites. He becomes a "marginal man," living on the fringes of both societies in a world largely of "make believe." This black person is urged to adopt American middle-class standards and values. As with the black African who had to become a "Frenchman" in order to be accepted, so to be an American, the black man must strive to become "white." To the extent that he does, he is considered "well adjusted"—one who has "risen above the race question." These people are frequently held up by the white Establishment as living examples of the progress being made by the society in solving the race problem. Suffice it to say that precisely because they are required to denounce—overtly or covertly—their black race, *they are reinforcing racism in this country.*

In the United States, as in Africa, their "adaptation" operated to deprive the black community of its potential skills and brain power. All too frequently, these "integrated" people are used to blunt the true feelings and goals of the black masses. They are picked as "Negro leaders," and the white power structure proceeds to talk to and deal only with them. Needless to say, no fruitful, meaningful dialogue can take place under such circumstances. Those hand-picked "leaders" have no viable constituency for which they can speak and act. All this is a classic formula of colonial co-optation.

At all times, then, the social effects of colonialism are to degrade and to dehumanize the subjected black man. White America's School of Slavery and Segregation, like the School of Colonialism, has taught the subject to hate himself and to deny his own humanity. The white society maintains an attitude of superiority and the black community has too often succumbed to it, thereby permitting the whites to believe in the correctness of their position. Racist assumptions of white superiority have been so deeply engrained into the fiber of the society that they infuse the entire functioning of the national subconscious. They are taken for granted and frequently not even recognized. As Professors Lewis Killian and Charles Grigg express it in their book, *Racial Crisis in America:*

> *At the present time, integration as a solution to the race problem demands that the Negro foreswear his identity as a Negro. But for a lasting solution, the meaning of "American" must lose its implicit racial modifier, "white." Even without biological amalgamation, integration requires a sincere*

acceptance by all Americans that it is just as good to be a black American as to be a white American. Here is the crux of the problem of race relations—the redefinition of the sense of group position so that the status advantage of the white man is no longer an advantage, so that an American may acknowledge his Negro ancestry without apologizing for it. . . . They [black people] live in a society in which to be unconditionally "American" is to be white, and to be black is a misfortune [pp. 108–9].

The time is long overdue for the black community to redefine itself, set forth new values and goals, and organize around them.

REFERENCES

Baran, Paul. *The Political Economy of Growth.* New York: Monthly Review Press, 1956.

Boorstein, Edward. *The Economic Transformation of Cuba.* New York: Monthly Review Press, 1968.

Chomsky, Noam. *American Power and the New Mandarins.* New York: Pantheon, 1969.

Hobson, J. A. *Imperialism.* Ann Arbor, Mich.: Ann Arbor Publishers, 1965.

Kemp, Tom. *Theories of Imperialism.* London: Dobson, 1967.

Magdoff, Harry. *The Age of Imperialism.* New York: Monthly Review Press, 1969.

Nearing, Scott, and Freeman, Joseph. *Dollar Diplomacy.* New York: Monthly Review Press, 1969.

Van Alstyne, R. W. *The Rising American Empire.* Chicago: Quadrangle Books, 1960.

Weinberg, Albert K. *Manifest Destiny.* Chicago: Quadrangle Books, 1963.

Williams, William A. *The Tragedy of American Diplomacy.* New York: Delta Books, 1962.

3/Empire and Revolution

A society which elevates market values over real values, which asserts the priority of property rights over human rights, which distributes wealth, privilege, and power on a grossly unequal basis and yet depends for its legitimation on a myth of popular sovereignty and political equality—such a society cannot in the long run be stable.

In the past, the equilibrium of American society has been shaken only once by an uncontainable crisis in the form of civil war. An expansive frontier, first domestically and then overseas, and an ocean-protected isolation have been the primary sources of this stability. Nonetheless, in the last 70 years radical fissures in American society have opened up on three occasions. Twice these domestic crises were healed by distant World Wars which left America in far better material condition than at their start, while fusing a patriotic conservative consensus on the political front.

Twenty-five years after the Second World War, however, America is deep into its third major crisis of this century. This time it is enmeshed in a losing war for its imperial frontier in Southeast Asia, with no convenient exit in sight. The last frontier has already been occupied and now the thrust of human history is in the other direction: the native populations of the world are developing a revolutionary counterthrust which has already taken on the character of an historically irrepressible force.

This is the central reality that one must bear in mind when dealing with the necessity and inevitability of revolutionary social change inside the United States. For there is no American society apart from or independent of the international society into which American economic and military power has extruded itself during the twentieth century. Nor can that very thrust of American political and social energies into the framework of the international economy and society be regarded as merely one option among several, to be continued or discontinued at will by American leaders. Through decades of planning and investment, that outward expansion has acquired all the institutional rigidity and conservatism of a genuine social system, with deep roots in America's internal order. Already the past expansions of white European societies onto the societies of color in Africa, Asia, and America are bearing "domestic" fruit. Black servitude in North America and Africa becomes black revolt in Africa and North America, the one liberation inspiring and preparing the ground of the other, just as Africa's oppression provided the basis for black America's centuries ago.

If revolutionary social change (meaning a radical redistribution of power and wealth, a drastic overhaul of existing social priorities, and a reallocation of social resources) is the historical necessity of the epoch, such change is not possible through piecemeal reform, as the analyses in Part 1 of this volume should demonstrate. For the allocation and distribution of social resources is determined by the ownership of the means of production and the consequent distribution of social power. Moreover, the state, to which liberal reformers look for representation of the "public interest" in balancing the so-called "private" power of corporate wealth, is a creation of private property for the protection of private property. Juridically, militarily, and politically, the state is the design of the ruling class of society for the preservation of its power and privileges. To radically change this order is only possible by means of a struggle which removes the ruling class forces from their bases of power in the economy and the state; it means therefore a necessary change in the whole legal basis of society, beginning with its Constitution. In short, it means a revolution.

Such a revolution, while based on the deep-seated structural forces of the social order, would be in its development and execution profoundly political, a fact which is not well understood by revolutionary theorists (as opposed to revolutionary leaders). Lenin once remarked that there is no economic crisis which is insoluble within the existing social framework. The revolutionary crisis is above all a political crisis and therefore it is affected by ideological factors, which are by no means simple reflections of an economic base. One consequence of this fact is that revolutionary breaks cannot be analyzed with anything like the precision with which the normal operation and evolution of the social order itself is analyzed.

Without question, the most brilliant description of modern socialist revolution, and the most classic formulation of the role of conscious factors in the dynamics of social change, is that of Leon Trotsky, whose History of the Russian Revolution is one of the supreme masterpieces of the Marxist tradition and of Western historiography in general. In the excerpts that follow, Trotsky outlines the complex dialectic of the encounter between the active agents of revolutionary change and the determinant forces of the social framework.

At this historical remove, however, Trotsky's determinism seems somewhat overstated and overconfident. The global political factors created by the Bolshevik revolution itself have served to make more complex and less determinate the revolutionary development and outcome of any given national dynamic. The selections by Eldridge Cleaver and Tom Hayden explore the dialectics of revolution in a thoroughly interdependent world order, where the social forces of "mother country" and "colony" are so intertwined as to raise the problem to a new level of complexity, and to give it a truly international dimension.

REVOLUTION AND INSURRECTION

LEON TROTSKY

During the first two months of 1917 Russia was still a Romanov monarchy. Eight months later the Bolsheviks stood at the helm. They were little known to anybody when the year began, and their leaders were still under indictment for state treason when they came to power. You will not find another such sharp turn in history—especially if you remember that it involves a nation of 150 million people. It is clear that the events of 1917, whatever you think of them, deserve study.

The history of a revolution, like every other history, ought first of all to tell what happened and how. That, however, is little enough. From the very telling it ought to become clear why it happened thus and not otherwise. Events can neither be regarded as a series of adventures, nor strung on the thread of some preconceived moral. They must obey their own laws. The discovery of these laws is the author's task.

The most indubitable feature of a revolution is the direct interference of the masses in historic events. In ordinary times the state, be it monarchical or democratic, elevates itself above the nation, and history is made by specialists in that line of business—kings, ministers, bureaucrats, parliamentarians, journalists. But at those crucial moments when the old order becomes no longer endurable to the masses, they break over the barriers excluding them from the political arena, sweep aside their traditional representatives, and create by their own interference the initial groundwork for a new régime. Whether this

From *History of Russian Revolution* by Leon Trotsky. © 1934. Reprinted by permission of University of Michigan Press.

is good or bad we leave to the judgment of moralists. We ourselves will take the facts as they are given by the objective course of development. The history of a revolution is for us first of all a history of the forcible entrance of the masses into the realm of rulership over their own destiny.

In a society that is seized by revolution classes are in conflict. It is perfectly clear, however, that the changes introduced between the beginning and the end of a revolution in the economic bases of the society and its social substratum of classes are not sufficient to explain the course of the revolution itself, which can overthrow in a short interval age-old institutions, create new ones, and again overthrow them. The dynamic of revolutionary events is *directly* determined by swift, intense and passionate changes in the psychology of classes which have already formed themselves before the revolution.

The point is that society does not change its institutions as need arises, the way a mechanic changes his instruments. On the contrary, society actually takes the institutions which hang upon it as given once for all. For decades the oppositional criticism is nothing more than a safety valve for mass dissatisfaction, a condition of the stability of the social structure. Such in principle, for example, was the significance acquired by the social-democratic criticism. Entirely exceptional conditions, independent of the will of persons or parties, are necessary in order to tear off from discontent the fetters of conservatism, and bring the masses to insurrection.

The swift changes of mass views and moods in an epoch of revolution thus derive, not from the flexibility and mobility of man's mind, but just the opposite, from its deep conservatism. The chronic lag of ideas and relations behind new objective conditions, right up to the moment when the latter crash over people in the form of a catastrophe, is what creates in a period of revolution that leaping movement of ideas and passions which seems to the police mind a mere result of the activities of "demagogues."

The masses go into a revolution not with a prepared plan of social reconstruction, but with a sharp feeling that they can not endure the old régime. Only the guiding layers of a class have a political programme, and even this still requires the test of events, and the approval of the masses. The fundamental political process of the revolution thus consists in the gradual comprehension by a class of the problems arising from the social crisis—the active orientation of the masses by a method of successive approximations. The different stages of a revolutionary process, certified by a change of parties in which the more extreme always supersedes the less, express the growing pressure to the left of the masses—so long as the swing of the movement does not run into objective obstacles. When it does, there begins a reaction: disappointments of the different layers of the revolutionary class, growth of indifferentism, and therewith a strengthening of the position of the counter-revolutionary forces. Such, at least, is the general outline of the old revolutions.

Only on the basis of a study of political processes in the masses themselves, can we understand the rôle of parties and leaders, whom we least of all are inclined to ignore. They constitute not an independent, but nevertheless a very important element in the process. Without a guiding organisation the energy of the masses would dissipate like steam not enclosed in a piston-box. But nevertheless what moves things is not the piston or the box, but the steam. . . .

* * *

The purely psychological school, which looks upon the issue of events as an interweaving of the free activities of separate individuals or their groupings, offers, even with the best intentions on the part of the investigator, a colossal scope to caprice. The materialist method disciplines the historian, compelling him to take his departure from the weighty facts of the social structure. For us the fundamental forces of the historic process are classes; political parties rest upon them; ideas and slogans emerge as the small change of objective interests. The whole course of the investigation proceeds from the objective to the subjective, from the social to the individual, from the fundamental to the incidental. This sets a rigid limit to the personal whims of the author.

When a mining engineer finds magnetic ore in an uninvestigated region by drilling, it is always possible to assume that this was a happy accident: the construction of a mine is hardly to be recommended. But when the same engineer, on the basis, let us say, of the deviation of a magnetic needle, comes to the conclusion that a vein of ore lies concealed in the earth, and subsequently actually strikes ore at various different points in the region, then the most cavilling sceptic will not venture to talk about accidents. What convinces is the system which unites the general with the particular.

The proof of scientific objectivism is not to be sought in the eyes of the historian or the tones of his voice, but in the inner logic of the narrative itself. If episodes; testimonies, figures, quotations, fall in with the general pointing of the needle of his social analysis, then the reader has a most weighty guarantee of the scientific solidity of his conclusions. To be more concrete: the present author has been true to objectivism in the degree that his book actually reveals the inevitability of the October revolution and the causes of its victory.

The reader already knows that in a revolution we look first of all for the direct interference of the masses in the destinies of society. We seek to uncover behind the events changes in the collective consciousness. We reject wholesale references to the "spontaneity" of the movement, references which in most cases explain nothing and teach nobody. Revolutions take place according to certain laws. This does not mean that the masses in action are aware of the laws of revolution, but it does mean that the changes in mass consciousness are not accidental, but are subject to an objective necessity which is capable of theoretic explanation, and thus makes both prophecy and leadership possible.

Certain official soviet historians, surprising as it may seem, have attempted to criticise our conception as idealistic. Professor Pokrovsky, for example, has insisted that we underestimate the objective factors of the revolution. "Between February and October there occurred a colossal economic collapse." "During this time the peasantry . . . rose against the Provisional Government." It is in these "objective shifts" says Pokrovsky, and not in fickle psychic processes, that one should see the motive force of the revolution. Thanks to a praiseworthy incisiveness of formulation, Pokrovsky exposes to perfection the worthlessness of that vulgarly economic interpretation of history which is frequently given out for Marxism.

The radical turns which take place in the course of a revolution are as a matter of fact evoked, not by those episodic economic disturbances which arise during the events themselves, but by fundamental changes which have accumulated in the very foundations of society throughout the whole preceding epoch. The fact that on the eve of the overthrow of the monarchy, as also between February and October, the economic collapse was steadily deepening, nourishing and whipping up the discontent of the masses—that fact is indubitable and has never lacked our attention. But it would be the crudest mistake to assume that the second revolution was accomplished eight months after the first owing to the fact that the bread ration was lowered during that period from one-and-a-half to three-quarters of a pound. In the years immediately following the October revolution the food situation of the masses continued steadily to grow worse. Nevertheless the hopes of the counter-revolutionary politicians for a new overturn were defeated every time. This circumstance can seem puzzling only to one who looks upon the insurrection of the masses as "spontanteous"—that is, as a herd-mutiny artificially made use of by leaders. In reality the mere existence of privations is not enough to cause an insurrection; if it were, the masses would be always in revolt. It is necessary that the bankruptcy of the social régime, being conclusively revealed, should make these privations intolerable, and that new conditions and new ideas should open the prospect of a revolutionary way out. Then in the cause of the great aims conceived by them, those same masses will prove capable of enduring doubled and tripled privations.

The reference to the revolt of the peasantry as a second "objective factor" shows a still more obvious misunderstanding. For the proletariat the peasant war was of course an objective circumstance—in so far as the activity of one class does in general become an external stimulus to the consciousness of another. But the direct cause of the peasant revolt itself lay in changes in the consciousness of the villages. Let us not forget that revolutions are accomplished through people, although they be nameless. Materialism does not ignore the feeling, thinking and acting man, but explains him. What else is the task of the historian?

* * *

THE ART OF INSURRECTION

People do not make revolution eagerly any more than they do war. There is this difference, however, that in war compulsion plays the decisive rôle, in revolution there is no compulsion except that of circumstances. A revolution takes place only when there is no other way out. And the insurrection, which rises above a revolution like a peak in the mountain chain of its events, can no more be evoked at will than the revolution as a whole. The masses advance and retreat several times before they make up their minds to the final assault.

Conspiracy is ordinarily contrasted to insurrection as the deliberate undertaking of a minority to a spontaneous movement of the majority. And it is true that a victorious insurrection, which can only be the act of a class called to stand at the head of the nation, is widely separated both in method and historic significance from a governmental overturn accomplished by conspirators acting in concealment from the masses.

In every class society there are enough contradictions so that a conspiracy can take root in its cracks. Historic experience proves, however, that a certain degree of social disease is necessary—as in Spain, for instance, or Portugal, or South America—to supply continual nourishment for a régime of conspiracies. A pure conspiracy even when victorious can only replace one clique of the same ruling class by another—or still less, merely alter the governmental personages. Only mass insurrection has ever brought the victory of one social régime over another. Periodical conspiracies are commonly an expression of social stagnation and decay, but popular insurrections on the contrary come usually as a result of some swift growth which has broken down the old equilibrium of the nation. The chronic "revolutions" of the South American republics have nothing in common with the Permanent Revolution; they are in a sense the very opposite thing.

This does not mean, however, that popular insurrection and conspiracy are in all circumstances mutually exclusive. An element of conspiracy almost always enters to some degree into any insurrection. Being historically conditioned by a certain stage in the growth of a revolution, a mass insurrection is never purely spontaneous. Even when it flashes out unexpectedly to a majority of its own participants, it has been fertilised by those ideas in which the insurrectionaries see a way out of the difficulties of existence. But a mass insurrection can be foreseen and prepared. It can be organized in advance. In this case the conspiracy is subordinate to the insurrection, serves it, smoothes its path, hastens its victory. The higher the political level of a revolutionary movement and the more serious its leadership, the greater will be the place occupied by conspiracy in a popular insurrection.

It is very necessary to understand the relations between insurrection and conspiracy, both as they oppose and as they supplement each other. It is especially so, because the very use of the word conspiracy, even in Marxian literature, contains a superficial contradiction due to the fact that it sometimes implies an independent undertaking initiated by the minority, at others a preparation by the minority of a majority insurrection.

History testifies, to be sure, that in certain conditions a popular insurrection can be victorious even without a conspiracy. Arising "spontaneously" out of the universal indignation, the scattered protests, demonstrations, strikes, street fights, an insurrection can draw in a part of the army, paralyse the forces of the enemy, and overthrow the old power. To a certain degree this is what happened in February 1917 in Russia. Approximately the same picture is presented by the development of the German and Austro-Hungarian revolutions of the autumn of 1918. Since in these events there was no party at the head of the insurrectionaries imbued through and through with the interests and aims of the insurrection, its victory had inevitably to transfer the power to those parties which up to the last moment had been opposing it.

To overthrow the old power is one thing; to take the power in one's own hands is another. The bourgeoisie may win the power in a revolution not because it is revolutionary, but because it is bourgeois. It has in its possession property, education, the press, a network of strategic positions, a hierarchy of institutions. Quite otherwise with the proletariat. Deprived in the nature of things of all social advantages, an insurrectionary proletariat can count only on its numbers, its solidarity, its cadres, its official staff.

Just as a blacksmith cannot seize the red hot iron in his naked hand, so the proletariat cannot directly seize the power; it has to have an organization accommodated to this task. The coordination of the mass insurrection with the conspiracy, the subordination of the conspiracy to the insurrection, the organisation of the insurrection through the conspiracy, constitutes that complex and responsible department of revolutionary politics which Marx and Engels called "the art of insurrection." It presupposes a correct general leadership of the masses, a flexible orientation in changing conditions, a thought-out plan of attack, cautiousness in technical preparation, and a daring blow.

Historians and politicians usually give the name of *spontaneous insurrection* to a movement of the masses united by a common hostility against the old régime, but not having a clear aim, deliberated methods of struggle, or a leadership consciously showing the way to victory. This spontaneous insurrection is condescendingly recognised by official historians—at least those of democratic temper—as a necessary evil the responsibility for which falls upon the old régime. The real reason for their attitude of indulgence is that "spontaneous" insurrection cannot transcend the framework of the bourgeois régime.

The social democrats take a similar position. They do not reject revolution at large as a social catastrophe, any more than they reject earthquakes, volcanic eruptions, eclipses and epidemics of the plague. What they do reject—calling it "Blanquism," or still worse, Bolshevism—is the conscious preparation of an overturn, the plan, the conspiracy. In other words, the social democrats are ready to sanction—and that only *ex post facto*—those overturns which hand the power to the bourgeoisie, but they implacably condemn those methods which might alone bring the power to the proletariat. Under this pretended objectivism they conceal a policy of defense of the capitalist society.

From his observations and reflections upon the failure of the many insurrections he witnessed or took part in, Auguste Blanqui derived a number of tactical rules which if violated will make the victory of any insurrection extremely difficult, if not impossible. Blanqui demanded these things: a timely creation of correct revolutionary detachments, their centralized command and adequate equipment, a well calculated placement of barricades, their definite construction, and a systematic, not a mere episodic, defense of them. All these rules, deriving from the military problems of the insurrection, must of course change with social conditions and military technique, but in themselves they are not by any means "Blanquism" in the sense that this word approaches the German "putschism," or revolutionary adventurism.

Insurrection is an art, and like all arts it has its laws. The rules of Blanqui were the demands of a military revolutionary realism. Blanqui's mistake lay not in his direct but his inverse theorem. From the fact that tactical weakness condemns an insurrection to defeat, Blanqui inferred that an observance of the rules of insurrectionary tactics would itself guarantee the victory. Only from this point on is it legitimate to contrast Blanquism with Marxism. Conspiracy does not take the place of insurrection. An active minority of the proletariat, no matter how well organized, cannot seize the power regardless of the general conditions of the country. In this point history has condemned Blanquism. But only in this. His affirmative theorem retains all its force. In order to conquer the power, the proletariat needs more than a spontaneous insurrection. It needs a suitable organisation, it needs a plan; it needs a conspiracy. Such is the Leninist view of this question.

Engels' criticism of the fetishism of the barricade was based upon the evolution of military technique and of technique in general. The insurrectionary tactic of Blanquism corresponded to the character of the old Paris, the semi-handicraft proletariat, the narrow streets and the military system of Louis Philippe. Blanqui's mistake in principle was to identify revolution with insurrection. His technical mistake was to identify insurrection with the barricade. The Marxian criticism has been directed against both mistakes. Although at one with Blanquism in regarding insurrection as an art, Engels discovered not only the subordinate place occupied by insurrection in a revolution, but also the declining rôle of the barricade in an insurrection. Engels' criticism had nothing in common with a renunciation of the revolutionary methods in favour of pure parliamentarism, as the philistines of the German Social Democracy, in co-operation with the Hohenzollern censorship, attempted in their day to pretend. For Engels the question about barricades remained a question about one of the technical elements of an uprising. The reformists have attempted to infer from his rejection of the decisive importance of the barricade a rejection of revolutionary violence in general. That is about the same as to infer the destruction of militarism from considerations of the probable decline in importance of trenches in future warfare.

The organisation by means of which the proletariat can both overthrow the old power and replace it, is the soviets. This afterwards became a matter of historic experience, but was up to the October revolution a theoretical prognosis—resting, to be sure, upon the preliminary experience of 1905. The soviets are organs of preparation of the masses for insurrection, organs of insurrection, and after the victory organs of government.

However, the soviets by themselves do not settle the question. They may serve different goals according to the programme and leadership. The soviets receive their programme from the party. Whereas the soviets in revolutionary conditions—and apart from revolution they are impossible—comprise the whole class with the exception of its altogether backward, inert or demoralized strata, the revolutionary party represents the brain of the class. The problem of conquering the power can be solved only by a definite combination of party with soviets—or with other mass organisations more or less equivalent to soviets.

When headed by a revolutionary party the soviet consciously and in good season strives towards a conquest of power. Accommodating itself to changes in the political situation and the mood of the masses, it gets ready the military bases of the insurrection, unites the shock troops upon a single scheme of action, works out a plan for the offensive and for the final assault. And this means bringing organised conspiracy into mass insurrection.

The Bolsheviks were compelled more than once, and long before the October revolution, to refute accusations of conspiratism and Blanquism directed against them by their enemies. Moreover, nobody waged a more implacable struggle against the system of pure conspiracy than Lenin. The opportunists of the international social democracy more than once defended the old Social Revolutionary tactic of individual terror directed against the agents of czarism, when this tactic was ruthlessly criticised by the Bolsheviks with their insistence upon mass insurrection as opposed to the individual adventurism of the intelligentsia. But in refuting all varieties of Blanquism and anarchism, Lenin did not for one moment bow down to any "sacred" spontaneousness of the masses. He thought out before anybody else, and more deeply, the correlation between the objective and subjective factors in a revolution, between the spontaneous movement and the policy of the party, between the popular masses and the progressive class, between the proletariat and its vanguard, between the soviets and the party, between insurrection and conspiracy.

But if it is true that an insurrection cannot be evoked at will, and that nevertheless in order to win it must be organized in advance, then the revolutionary leaders are presented with a task of correct diagnosis. They must feel out the growing insurrection in good season and supplement it with a conspiracy. The interference of the midwife in labour pains—however this image may have been abused—remains the clearest illustration of this conscious intrusion into an elemental process. Herzen once accused his friend Bakunin of invariably in all his revolutionary enterprises taking the second month of pregnancy for the ninth. Herzen himself was rather inclined to deny even in the ninth that pregnancy existed. In February the question of determining the date of birth hardly arose at all, since the insurrection flared up unexpectedly without centralised leadership. But exactly for this reason the power did not go to those who had accomplished the insurrection, but to those who had applied the brakes. It was quite otherwise with the second insurrection. This was consciously prepared by the Bolshevik Party. The problem of correctly seizing the moment to give the signal for the attack was thus laid upon the Bolshevik staff.

Moment here is not to be taken too literally as meaning a definite day and hour. Physical births also present a considerable period uncertainty—their limits interesting not only to the art of the midwife, but also the casuistics of the Surrogate's Court. Between the moment when an attempt to summon an insurrection must inevitably prove premature and lead to a revolutionary miscarriage, and the moment when a favourable situation must be considered hopelessly missed, there exists a certain period—it may be measured in weeks, and sometimes in a few months—in the course of which an insurrection may be carried out with more or less chance of success. To discriminate this comparatively short period and then choose the definite moment—now in the more accurate sense of the very day and hour—for the last blow, constitutes the most responsible task of the revolutionary leaders. It can with full justice be called the key problem, for it unites the policy of revolution with the technique of insurrection—and it is needless to add that insurrection, like war, is a continuation of politics with other instruments.

Intuition and experience are necessary for revolutionary leadership, just as for all other kinds of creative activity. But much more than that is needed. The art of the magician can also successfully rely upon intuition and experience. Political magic is adequate, however, only for epochs and periods in which routine predominates. An epoch of mighty historic upheavals has no use for witch-doctors. Here experience, even illumined by intuition, is not enough. Here you must have a synthetic doctrine comprehending the interactions of the chief historic forces. Here you must have a materialistic method permitting you to discover, behind the moving shadows of programme and slogan, the actual movement of social bodies.

The fundamental premise of a revolution is that the existing social structure has become incapable of solving the urgent problems of development of the nation. A revolution becomes possible, however, only in case the society contains a new class capable of taking the lead in solving the problems presented by history. The process of preparing a revolution consists of making the objective problems involved in the contradictions of industry and of classes find their way into the consciousness of living human masses, change this consciousness and create new correlations of human forces.

The ruling classes, as a result of their practically manifested incapacity to get the country out of its blind alley, lose faith in themselves; the old parties fall to pieces; a bitter struggle of groups and cliques prevails; hopes are placed in miracles or miracle workers. All this constitutes one of the political premises of a revolution, a very important although a passive one.

A bitter hostility to the existing order and a readiness to venture upon the most heroic efforts and sacrifices in order to bring the country out upon an upward road—this is the new political consciousness of the revolutionary class, and constitutes the most important active premise of a revolution.

These two fundamental camps, however—the big property holders and the proletariat—do not exhaust the population of a country. Between them lie broad layers of the petty bourgeoisie, showing all the colours of the economic and political rainbow. The discontent of these intermediate layers, their disappointment with the policy of the ruling class, their impatience and indignation, their readiness to support a bold revolutionary initiative on the part of the proletariat, constitute the third political premise of a revolution. It is partly passive—in that it neutralizes the upper strata of the petty bourgeoisie—but partly also active, for it impels the lower strata directly into the struggle side by side with the workers.

That these premises condition each other is obvious. The more decisively and confidently the proletariat acts, the better will it succeed in bringing after it the intermediate layer, the more isolated will be the ruling class, and the more acute its demoralisation. And, on the other hand, a demoralisation of the rulers will pour water into the mill of the revolutionary class.

The proletariat can become imbued with the confidence necessary for a governmental overthrow only if a clear prospect opens before it, only if it has had an opportunity to test out in action a correlation of forces which is changing to its advantage, only if it feels above it a far-sighted, firm and confident leadership. This brings us to the last premise—by no means the last in importance—of the conquest of power: the revolutionary party as a tightly welded and tempered vanguard of the class.

Thanks to a favorable combination of historic conditions both domestic and international, the Russian proletariat was headed by a party of extraordinary political clarity and unexampled revolutionary temper. Only this permitted that small and young class to carry out a historic task of unprecedented proportions. It is indeed the general testimony of history—the Paris Commune, the German and Austrian revolutions of 1918, the Soviet revolutions in Hungary and Bavaria, the Italian revolution of 1919, the German crisis of 1923, the Chinese revolution of 1925–1927, the Spanish revolution of 1931—that up to now the weakest link in the chain of necessary conditions has been the party. The hardest thing of all is for the working class to create a revolutionary organization capable of rising to the height of its historic task. In the older and more civilized countries powerful forces work toward the weakening and demoralisation of the revolutionary vanguard. An important constituent part of this work is the struggle of the social democrats against "Blanquism," by which name they designate the revolutionary essence of Marxism.

Notwithstanding the number of great social and political crises, a coincidence of all the conditions necessary to a victorious and stable proletarian revolution has so far occurred but once in history: in Russia in October 1917. A revolutionary situation is not long-lived. The least stable of the premises of a revolution is the mood of the petty bourgeoisie. At a time of national crisis the petty bourgeoisie follows that class which inspires confidence not only in words but deeds. Although capable of impulsive enthusiasm and even of revolutionary fury, the petty bourgeoisie lacks endurance, easily loses heart under reverses, and passes from elated hope to discouragement. And these sharp and swift changes in the mood of the petty bourgeoisie lend their instability to every revolutionary situation. If the proletarian party is not decisive enough to convert the hopes and expectations of the popular masses into revolutionary action in good season, the flood tide is quickly followed by an ebb: the intermediate strata turn away their eyes from the revolution and seek a saviour in the opposing camp. And just as at flood tide the proletariat draws after it the petty bourgeoisie, so during the ebb the petty bourgeoisie draws after it considerable layers of the proletariat. Such is the dialectic of the communist and fascist waves observable in the political evolution of Europe since the war.

Attempting to ground themselves upon the assertion of Marx that no régime withdraws from the stage of history until it has exhausted all its possibilities, the Mensheviks denied the legitimacy of a struggle for proletarian dictatorship in backward Russia where capitalism had far from exhausted itself. This argument contained two mistakes, both fatal. Capitalism is not a national but a world-wide system. The imperialist war and its consequences demonstrated that the capitalist system had exhausted itself on a world scale. The revolution in Russia was a breaking of the weakest link in the system of world-wide capitalism.

But the falsity of this Menshevik conception appears also from a national point of view. From the standpoint of economic abstraction, it is indeed possible to affirm that capitalism in Russia has not exhausted its possibilities. But economic processes do not take place in the ether, but in a concrete historical medium. Capitalism is not an abstraction, but a living system of class relations requiring above all things a state power. That the monarchy, under whose protection Russian capitalism developed, had exhausted its possibilities is not denied even by the Mensheviks. The February revolution tried to build up an intermediate state régime. We have followed its history: in the course of eight months it exhausted itself completely. What sort of state order could in these conditions guarantee the further development of Russian capitalism.

"The bourgeois republic, defended only by socialists of moderate tendencies, finding no longer any support in the masses . . . could not maintain itself. Its whole essence had evaporated. There remained only an external shell." This accurate definition belongs to Miliukov. The fate of this evaporated system was necessarily, according to his words, the same as that of the czarist monarchy: "Both prepared the ground for a revolution, and on the day of revolution neither could find a single defender."

As early as July and August Miliukov characterized the situation by presenting a choice between two names: Kornilov or Lenin? But Kornilov had now made his experiment and it had ended in a miserable failure. For the régime of Kerensky there was certainly no place left. With all the varieties of mood, says Sukhanov, "the one thing upon which all united was hate for the Kerensky régime." Just as the czarist monarchy had toward the end become impossible in the eyes of the upper circle of the nobility and even the grand dukes, so the government of Kerensky became odious even to the direct inspiritors of his régime, the "grand dukes" of the compromisist upper crust. In this universal dissatisfaction, this sharp political nerve-tension of all classes, we have one of the symptoms of a ripe revolutionary situation. In the same way every muscle, nerve and fibre of an organism is intolerably tensed just before an abscess bursts.

The resolution of the July congress of the Bolsheviks, while warning the workers against premature encounters, had at the same time pointed out that the battle must be joined "whenever the general national crisis and the deep mass enthusiasm have created conditions favorable to the going over of the poor people of the city and country to the side of the workers." That moment arrived in September and October.

The insurrection was thenceforth able to believe in its success, for it could rely upon a genuine majority of the people. This, of course, is not to be understood in a formal sense. If a referendum could have been taken on the question of insurrection, it would have given extremely contradictory and uncertain results. An inner readiness to support a revolution is far from identical with an ability clearly to formulate the necessity of it. Moreover, the answer would have depended to a vast degree upon the manner in which the question was presented, the institution which conducted the referendum—or, to put it more simply, the class which held the power.

There is a limit to the application of democratic methods. You can inquire of all the passengers as to what type of car they like to ride in, but it is impossible to question them as to whether to apply the brakes when the train is at full speed and accident threatens. If the saving operation is carried out skillfully, however, and in time, the approval of the passengers is guaranteed in advance.

Parliamentary consultations of the people are carried out at a single moment, whereas during a revolution the different layers of the population arrive at the same conclusion one after another and with inevitable, although sometimes very slight, intervals. At the moment when the advanced detachment is burning with revolutionary impatience the backward layers have only begun to move. In Petrograd and Moscow all the mass organizations were under the leadership of the Bolsheviks. In Tamboy province, which has over three million population—that is, a little less than both capitals put together—a Bolshevik faction first appeared in the Soviet only a short time before the October revolution.

The syllogisms of the objective development are far from coinciding—day by day—with the syllogisms of the thought process of the masses. And when a great practical decision becomes unpostponable, in the course of events, that is the very moment when a referendum is impossible. The difference is level and mood of the different layers of the people is overcome in action. The advance layers bring after them the wavering and isolate the opposing. The majority is not counted up, but won over. Insurrection comes into being at exactly that moment when direct action alone offers a way out of the contradictions.

Although lacking the power to draw by themselves the necessary political inferences from their war against the landlords, the peasants had by the very fact of the agrarian insurrection already adhered to the insurrection of the cities, had evoked it and were demanding it. They expressed their will not with the white ballot, but with the red cock—a more serious referendum. Within those limits in which the support of the peasantry was necessary for the establishment of a soviet dictatorship, the support was already at hand. "The dictatorship"—as Lenin answered the doubters—"would give land to the peasants and all power to the peasant committees in the localities. How can you in your right mind doubt that the peasant would support that dictatorship?" In order that the soldiers, peasants and oppressed nationalities, floundering in the snow-storm of an elective ballot, should recognize the Bolsheviks in action, it was necessary that the Bolsheviks seize the power.

But what correlation of forces was necessary in order that the proletariat should seize the power? "To have at the decisive moment, at the decisive point, an overwhelming superiority of force," wrote Lenin later, interpreting the October revolution, "—this law of military success is also the law of political success, especially in that seething and bitter war of classes which is called revolution. The capitals, or generally speaking, the biggest centres of trade and industry . . . decide to a considerable degree the political fate of the people—that is, of course, on condition that the centres are supported by sufficient local rural forces, although this support need not be immediate." It was in this dynamic sense that Lenin spoke of the majority of the people, and that was the sole real meaning of the concept of majority.

The enemy democrats comforted themselves with the thought that the people following the Bolsheviks were mere raw material, mere historic clay. The potters were still to be these same democrats acting in co-operation with the educated bourgeoisie. "Can't those people see," asked a Menshevik paper, "that the Petrograd proletariat and garrison were never before so isolated from all other social strata?" The misfortune of the proletariat and the garrison was that they were "isolated" from those classes from whom they intended to take the power!

But was it really possible to rely upon the sympathy and support of the dark masses in the provinces and at the front? "Their Bolshevism," wrote Sukhanov scornfully, "was nothing

but hatred for the coalition and longing for land and peace."
As though that were little! Hatred for the coalition meant a
desire to take the power from the bourgeoisie. Longing for land
and peace was the colossal programme which the peasant and
soldier intended to carry out under the leadership of the workers.
The insignificance of the democrats, even the most leftward,
resulted from this very distrust—the distrust of "educated" scep-
tics—in those dark masses who grasp a phenomenon wholesale,
not bothering about details and nuances. This intellectual, pseu-
do-aristocratic, squeamish attitude toward the people was
foreign to Bolshevism, hostile to its very nature. The Bolsheviks
were not lily-handed, literary friends of the masses, not pedants.
They were not afraid of those backward strata now for the first
time lifting themselves out of the dregs. The Bolsheviks took
the people as preceding history had created them, and as they
were called to achieve the revolution. The Bolsheviks saw it
as their mission to stand at the head of that people. Those against
the insurrection were "everybody"—except the Bolsheviks. But
the Bolsheviks were the people.

THE LAND QUESTION

ELDRIDGE CLEAVER

The first thing that has to be realized is that it is a reality when people say that there's a "black colony" and a "white mother country." Only if this distinction is borne clearly in mind is it possible to understand that there are two different sets of political dynamics now functioning in America.

From the very beginning, Afro-America has had a land hang-up. The slaves were kidnapped on their own soil, transported thousands of miles across the ocean and set down in a strange land. From sunup to sundown, they worked the land: plowing, sowing and reaping crops for somebody else, for a profit they would never see or taste themselves. This is why, even today, one of the most provocative insults that can be tossed at a black is to call him a farm boy, to infer that he is in any way attached to an agrarian situation. In terms of seeking status in America, blacks—principally the black bourgeoisie—have come to measure their own value according to the number of degrees they are away from the soil.

Considered subhuman by the founders of America, black people have always been viewed by white Americans as un-American, as not really belonging here. Thus, it is not surprising that the average black man in America is schizoid on the question of his relationship to the nation as a whole, and there is a side of him that feels only the vaguest, most halting tentative and even fleeting kinship with America. The feeling of alienation and dissociation is real, and black people would have

From *Eldridge Cleaver: Post-Prison Writings and Speeches* edited by Robert Scheer. © 1967, 1968, 1969 by Eldridge Cleaver. Reprinted by permission of Random House and Jonathan Cape, Ltd.

long ago readily identified themselves with another sovereignty had a viable one existed.

THE MOTHER COUNTRY'S SOLUTION

Integration was the solution to the land question offered by the mother country—i.e., by the white liberals, white radicals and black bourgeoisie, working hand in glove with the Imperialists.

This is not to imply that white liberals, radicals and the black bourgeoisie were actively involved in a conscious conspiracy with the Imperialists. Particularly in the case of white radicals, the last thing they want to do is to help the Imperialists remain in power. Rather, we speak here of a coalescence of interests and goals. The domestic conflict over segregation was creating for the Imperialists problems on the international plane, particularly in their dealings with the new black African governments. Therefore, when the federal government "joined" the civil rights movement, the Imperialists in control of the government actually strengthened their own position and increased their power. Internationally, U.S. imperialism improved its image, making the con game it plays on the world—its pose as the champion of human freedom—easier. When President Johnson, the arch-hypocrite warmonger of the twentieth century, stood before the nation and shouted "We Shall Overcome," white liberals, radicals and the black bourgeoisie experienced a collective orgasm. What Johnson really wanted was peace and quiet at home and an integrated army to defend "democracy" abroad.

White radicals, liberals and the black bourgeoisie acted from completely different motivations, but the logic of the situation threw them into a coalition with the Imperialists, and the game that was run on them was so successful that they became some of the most ardent workers for LBJ in the election of 1964. Their motivation was to implement the American dream and the conception of America as a huge melting pot. All that remained to be done, in their view, was to integrate the black ingredient into the American stew and thus usher in the millennium of black/white solidarity wherein the white working class of the mother country would join hands with the black workers from the colony and together they would march forward to the Garden of Eden.

March forward they did, not to Eden but to Detroit and armed urban guerrilla warfare. The basic flaw in the analysis and outlook of the white liberals, radicals and the black bourgeoisie was that the concept of the American melting pot completely ignored the distinction and the contradiction between the white mother country and the black colony. And the solution of Integration, based on this false outlook, was doomed from the beginning to yield only a deceptive and disillusioning result. *Black people are a stolen people held in a colonial status on stolen land, and any analysis which does not acknowledge the colonial status of black people cannot hope to deal with the real problem.*

As an ideological tenet, Integration embodies the dream of the mother country which sees America as a huge melting pot. It seeks to pull the black colonial subjects into America and citizenize them. The mother country's euphemism of "second class citizenship" is a smokescreen that seeks to obscure the colonial status of black people in America.

Viewed on the international plane, Integration represents an attempt by the white mother country to forestall the drive for national liberation by its colonial subjects in precisely the same manner as France sought to hold onto its colonial spoils by defining its holdings as "overseas provinces," or as Britain tried to do with its Commonwealth, or as Portugal tried to do with its "overseas provinces." France, England and Portugal have all failed in attempts to keep their colonial possessions by trying to get the colonial subjects themselves to stop short of taking complete sovereignty in their drive for a better life. And America is also doomed to failure in this respect.

Until Detroit, America absolutely refused to even consider the true nature of the domestic crisis. But Detroit forced a confrontation with the facts through sheer military necessity: President Johnson was forced to place the problem in the hands of the Pentagon so that a war of suppression could be properly carried out by the same entity charged with carrying out the war of suppression against the national liberation struggle in Vietnam. But even after Detroit, after the shooting stopped, the minions of the power structure returned to their old, hackneyed rhetoric, as though Integration were still the operating slogan in the black colony.

EARLY BLACK SOLUTIONS:
MARCUS GARVEY & ELIJAH MUHAMMED

Nevertheless, there is a deep land hunger in the heart of Afro-America. It has always been there, just as much so as in any other people. Even to waste time asserting this factor is to yield to racism, to argue with the racist assertion that blacks just aren't like other people. Suffice it to say that Afro-Americans are just as land hungry as were the Mau Maus, the Chinese people, the Cuban people; just as much so as all the people of the world today who are grappling with the tyrant of colonialism, trying to get possession of some land of their own.

When he projected his program for black people some 50 years ago, Marcus Garvey tapped black land hunger by claiming the continent of Africa for black people and reasserting black identification with an ancestral homeland. This marked an historic shift in the psyche of black people. It got them over a crucial hump in their struggle up from the white light of Slavery into knowledge of themselves and their past.

However, the practical prospect of Garvey actually physically transporting blacks to Africa turned most black people off because of a world situation and balance of power that made such a solution impossible. And as Garvey's fleet of ships, the Black Star line—which was supposed to provide transportation for blacks back to Africa—sank in the quicksand set at his feet by the white racist power structure and the bootlickers of his era, Afro-America's land hunger became more acute, more desperate.

Learning from Garvey's failure, Elijah Muhammed knew that he had to deal with Afro-America's land hunger, but he also knew that it would be tactically wise for him to be a little more abstract, in order to more closely approximate the true historical relationship of Afro-Americans to the land beneath their feet. He therefore was very careful never to identify any specific geographical location when he issued his call for land for Afro-America. "We must have some land! Some land of our own, or else!"—is the way Elijah Muhammed posed the land question to his people. And it is a fact that black Americans could relate to that particular formulation.

However, there is something inadequate, something lacking in that particular slogan because in practice it impeded rather than enhanced movement. In the first place, it is merely a protest slogan; there is nothing revolutionary about it, because it is asking the oppressor to make a gift to black people. The oppressor is not about to give niggers a damn thing. Black people know this from bitter experience. In a land where the racist pigs of the power structure are doing every dirty thing they can to cut off welfare payments, where they refuse medical care to sick people, where they deliberately deprive black people of education and where they leave black babies to die from lack of milk, no black person in his right mind is going to stand around waiting for those same pigs to give up some of this land, say five or six states!

A REVOLUTIONARY SOLUTION: BLACK POWER

But black people waited. They awaited a revolutionary formulation that would be suited to their relationship to America. Stokely Carmichael provided this formulation with his thesis of Black Power. The ingeniousness of this slogan derives precisely from a clear understanding of Afro-American history and a clear perception of the relationship of black people to the land.

Black Power as a slogan does not attempt to answer the land question. It does not deny the existence of that question, but rather very frankly states that at the present moment the land question cannot be dealt with, that black people must put first things first, that there are a few things that must be done before we can deal with the land question. We must first get some power so that we will be in a position to *force* a settlement of the land question. After black people put themselves, through revolutionary struggle, into a position from which they are able to inflict a political consequence upon America, to hit them where it hurts, then the land question can be brought out.

At a rally in Roxbury, the black colonial enclave of Boston, Stokely Carmichael told an enthusiastic throng of 4000 blacks: "We are poor, we have no money, but we don't have to pay for the land—we already own it; we paid for it with 400 years of our sweat, our blood, and our suffering. . . . We need a revolution so we can live like proud human beings. Our revolution is for land and until we take the land we are gonna stay poor. If you're poor and if you're black, you've got no rights. We want a redistribution of wealth in this country. We don't want any handouts."

It can be said that Stokely Carmichael has made a contribution of historic proportions to the national liberation struggle of Afro-America by hurling forth the thesis of Black Power. The necessity upon Afro-America is to move, now, to begin functioning as a nation, to assume its sovereignty, to demand that that sovereignty be recognized by other nations of the world. Stokely Carmichael was received in Havana as a representative of a people, of a nation, and, in principle, the assembled revolutionaries were recognizing the sovereignty of Afro-America. This lesson was first driven home by Malcolm X's trips to Africa, where he was received by heads of state as an ambassador of Afro-America.

Black Power must be viewed as a projection of sovereignty, an embryonic sovereignty that black people can focus on and through which they can make distinctions between themselves and others, between themselves and their enemies—in short, between the white mother country of America and the black colony dispersed throughout the continent on absentee-owned land, making Afro-America a decentralized colony. Black Power says to black people that it is possible for them to build a national organization on somebody else's land.

BLACK LIBERATION AND
THE BLACK MAN'S LAND

The parallel between the situation of the Jews at the time of the coming of Theodor Herzl and the present situation of black people in America is fascinating. The Jews had no homeland and were dispersed around the world, cooped up in the ghettos of Europe. Functionally, a return to Israel seemed as impractical as obtaining a homeland for Afro-America seems now.

The gravitational center of the Jewish population at that time was in Eastern Europe. With the outbreak of massive pogroms in that area near the end of the nineteenth century, the Jewish people were prepared psychologically to take desperate and unprecedented action. They saw themselves faced with an immediate disastrous situation. Genocide was staring them in the face, and this common threat galvanized them into common action.

Psychologically, black people in America have precisely the same outlook as the Jews had then, and they are therefore prepared to take common action for the solution to a common problem. Oppressed because of the color of their skin, black people are reacting on that basis. A nationalist consciousness has at last awakened among the black masses of Afro-America. One would have to search far and wide in the annals of history to find a case where such a tide of nationalism did not continue to sweep the people forward into nationhood—by any means necessary. Given the confusion in America over the distinction between the white mother country and the black colony, and the rapidly developing national consciousness of Afro-America, it is easy to see that unless these titanic forces are harnessed and channeled into creative outlets, such as some of those proposed by black revolutionaries, America is headed for a catastrophe of unprecedented proportions.

The facts of history show that the Jews were able to do precisely the same thing that Afro-America must now do. When Theodor Herzl founded the National Jewish Congress, he virtually founded a government in exile for a people in exile. They would build their organization, their government, and then later on they would get some land and set the government and the people down on the land, like placing one's hat on top of one's head. The Jews did it. It worked. Now Afro-Americans must do the same thing.

In fact, when Malcolm X moved to found the Organization of Afro-American Unity, this is precisely what he was doing—founding a government in exile for a people in exile. Stokely Carmichael and Rap Brown are now speaking in the name of that sovereignty, in the name of a nation. "I am not bound by the laws or the morals of America!" Rap Brown stated in Newark, New Jersey. And in California, the Black Panther Party for Self Defense has begun calling for U.N. membership for Afro-America.

Another proposal of the Black Panthers that is winning more and more support in the black colony is the call for a U.N.-supervised plebiscite in black communities across the nation. The purpose of the plebiscite is to answer the question once and for all as to just what the masses of black people want. Do the masses of black people consider themselves a nation? Do they want U.N. membership? The viability of this proposal consists in the fact that it does not call for a response beyond the means of black people. All that they are asked to do is answer yes or no—about all that they can do in America.

The mere widespread agitation for such a plebiscite will create a major crisis for U.S. imperialism. Internationally, America's enemies can be counted upon, in some cases, to endorse the proposal. In other cases, countries which are not willing to go all the way with the idea of a plebiscite will at least give an equivocal response.

Domestically, America will be placed in the peculiar position of arguing to black people that they do not need U.N. membership because they are American citizens. The blacks in the ghettos will respond with, Oh yeah? Well, if I'm an American citizen, why am I treated like a dog? The entire problem will be decisively internationalized and raised to a higher level of debate. The forces of reaction will be placed squarely on the defensive, and it will be obvious to all that fundamental changes in the status of black people in America can no longer be postponed or avoided.

So we are now engaged openly in a war for the national liberation of Afro-America from colonial bondage to the white mother country. In our epoch, guerrilla warfare is the vehicle for national liberation all around the world. That it would soon come to America could have been predicted. The spirit has always been there. Only the racist underestimation of the humanity of black people has blinded America to the potential for revolutionary violence of Afro-America. Nat Turner, Gabriel Prosser and Denmark Vesey, black men who led the most successful slave revellions in the U.S., are the spiritual fathers of today's urban guerrillas.

Robert Williams and Malcolm X stand as two titans, even prophetic figures, who heralded the coming of the gun, the day of the gun, and the resort to armed struggle by Afro-America. The fate of these two prophetic figures is of paramount interest: Robert Williams actually picked up the gun against the racist cops of North Carolina, while Malcolm X did not actually pick up the gun but spread the word to an audience that Robert Williams never reached. Malcolm X caused the power structure more public concern than Williams ever did, but in the cloak and dagger world of the CIA and the FBI, Williams has made just as much impact as Malcolm, because Williams hurled a challenge at both the white mother country and the black colony: let the issue be settled by war; let the black colony take up arms against the mother country!

Today Malcolm X is dead and Robert Williams is still alive. Now in China, the guest of the Prophet of the Gun, Mao Tse-tung, Williams is coming into his own because his people have at last risen to his level of consciousness and are now ready for his style of leadership.

The black urban guerrillas have already accepted Williams' challenge. The white power structure, when LBJ placed the black colonial problem under the tender mercies of the Department of Defense, also served warning that it would meet Williams' challenge blow for blow, in open military terms. Black urban guerrillas now dream of liberating black communities with the gun by eliminating America's police power over black people, i.e., by breaking the power of the mother country over the black colony.

The dream is to bring Robert Williams home. Black people know that they will not have achieved success in this goal until they can bring Robert Williams home and guarantee him safe conduct; until Williams can stand up in the center of Harlem and deliver a speech and the black people can prevent the troops of the occupying army from coming in and taking him prisoner; until Rap Brown and Stokely Carmichael can speak before any audience of assembled black people without fear of arrest by the gestapo of the mother country.

In order to bring this situation about, black men know that they must pick up the gun, they must arm black people to the teeth, they must organize an army and confront the mother country with a most drastic consequence if she attempts to assert police power over the colony. If the white mother country is to have victory over the black colony, it is the duty of black revolutionaries to insure that the Imperialists receive no more than a Pyrrhic victory, written in the blood of what America might have become.

COLONIALISM AND LIBERATION

TOM HAYDEN

In July 1967, after the Newark uprising, I wrote: "This country is experiencing its fourth year of urban revolt, yet the message from Newark is that America has learned almost nothing since Watts."

There is no reason to revise that conclusion today. America is nearly bankrupt in its ability to find social, economic or political answers to racism. The "solutions" being prepared are military ones increasingly.

If there are no answers, it is because men concentrate on the wrong questions. We should abandon the notions that America is a melting pot, that the welfare state is progressive, that revolution is impossible because black people are a minority. We must look at America as a new and violent form of colonial society, and we must draw the consequences.

There are three continual objections made to the use of "colonialism" as a term to describe the ghetto conditions in the United States. The first is that black people are nationalized Americans, not people of a separate identity governed by a foreign power. The second is that the Constitution supports equal citizenship for all people rather than a principle of second-class status. The third is that racism is based on historical prejudice rather than economic profit. Each of these objections contains an important point. Taken together they make it necessary to go beyond the traditional definition of colonialism as a system of economic exploitation based on political control of one people by another. But they do not erase the essential similarities between American racism and the historical colonialism of the Western European powers. America is a colonial society in a new sense. Let us examine these objections to using the term "colonialism" one by one:

Objection 1: *that black people are American, not foreign.* In the obvious sense of "citizenship" no one can dispute this assertion. However it is assumed mistakenly that black people are an assimilated people like the European immigrants who were integrated into the American society. The falseness of this view is obvious. The African slaves did not choose to live in America as did the immigrants; they were forcibly taken here. Once here, the chattel slavery system violated their family structure and culture, while the Europeans, on the other hand, drew their greatest strength from the traditions they preserved. With the passing of slavery, black people faced a permanent situation of under-employment, while the Europeans moved into a system of expanding economic opportunities. And, of course, the policy of discrimination was a deterrent against progress which the Europeans faced in a far milder and less universal sense than the "emancipated" blacks. Thus the separate status of black people in the midst of American society has always been a fact. That black people identify themselves as Americans, that they express loyalty to the country as a whole, should blind no one to the essential differences between their experience and that of the more assimilated white immigrants. The nationalist concept of blacks as "overseas Africans" refers to an important reality which the concept of the "melting pot" fails to explain.

Objections 2: *black people have equal consitutional rights with whites.* As with the first objection, no one can disagree that there is a significant difference between this constitutional reality and that of colonial societies where entire classes are disenfranchised. Yet no one can deny that the constitutional promise has never materialized for black people as a whole class. Legal barriers to voting and other forms of social participation, presumably outlawed by the Constitution itself, are still the subject of heated controversy in the southern states and part of the North. When looked at from a wider perspective than that of technical rights, moreover, there appears a systematic pattern of under-representation of black people in every decision-making sphere that affects their lives. Tenants in slum housing or federally-constructed public housing projects have no meaningful power over their rents or living conditions. Mothers on welfare have no meaningful voice over the administration and rules governing them. The citizen of the ghetto has no meaningful procedure for deterring police abuse. Black workers are employed in conditions—for example, domestic work—which offer few opportunities for unionization. The possession of the vote is of little value in offsetting these denials of power over one's life. Having ten percent of the votes in a system of institutionalized racism guarantees nothing.

Objection 3: *the black population in America is not a source of raw materials and cheap labor in the way that colonized peoples are.* While this objection falsifies history, for the present day it suggests an unwitting truth which may be more ominous than economic servitude. Certainly the slaves were brought here as cheap labor. After "emancipation" blacks have either been exploited or underemployed so consistently that we must suppose our competitive economic system needs a degree of joblessness. Today, in fact, it is possible to view the black population as surplus or irrelevant manpower, from which alarming conclusions can be drawn. In the old forms of colonialism, brutality rarely became genocidal because the colonialist needed the slaves for production; but in a new form in which slaves are economically useless, what is to prevent genocide when the colonialist becomes irritated by the slaves' demands?

These objections in no way change the fact that black people, as a group, are blocked from participating in the "mainstream" of American society. They live and work within frameworks established by the racial majority. They are subjected to a combination of racism and economic exploitation. This is the substance of a colonial situation although the forms are distinctly American.

One implication of this perspective is that solutions to the problem will not be of a traditional kind. The channels of mobility open to the white immigrants are closed to black people. Opportunities to rise in the economic system do exist for the black individual, but not for his social group as a whole. The individual who "succeeds" usually does so in terms entirely defined by the white community. He becomes a token or marginal person in an alien system, losing his identification with any group of his own. The long-term solution, viewed from this perspective, would be culturally genocidal: Negroes would have to become "whites" in all respects to gain majority acceptance.

Stokely Carmichael points out that black people *have* adapted to the Puritan ethic—hard work brings personal reward—but that generations of labor in the cotton fields brought no gains. If the Protestant ethic were true for all, black people would be millionaires. The problems of black people are not individual problems. The problems are collective. Self-help cannot build houses, schools, hospitals, or modernize whole urban areas. These problems require structural change and public resources.

The other common avenue of change in America, besides individual entrepreneurship, is pressure-group politics. This too can be of value to individuals and, at certain times, to the group as a whole. Wage increases, housing reform, city services and due process of law can all be achieved to some extent. Veto power can be achieved as well: the prevention of discriminatory laws, rent increases, welfare cuts, certain political abuses. The problem is that the achievements are impossible to make secure in a racist colonial society. The period of Reconstruction is the best historical example of this reversal of gains. But the 1960's are full of new examples. The Mississippi Freedom Democratic Party in 1964 was the most representative group of black Mississippians ever organized, yet they were rejected in their bid for representation by the decision of the national Democratic Party. Adam Clayton Powell is one of the most popular congressmen in the country, yet he was stripped of his rank by the decision of the Congress. Any organized black force, if it fights according to the traditions of pressure groups, finds itself able only to make temporary coalitions with different elements in the majority. Other pressure groups have succeeded in their aims because they were able to include themselves into the dominant society.

Black people cannot be included in the same way. (This is precisely the inadequacy of traditional socialist proposals for alliances between blacks and white workers in a political movement. The value of the socialist formulation is in the emphasis on alliances and struggles as crucial to change. But the formulation overemphasizes the class struggle without recognizing the colonialist nature of American capitalism. Racism is the factor which keeps black workers behind whites within the structure of the economy and even within the trade unions.)

Nor can the situation be changed by the Federal government or by national coalitions of business, labor, the churches and other groups. The interests of these groups cannot coincide with the interests of ghetto dwellers. Investment in the slums, as even David Rockefeller admits, is a bad business risk. The alternative—planned development under government direction—is opposed as socialism. The main reason elites are concerned now with the slum is the need to maintain "order"—which is to say, to maintain the essentials of an institutional system which excludes black people as a group. Influential groups may support reforms of a minor kind within this framework of order, either from a sense of humanitarianism or a desire to maintain the system as a whole. Thus a welfare and unemployment insurance program has been adopted, individual rights tend to be respected, groups are permitted a wide freedom to peacefully protest injustices, and occassionally token material improvements are made in housing or other fields.

The value of these liberties and welfare state reforms should not be underestimated, but the greater danger in America is in the exaggeration of their scale. The priorities of the majority, and the reason that black people cannot count on that majority, are revealed sharply in attitudes toward the welfare state. The average white taxpayer typically feels that his earnings are being poured out in support of the "shiftless" underclass, but does not object to the fact that, in reality, nearly all his taxes go toward the expansion of the military establishment. In large measure the American welfare state is a myth. The people at the bottom tend to survive because America is prosperous, not because it is just.

The people with fewest illusions about the welfare state are the poor who are served by it. When they protest, usually in the name of recognized American ideals, a typical reaction follows. Some among the majority react sympathetically, but a sufficient number of opposing interests are aroused to prevent any drastic change, and often even moderate changes are blocked. The poor, who in most cases begin by politely petitioning their governors, soon take more dramatic steps, thinking they can perhaps awaken the conscience of the majority or at least of higher authorities. They do awaken the conscience of some people, and to some extent they force elites to concede token changes. But at the same time, a "counter-revolution" is triggered. The system as a whole becomes deadlocked. No more than token reforms, crumbs, result for the protestors. Their scale of protest increases as they realize appeals to conscience are inadequate. They look for methods of transcending the rules of pressure politics which have not worked. They begin civil disobedience and disruption. The immediate reaction of the power structure is to maintain order. The police are brought into the conflict. Considerations of social, economic or political solutions to the conflict gradually are replaced by the emphasis on law and order. Violent repression becomes routine.

This pattern is concretely illustrated by events in Newark during the last year. Official Newark (the business and political elite) had documented reports on the magnitude of poverty in the city long before the rebellion of July 1967. The power structure knew, too, that it was "sitting on a powder keg." Yet those in power could not and would not make changes. When the revolt finally occurred, there were no further references by officials to the longstanding injustice at the root of the problem. The only question for officials was that of "law and order." The police, guardsmen, and troopers went to work. It was legitimate to shoot looters after calling "halt." Policemen carried their private guns into the battle (thus there could be no official ballistics check later). Sniping incidents were fabricated. Mass arrests were made. Newark fell under military occupation.

In the wake of the rebellion Governor Hughes took no action but appointed a commission. Their report ultimately was critical of police behavior and of Newark's political insensitivity, though in the framework of calling for a more rational system of putting down rebellions. Not only was the report modest, but the commission was without legislative power to implement its proposals. Yet the report was explosive enough to make Hughes suppress it after printing 4,000 copies and refuse publication rights to a paperback company. In the meantime, the County Grand Jury investigating the 26 killings that occurred in the rebellion returned only one indictment: on a black man for supposedly shooting a black woman. John Smith, the cab driver whose brutal beating by the police triggered the rebellion, was found guilty in Municipal Court of having assaulted the police officers. The Newark Police Department has been exonerated, has received $250,000 in City Council appropriations for additional weapons, and has hooked up informally with an armed white vigilante organization from an Italian ward.

The same process is apparent at the national level, especially in the events following the assassination of Martin Luther King. The immediate worry of the power structure was not that America was a violent and sick society, but that blacks would rebel at the slaying of their leader. Despite the Vietnam war and the annual $80 billion spent for defense, despite the massive preparation of police for the coming summer, despite the repeated killing of civil rights leaders, President Johnson could still implore the black people not to follow the road of "blind violence." The bankruptcy of America was most exposed in the fact that no major leader dared express anger at the killing of King, for there was nothing to do with anger but burn. No demonstration was going to change policy, just as King's demonstrations had not before. The "constructive ways" had been tried before and failed; now there was no "constructive outlet" for rage left. This bankruptcy was proven most finally in the "civil rights" legislation that Congress passed as a tribute to Dr. King. The law is known euphemistically as an "open housing law" but in reality it is a fantastic police-state plan. The open housing provisions are meaningless because sufficient legislation is on the books from Reconstruction, because the procedures for complaint read like an obstacle course, because only 80%

of housing is covered, and even then it is covered only in stages until 1970. The other provisions of the act are unreported and more lethal:

1. the civil rights protection part does not cover economic intimidation;
2. interfering with the operation of a store during a riot becomes a felony;
3. teaching how to make an explosive device with reason to know it might be used in a riot becomes a felony;
4. interfering with firemen or policemen during a riot becomes a felony, and all law enforcement personnel are made exempt from prohibitions against violating the civil rights of citizens;
5. a riot is defined as a public disturbance involving three or more people together with either an act or threat of violence (so it becomes a crime to defend rebellion as a right);
6. the penalties for any of the above are far more severe than those which might be imposed on a realtor if he is found guilty of discrimination in the sale of housing.

The trend is clear. During times of relative social peace, the issue of race goes unresolved. When the issue is forced by black people for reasons of dignity and survival, the answer is to suspend politics and restore order. When the streets are occupied by troops the ultimate colonial substance of the system is revealed.

American foreign policy differs very little in essentials from the domestic colonial policy. In the Third World a very clear pattern stands out. In countries where there is thoroughgoing corruption and poverty, the United States is doing little more than developing the "infrastructure" of transportation routes which makes American business expansion more efficient. Foreign aid, opposed as "charity," is defended primarily as insurance against revolution. The greatest amounts of American aid go to countries which are unstable because of insurgent or revolutionary movements. Invariably this aid is military in character, doing little if anything about the underlying social crises. In countries where a revolutionary movement threatens to replace pro-Western ruling elites, the United States intervenes with force. In all of these cases, the problems of poverty and under-development are not considered from the point of view of injustice and social need, but from the viewpoint of U.S. strategic interests. These interests now are counterrevolutionary.

What has happened in Vietnam is a perfect case of this pattern evolving. After considering whether it could replace the French in the Southeast Asian "sphere of influence" in the 1940's, the U.S. decided to supply money and arms to help the French reconquer Vietnam from the victorious Vietminh. Following the defeat of the French at Dienbienphu and the Geneva Accords, the U.S. chose and backed the reactionary Diem dictatorship in South Vietnam. Diem was supplied with weapons and his police administration was modernized. In addition, "social re-form" was proposed as a method of stabilizing the regime. But the reforms proposed actually constituted a counterrevolution in the literal sense of the word. Landlords were retitled to property taken from them in the revolutionary war; peasants were then charged "controlled rents" for lands they already tilled as their own. Even if the American-inspired programs had been more realistic, they would have failed—as they continue to fail today—because the U.S. sought reforms while restoring the old order of mandarins who had already lost the revolution. The U.S. chose the preservation of order rather than the risk of reforms which might alienate the most solid anti-communists and entrenched bureaucrats. The result, of course, was not order but the escalation of force in a futile effort to establish it. Today we are witnessing an extreme form of the basic pattern: the gradual destruction of Vietnam as a society because the Viet-namese will not accept the American prescription for their development.

This is essentially the same policy which prevails in American ghettos, carried to a destructive extreme. In the beginning, a long period of neglect while the poor struggle as second-class humans. Then the initiation of protest, followed by the mixture of palliatives and violence. Then insurrection. Frenzied counter-revolution. Finally: Promises of a Great Society, in Asia and Harlem, after the napalming. Doves and Hawks are part of the same system.

The evidence is growing that the only way out of under-development is through revolution.

The haves will not help the have-nots. Those who have (money, status, security, privilege) define what they have as limited. There is not enough to go around, they think, no matter if we are the richest country in the world. In addition, there is a sense of guilt, of having stolen someone else's property, a sense that there will be debts to pay if the rebels (the blacks, the yellows) take over. The haves may be right. An entire system, of international proportions, is at stake. It is an empire of property, of military machinery, of political domination. When protest begins, the haves draw together sufficiently to prevent effective reform. The have-nots are left to choose between submission and more militant protest. There is no basis for hope unless the struggle is begun.

There is no way to begin the struggle unless what Oscar Lewis calls "the culture of poverty" is thrown off. This is the mood of despair, the sense of personal ineffectiveness, the loss of morale and self-esteem which, in Lewis' view, seems to be characteristic of the poor in colonial and certain capitalist societies. This culture, which appears to the more privileged class as a sign of innate inferiority and laziness, grips a people threatened with the loss of identity and decision-making power. The only apparent way to break out of the culture is not by copying the terms of the dominant, stultifying culture, but by rebellion. The act of rebellion requires a new appraisal of self, a rejection of the dominant cultural styles on behalf of more authentic or natural ones. It requires a realization that the blame for poverty falls not on oneself but on others who are responsible. It requires a sense that misery is not the result of God's inscrutable will but the result of a concrete power structure's priorities. The act of rebellion is the beginning of a man's making history and the end of his being its object.

We are witnessing this process in the ghettos. There is an order, a logic, about the seemingly chaotic "riots" taking place in most American cities. American society has had its chance to solve the racial problem in the context of peace, and failed. Hard puritan work has failed. Petitions organized lobbying, voting, and demonstrations have failed. The civil rights leadership—good moral men seeking to make America's words and laws take effect—has failed. Suddenly, however, people jam the streets. The people commit revolutionary violence, primarily against property. Their act is selective and concrete: to steal back some material goods from the society which has stolen from them. The act is profoundly unifying for the community, and a sense of power and pride runs through a majority of the people. The police violence naturally causes fear and intimidation, but also hatred and shock. Things will never be the same again. A sense of self-determination is born. Those who believe this is simply an aggressive desire to have what white Americans have should recall that the first American revolutionaries were fighting for their rights as Englishmen.

Many will agree that development of a revolutionary consciousness to replace the "culture of poverty" is desirable, but will ask: what kind of revolution, indeed what kind of change at all, can a group make which is irrelevant to economic production and counts for only ten percent of the population? Revolutions can only be made by groups which are relevant to the social structure they wish to change; since black people are marginal economically and numerically, what is their relevance?

The answer is that black people may very well have the power to destroy America's position in the world. America is looking for trade opportunities and other forms of influence in a world in which colored nations are assuming power. Dean Rusk himself once acknowledged (before the Vietnam war) that the American racial crisis is the country's leading foreign policy problem. As long as there remains the racial crisis, U.S. foreign policy will be looked upon as hypocritical. Allied nations will lack confidence about the stability of America's future. The U.S. will be over extended: unable to find the resources to deal with crises around the world and at home. And black organizations here will find increasing support for their struggle—and opposition to suppression—from nations of the Third World. The black minority at home is part of a colored majority in the world.

But black people occupy a relevant position inside the American social structure as well. The "sharpest contradiction" in this situation, as it takes shape at home, is between the oppressed and concentrated people of the ghettos and the centers of commerce they surround. If black people follow the road of the last few summers, they can do immense damage to some of America's most vital insitutions, especially if spontaneous rebellion takes on a more organized form. The cities are the "jungles" in which armed guerrillas, with popular support, can carry out disruption of commerce and communication with great success. The climate of terror created is already driving greater numbers of whites from the cities, abandoning them to the growing black populations.

A related possibility is that the period of spontaneous rebellion will lead into a more organized and political period. The failure of the government to deliver change, the violence of the police, and other signs of American racism are showing black people the need for unity and struggle in a more concrete way than any nationalist ideology by itself could do. It is likely that united political organizations, of a coalition character, will develop in urban areas. These will be more or less militant depending on leadership and local conditions. They would serve as institutional centers for protest and service in the community. They would teach people organizing skills and develop programs for change. Their emphasis might vary—organization of tenants, welfare mothers, youth groups, educational workshops, self-defense and electoral campaigns—but they will have a grass-roots, black power orientation. They will be supported and sometimes staffed by black students—now the most revolutionary leadership group—from nearby campuses.

If there is success in the search for independent political power, such power could be used to gain resources through taxation, building up voting power for bargaining purposes, and developing community-controlled police power as a deterrent to white racism. There would be a possibility of bargaining for change without bargaining away independence.

Having pointed out these possibilities, it is important to add that there is no inevitability about the development of revolutionary change. America's rulers somehow may yet pull themselves together to expand welfare programs on a "New Deal" scale for blacks, within the framework of imperialism and through a combination of pressure and material rewards. Or governmental and business leaders, seeing the threat, may move to reorganize city boundaries to prevent black political majorities. This would be an unspoken consequence of programs to reconstitute cities as planned metropolitan areas. The difficulty in achieving such an alteration, however, should not be underestimated. Much as various sophisticated planners desire metropolitan reorganization, their dreams are exactly contrary to those of the white suburbanites. The suburbanites, having left the cities to avoid their crises, will not be easily persuaded that they should be reintegrated into a metropolitan area with a large black population.

The other possible means of softening the crisis, more achievable in the short run, is through business and foundation support of moderate black political leaders. This seems to have happened in Cleveland and perhaps Gary. In Cleveland the downtown business community, linked with the Ford Foundation, supported a civil rights campaign that elected a black Mayor. The new Mayor, however, tends to represent the interests of the black and white middle class, professional and commercial communities. He opposes insurrection. He supports the Johnson-Humphrey Administration and the Vietnam war, presumably expecting to win federal funds for Cleveland. The evidence is that he has given people some degree of hope or at least the possibility of communication with their government. However, the Stokes strategy is faced with enormous obstacles: the indifference of the Congress to ghetto needs, the lack of incentive for business to invest in the slums, the lack of other black or white power groups with whom Stokes might ally. If the strategy fails to deliver concrete changes, as it no doubt will, the result will be a more explosive ghetto. Time will have been gained, people's sense of expectation will have increased, but a solution will not have been found.

Some expect that the most likely scenario of the future is neither revolution nor partial reform, but a repression which would set back all opportunities for change. Part of this view is that the white power structure should not be provoked by mass rioting or threats of violence. This fear of repression has been invoked by moderates at every new tactical stage of the civil rights movement since 1960. There has been repression and political intimidation at every new point of development, but never sufficient to prevent the movement's growth. Undoubtedly, the U.S. desire to keep a democratic image contributes to its hesitation in repressing insurgents. Moreover, there are divisions of opinion in high circles over the effectiveness of repression—whether, for instance, Stokely Carmichael would be more important as a martyr in jail than as an agitator in the streets. There are practical risks which befall repressors also. If black resistance grew against the occupying police, the cities might have to be destroyed or become permanently insecure.

No rebel wants repression. He prefers a legal and peaceful method of change. But the characteristic of a rebel is that he does not give up if such change is blocked. He finds new forms. His beliefs are too deep to surrender. He insists on the ultimate legality of his actions—as expressed in the Declaration of Independence and Constitution—even if at present he goes to jail for them. He risks repression without welcoming it.

Those who fear repression tend to lecture militants when they should be proving with deeds that meaningful change can be accomplished within the present framework of society. From a theoretical viewpoint, America seems to possess the wealth and constitutional flexibility necessary to permit change to occur in a relatively peaceful way. The question is whether it is possible to define a set of goals which are achievable without requiring an immediate transformation of American society, but at the same time goals consistent with the need to liberate the society from racism. The simplest way of stating the goals and the issues is: can self-determination for black people be created even partially within the framework of American society?

There has been confusion—legitimate as well as the breast-beating variety—on the meaning of "self-determination." A narrow perspective has assumed that only two outcomes of the black-white struggle are possible, integration or separation. But neither of these concepts has clear meaning now. The issue now is power, the idea that black people should control the communities and institutions which now control them. This emphasis points toward certain goals, among them:

—predominantly black political parties;
—black labor organizations or caucuses within unions;
—cultural institutions developing awareness of Afro-American history; participation in control of ghetto schools by parents, teachers and students;
—abolition of the social work profession; recognition of "welfare rights" unions as bargaining agents in matters pertaining to the scale and administration of public assistance;
—public housing administered and owned by a combination of tenants and community housing corporations;
—reduction or abolition of private absentee ownership of housing; in the interim, establishment of tenant unions with recognized powers to negotiate contracts and grievances; initiation of individual and collective ownership of housing by residents themselves;
—community control of police: police chosen from the community they patrol, elected civilian review boards in each precinct with powers to investigate, subpoena, and initiate proceedings for the removal of officers or changes in department policy;
—transfer of municipal court system: community selection of judges, abolition of bail, trial by juries from the community, and release of prisoners not convicted by their peers;
—establishment of cooperatively-owned stores; management of national chain stores by local business associations; taxation of chain stores for community needs.

This emphasis in no way underestimates the need for money from the government as part of the solution. Rather, the issue of funding should be seen in a new perspective. The present public expenditures for "welfare" are not only too small but, more important, are administered through a machinery which perpetuates colonial domination. The idea of self-determination, however, supposes that new institutions must be constructed, from the bottom up, before funds can be distributed according to need. Undoubtedly, this institutional change in the ghetto would have broad national effects. For instance, some form of national economic planning would necessarily come into effect.

This perspective is not utopian. The logic of the present crisis points towards the eventual adoption of toleration of these changes out of necessity. The present administrative machinery of the ghetto is being challenged and undermined. Most police departments find it difficult to recruit new men; many policemen are departing the ghettos to take safer jobs with fire departments or county government. Caseworkers are equally difficult to recruit; they fear going into the "field" and in many places are not insured by their employers after mid-afternoon. The same pressures affect teachers in ghetto schools; they fear the students and the hostile ghetto. Landlords now take physical risks by attempting to collect rent from angry tenants. City services in general are becoming impossible to manage.

A more repressive municipal machinery would be useless. The tension between people and the agencies would increase, and recruiting, management problems, and costs would multiply. A more "modern" administrative approach—creating higher wages and incentives for personnel to staff the current machinery—is not working where it is being tried. There are safer jobs which pay as well. The more liberal elements of ghetto administration, such as VISTA and anti-poverty agencies, are also in crisis. People who want to "fight City Hall" are blocked or weeded out, leaving control in the hands of mediocre anti-poverty careerists dependent on the local government.

This movement for self-determination and "black control of black communities" will not obscure class and political conflicts within black society. There are those who seem to feel that "black power" in itself is revolutionary, leading toward national liberation and socialism; others predict that "black power" can be fit within the framework of liberal pluralism as with other ethnic movements. Neither of these extreme tendencies of analysis seems quite realistic. There surely will emerge ideological differences among black intellectuals and leaders, and sharp differences along class lines will continue to grow—struggle between the black burgeoisie and black masses may in time be modified through a process of black intellectuals returning "home" to their community. The only viable way to make such a return is through identification with the class needs of the ghetto poor. On the other hand, white society will continue to encourage the growth of the classic "comprador bourgeoisie" of blacks to administer the colony for the mother country. In the end, the intransigent nature of racism and exploitation in American society, plus the growth of new revolutionary leadership, seem certain to necessitate a black liberation movement in the process of steady—but not automatic—radicalization.

The movement for self-determination and control is the beginning of a new stage in the politics of black liberation. The possibility of revolution first requires a struggle for structural change to place power in the community.

A new perspective is required of white Americans:

First, America must be seen as a colonial society, not a melting pot in which integration can be realized.

Second, the issue of race must be recognized as an issue of self-determination.

Third, it must be accepted that self-determination cannot be "granted." It is always wrested from those who oppose it. People first win self-determination, then their former oppressors "grant" it.

Fourth, the battle for self-determination should be understood as either long or short, peaceful or bloody, according to the degree of vested interest and determination of the oppressors. It is possible, theoretically at least, for a process of challenge-and-concession to gradually cripple racism with a minimum of destruction to the framework of due process and law—though the present prospects for this are unlikely.

Fifth, the establishment of self-determination for blacks will have deep effects on the total society. A revolution would not only have to occur *against* white America but *within* white America as well.

The deepest effect on American society would be in the area of policy priorities. The spending for Vietnam and national defense would have to be reallocated to domestic need. It is impossible to have a policy of "guns and butter." The political will does not exist. Congressmen and taxpayers who favor an arms race, a military establishment surpassing that of any country in the world, and a genocidal war in Vietnam, are not capable of understanding or acting on the social needs of the poor in America. It is impossible to maintain a foreign policy of violent counterrevolution with a policy of reform at home. Foreign and domestic policy flow from the same structure of interests. Policy cannot be modified without a movement so massive that it at least threatens those interests; and policy cannot be fundamentally changed without the political defeat of those interests. At a minimum this would mean breaking the power of urban machines and southern congressmen, and placing effective public demands on the major corporations. Without a major change in political leadership, and without the harnessing of business to the achievement of public policy objectives, there can be no meaningful talk of abolishing slums and racism.

But white Americans must also recognize how they themselves are oppressed by colonialism. Racial guilt is inadequate; a revolutionary politics cannot stem from white "shame" but from recognition of one's own oppression.

Because of American racism, whites can be dehumanized and made into beasts. Because of American racism, the society makes "law and order" its paramount objective, preventing social progress—for whites or blacks—in urban development, in education, in medical research, in countless areas of human need. Because of American racism, whites are paying taxes for a government which is less and less able to deal with social problems. And even if America could be imagined without racism, the society would be ridden with problems because of its commitment to the growth of private enterprise and consumption at the expense of social needs. Our cities are unliveable. Our mass media are base. Advertising corrupts the ability for independent thought. Meaningless, hard work is still done by millions of people to support the private luxuries for a few. America progressively becomes a military state, and its citizens are able to achieve progressively less security. The technological capacity of this society allows for revolutionary changes in the way men can live, but the American imagination for change is underdeveloped and poisoned by passivity and fear. The point is that while the blacks are the most brutally oppressed and rebellious group in America, and while whites must remain abreast of the black revolt to be relevant, whites need not wait for blacks to provide a reason for outrage. White people have enough to rebel against on their own.

When a white American moves beyond guilt to a recognition that he is a brainwashed victim of exploitation, then on the basis of self-interest he can begin to work against the colonial status quo. If he is motivated only by "shame" then he will be limited to asking what he can do "for" black people. If he is motivated by personal indignation, however, he will be more able to view black people as possible *allies* in a struggle for change.

The role of whites in the racial crisis can take several forms. First, a white can work inside, or in close relation with, organizations in the black community; for example, as a lawyer, journalist, fund-raiser, even as a participant. But this is only possible where the white is operating within the approval or discipline of black leadership. Second, the white can work inside the white community directly against racism. This might be educational work (organizing confrontations between ghetto rebels and white church congregations), emergency aid groups to help with fund-raising, legal defense, medical needs in times of crisis, or political protest work (exposure of "respectable" suburbanites who profit from racism as slum-landlords or in other roles). During police suppression of rebellions whites can carry out diversionary demonstrations to make the military occupation more costly and difficult. If racists intend to spill blood they should be made to realize that it will not be the blood of blacks alone, but of white radicals and perhaps of the racists as well.

Finally, and most importantly, whites can organize movements which have certain common interests with the black community. These movements can be organized among poor whites (demand economic changes, such as new housing, which would also benefit blacks), professionals (who want to develop imaginative new roles in the "public sector" free of top-down control), students (who want to reorganize power and purpose in the universities), and the broad cross-section of people who oppose the Vietnam war, the draft, and the growing military budget.

Perhaps the chief problem for whites lies in their need to overcome their privileged position in white society. Students, young professionals and industrial workers are exploited in different ways for the needs of advanced capitalism, but they are among the more contented victims of exploitation in history. Overcoming privilege does not necessarily mean that all whites should become John Browns, and most certainly it does not mean that whites should drop out only to drop into black culture. But neither does it mean that whites can expect to be relevant any longer in conventional slots within the productive system and cultural establishment. Whites must have at the very least one foot outside the conventional roles assigned them, and their main weight should be on that foot.

A hopeful recent case of such politics is the Columbia University strike. There the students went beyond the simple demand for "student power" for themselves in a corrupt university. They voiced and stuck by demands in behalf of the people in Harlem and Vietnam who are exploited by American universities. The striking students were willing to accept police repression, loss of their student status and exposure to the draft. Their action helped to re-open an issue which was nearly closed two years ago when Stokely Carmichael advised whites to go into the white community. Stokely's suggestion tended to paralyze many whites not only by causing feelings of "rejection" but because Stokely also argued that the white community was racist "from top to bottom." Thus working in the white racist community seemed only to include working "for" flacks once again but under largely futile conditions. But now the white radicals are into the white community, at least on the campuses, and are finding revolutionary roles for themselves. There has developed the possibility of coalitions on a new basis coordinating the black liberation struggle with those whites who are ready and able to break down the mother country from within. The new coalition, if it materializes, will not be based simply on whites "helping" or supporting blacks but on whites taking a frontline position in behalf of their own liberation. The struggle of the blacks has helped whites to discover their own oppression.

The prospects for such radicalism among whites will increase with the intensification of the racial crisis, and especially with the prolongation of the Vietnam war and new Vietnams. The most visible awakening so far is among the students: they are freest of the weight of the past, and temporarily independent of the conservative pressures of family and job. Their growing rebellion in large part has been motivated by shame—shame at the brutality committed by the United States in Mississippi and Vietnam. But their movement is motivated also by an authentic revulsion at their own condition: their sense of being "processed" and channeled" by parents, draft boards, high school and university administrations and the big corporations. Some are coming to the understanding that their passions, imagination and skills cannot find an outlet in the present context of the society.Their protest movement, as well as the black liberation movement, has triggered a widespread reexamination of purposes throughout the society, particularly among the clergy, intellectuals and educated professionals.

It is not possible to predict now what this youth and student revolt will become. All that is clear is that the student protest is moving from liberal humanitarianism to a class-conscious opposition movement. The American empire, instead of creating welfare and security for the American people, is beginning to impose costs which people are unwilling to pay. These naturally include endless taxes and blood for the military machine. But there is a greater price, the sentencing of people to meaningless, exploited lives at a time when human possibilities should be expanding. Men are capable of spending their taxes and their blood when the purpose inspires them. But gradually the American ethic of anti-communism and the fast buck is losing its ability to inspire, and therefore its legitimacy, especially among young people. It may become increasingly difficult to pursue empire and war when large numbers of Americans are experiencing such confusion. It is faint, but here is the hope for undermining, and eventually transforming, the system of American oppression.

No nation can be free if it oppresses other nations.
KARL MARX

IMPERIALISM AND REVOLUTION

DAVID HOROWITZ

By the end of the second decade of cold war, developments within both world camps were ushering in a new era of relations between imperialism and revolution. The chief characteristic of this new period, distinguishing it from the preceding one of confrontation between national power blocs, was the increasingly clear polarization between international class forces—between the world socialist revolution on the one side and the imperialist-dominated bourgeois *counter*revolution on the other.

This polarization was partly a result of the post-independence radicalization of nationalist movements in the underdeveloped world, their adoption of "class" programs linking economic exploitation with national dependence, and socialist revolution with national liberation. In part, it reflected the advances made within the socialist camp itself, and in part, it represented a final conservative shift in the orientation of the leading bourgeois power, the United States, which had consolidated and completed its ascendancy in the postwar period.

In one sense, the liberalization within the Soviet bloc and the newly apparent conservatism of bourgeois power were closely related. Thus, the recent developments within the Soviet camp and the emergence of new revolutionary censors of power had the effect not only of releasing the revolution from its national Russian confines, and of accelerating socialist development in the direction of its democratic and internationalist ideals, but also of lifting the veil on the bankruptcy of the bourgeois revolution in the coming epoch.

For whereas the democratic rhetoric of the "free world" camp had previously been given resonance by Soviet domination and exploitation of the East European countries within its "security" zone, the partial self-liberation of these countries in the mid-fifties and the immobility of the NATO powers during the East European revolts deprived this cause of much of its substance. As a result the international confrontation between exploited and exploiting classes was seen to run that much more clearly from East to West, from the rising revolutions in the underdeveloped world to the colonial and neo-colonial powers of the NATO alliance. The basic character of the postwar conflict was increasingly recognized, even by the Western peoples, to be reflected in the fact that these same NATO powers had killed more than four million inhabitants (mostly peasants) of the underdeveloped world in counterrevolutionary actions in the first two postwar decades, and that in the third decade these actions were continuing as strongly as ever.

To be sure, the continuing confinement of the socialist revolution to the economically and culturally backward regions, the maintenance of the single-party monolith in the Soviet Union and the Communist bloc generally, and the unbroken Russian domination of the East European states still reserved to the advanced bourgeois democracies—at least in some eyes—a semblance of that progressiveness which had hitherto prevented the historical polarization from attaining completeness. Nonetheless, developments within the capitalist camp itself were rapidly combining with the changes in the East to reveal the tenuousness of the bourgeois commitment to bourgeois ideals and the primacy of its commitment to bourgeois power and survival—and thus were serving to accelerate and deepen the historical trend.

Previously, the basic conservatism of the capitalist West had been somewhat obscured both by the unfinished struggle between feudal-fascist and liberal-imperialist powers and by Washington's ambiguous opposition to the vestiges of European colonialism. The defeat of the Nazi Axis, however, the decolonization of most of the old empires, the emergence of the United States to undisputed global predominance and the general adoption of its own *neo*-colonial system by the other imperial powers all served to bring about a change in the balance of international forces. Where, since the turn of the century the United States had appeared in the guise of a liberalizing force among the dominant world powers in the new framework created by these developments, this most advanced, most democratic and most powerful of the capitalist states stood revealed more and more unambiguously as the conservative guardian of the international status quo.

Symbolic of this change and transformation was Washington's support for the fascist coup in Greece in April 1967. As a result of the recent U.S. détente with Moscow and the centrifugal developments in the Communist world, this coup appeared in a very different light from the previous U.S. intervention in behalf of Greek reaction and monarchism in 1947. For in the changed international context, the coup could not be portrayed, with the slightest degree of plausibility, as a necessary if deplorable defense against Russian expansionism. Rather it openly revealed itself as a classic fascist attempt to close the liberal door to potential *internal* socialist and Communist revolution. The United States' tacit but crucial support for the coup—against those same "liberal" forces that had fought the Communists in 1947—without the traditional justification of containing an external expansionism, expressed eloquently the changes which the new correlation of international forces had wrought.

America's readiness to abandon the bourgeois-democratic revolution in order to preserve the propertied status quo was even more decisively indicated by the failure of the Alliance for Progress, which Washington had initiated in 1961 to spur the "democratic revolution" in Latin America as an alternative to Cuban socialism. For not only were most of the existing dictatorships of the continent included by Washington in its self-proclaimed "alliance of free governments," but U.S. support was given in the ensuing years to every military coup (without exception) against the remaining constitutional regimes. The conservative outlook underlying this policy was well exemplified by a U.S. Embassy official explaining U.S. support for the brutal dictatorship in Paraguay, one of the most desperately poor and exploited countries in Latin America. "In the last analysis," commented the official, "our policy is one of *survival*. Thus a sure anti-Communist, no matter how despicable, is better than a reformer, no matter how honest, who might turn against us." (Emphasis added.)

Not surprisingly, before the end of the first five years of the Alliance, Washington had openly abandoned what it had never really in practice been ready to maintain, namely its support for bourgeois social reform and political democracy and its commitment to a policy of nonintervention in Latin American countries, at least at the overt military level. Henceforth, in pursuit of its real objectives as imperial guardian, Washington was to put far less stock in what were in the end only tactical concessions to democratic sentiment. These objectives were: internal political and economic stabilization in the satellite countries, coordinated intervention and counterrevolution to preserve the hemispheric status quo.

The failure of the ambitious Alliance program of economic, social and political reform within Washington's prototype neocolonial system testified eloquently to the futility of the hope of progress for the dependent nations within the capitalist orbit in the present historical epoch, the utter utopianism of attempting to resurrect the corpse of the bourgeois revolution with the aid of the bourgeois imperialist powers.

The depth of U.S. commitment to the status quo, however, was nowhere more poignantly manifested than in Washington's massive military intervention in Vietnam. While not entirely unique among U.S. actions in the cold war decades, this savage aggression showed more vividly than anything previously the lengths to which Washington was prepared to go to defeat a social revolution that threatened to breach its international system. Wholly indifferent to the claims of national sovereignty and the rights of self-determination, Washington showed itself willing to wage a war of unparalleled ferocity, even to the point of obliterating a poor and underdeveloped society, rather than allow its people to pursue their independent course.

This virtually unprecedented assault by the world's greatest industrial power on a small and impoverished peasant country impressed for the first time on the consciousness of millions the real character of U.S. imperialism, which had previously been concealed by its geographical isolation and the background role which it had been able to play during the twilight years of European power. Thus, as Trotsky noted long ago, "American imperialism is in essence ruthlessly rude, predatory in the full sense of the word, and criminal. But owing to the special conditions of American development, it has the possibility of draping itself in the toga of pacifism."

By the middle of the second decade of cold war, these special conditions no longer continued to prevail. In the wanton destruction of Vietnam, the brutality of American imperialism and its triumph over America's liberal ideals were starkly revealed: "Every bomb that falls on helpless peasants destroys the clearest claim upon humanity's allegiance that Western democracy once could make: that it was not terrorist society, that for all its defects it has a way of solving problems peacefully, and for that reason well worth defending. At bottom, this was perhaps always an allusion. Now, at any rate, each day's headlines shatter it." "There is a growing belief," reported Walter Lippmann after a tour of Europe in 1967, "that Johnson's America is no longer the historic America, that it is a bastard empire which relies on superior force to achieve its purposes, and is no longer providing an example of the wisdom and humanity of a free society. There is, to be sure, envy, fear, rivalry in the worldwide anti-Johnsonism. But the inner core of this sentiment is a feeling of betrayal and abandonment. It is a feeling that the American promise has been betrayed and abandoned."

It might be contended, however, that the Vietnam war represents merely a dreadful episode, rather than the magnified expression of a real historical trend, that the polarization which is visible in this conflict and in other areas represents only a temporary sharpening of the class struggle, rather than a long-term development and prospect. Such a hypothesis would carry more conviction if it were not for the cumulative historical experience of counterrevolutionary interventions by the imperialist powers and their inevitable continuing commitment to the social status quo. Moreover, it can be seen that underlying this historical experience and this commitment are powerful structural forces operating at the heart of the present epoch which will, in the long run, intensify, the developing conflict and force the confrontation between the socialist world revolution and the imperialist-dominated bourgeois counterrevolution.

The unprecedented expansionist drive of U.S. imperialism in the postwar period is undoubtedly the most important of these forces. Usually expressed in political terms as marking the end of U.S. "isolationism" and measured militarily in the acquisition of thousands of bases across the globe, this expansion has been supported economically by an equally impressive and in the long run even more significant program of overseas financial and industrial investment.

U.S. direct foreign investments alone increased more than sevenfold between 1946 and 1966—from $7.2 billion to $54.6 billion. By 1964, sales of U.S. goods abroad had tripled since 1950, and the size of the foreign market for U.S.-owned firms in 1965 was equal to approximately 40 percent of the domestic U.S. output of farms, factories and mines. Indeed, U.S. firms abroad constituted the third largest economic unit after the U.S. and Soviet domestic economies.

Not only was U.S. overseas investment expanding on an unprecedented scale in the postwar period, it was becoming more and more vital to the prosperity of the domestic economy itself. Thus, in 1964, in the crucial capital-goods sector, the combined support given by exports and military-investment demand (an obviously related factor) ranged from 20 percent to 50 percent of total output. U.S. leaders guiding this postwar overseas expansion were, of course, not ignorant of its important role vis-à-vis the domestic economy. In fact, in approaching the postwar period they had put this consideration at the very center of their calculations. For, like their predecessors, U.S. leaders during the Great Depression saw the solution to the domestic economic problem not in terms of internal structural changes, but in terms of staking out ever new, externally situated frontiers.

Mincing no words in describing the grave implications of the economic crisis, Undersecretary of State Dean Acheson had told a Congressional audience in November 1944, on the very eve of the postwar expansion: "We cannot go through another ten years like the ten years at the end of the twenties and the beginning of the thirties without having the most far-reaching consequences upon our economic and social systems. . . . We have got to see that what the country produces is used and sold under financial arrangements which make its production possible."

Analyzing the options available, in a fashion wholly orthodox for Washington and the leadership of America's corporate ruling class, Acheson held that so long as the United States maintained a capitalist economic system domestic markets would not suffice to absorb production on a profitable-enough basis to keep up the level of output and employment. "Under a different system," Acheson observed, "you could use the entire production of the country in the United States." However, to introduce such a system, namely, socialism, "would completely change our Constitution, our relation to property, human liberty, our very conception of law. And nobody contemplates that. Therefore, you must look to the other markets and those markets are abroad."

Acheson's remarks, which only expressed a consensus among the U.S. leadership at the time, reflect the consistency of the ideology of U.S. imperialism. In the calculations of U.S. leaders—from William McKinley to Franklin Roosevelt, from Woodrow Wilson to John F. Kennedy and Lyndon Johnson—the preservation of American prosperity and institutions and of "the American way of life" has been predicated on the preservation and extension of U.S. control of foreign markets, and thus the inevitable expansion of U.S. power overseas. Viewed in this perspective, the cold war can be seen as the U.S. ruling class evidently sees it, namely, as a war for the American frontier.

Of course, "frontier" in this usage is not to be understood in a territorial sense but in terms of a set of political institutions and ideological attitudes based, as they can only be based in this conception, on an international "free enterprise" economic system open to penetration and domination by United States capital. The security of these institutions at home is firmly believed to be dependent on the preservation and expansion of their outposts overseas—in short, of the United States' extra-geographical frontier, the "free world."

At this point it may be suggested, however, that this traditional expansionist outlook of the American ruling class is mainly based on a Hobsonian misconception of capitalist economics, and hence is bound to change and lead to a redirection of American energies from the enterprise of expansion and control in external frontiers to a much needed program of social reconstruction and rehabilitation at home. For with the development and acceptance of Keynesian doctrine, it is apparent that capitalist governments can, by their own action, raise the level of effective domestic demand, and thus, presumably, mitigate the necessity of an expansionist economics and politics.

However, even if insufficient demand at the national level were the fundamental cause of America's overseas expansion, there would be little historical basis for expecting such a revision of national priorities through the application of the Keynesian remedies. For it was precisely the two post-war decades which witnessed the increasing acceptance of the Keynesian analysis and techniques that at the same time marked the unprecedented expansion of U.S. foreign investment. Moreover, as previously noted, such expansion of the federal budget as did take place was primarily directed toward military investment (more than $904 billion since 1946, or 57 percent of the total). In fact, since 1929 there has been relatively no change in the level of federal nonmilitary expenditures as a fraction of GNP. In other words, given the class structure of U.S. monopoly capitalism with its intense resistance to redistributive measures and to any allocation of resources which runs against or circumvents the channels of the existing market, the only way demand can be significantly raised is by creating and supplying a huge military machine. Far from making possible a disengagement from the external frontier, Keynesian policy in practice has created a new and immensely powerful bureaucracy, which, with its corporate allies, has a vital and increasing stake in the maintenance and expansion of that overseas empire.

In other words, the net effect of the application of the Keynesian prescriptions has been to intensify the expansionist bias in American policy rather than lessen it. However, even if federal outlays could be allocated to meet domestic needs at a level adequate to sustain demand—despite all historical experience to the contrary—this still would not arrest the outward pressure of American imperialism. For the fundamental pressure behind imperialist expansion is not the overall level of demand (though it is influenced by that level) but the pressure of the system itself: the competitive struggle for the control of markets, or, as Lenin put it, for the completion of monopoly not only at home but internationally as well.

Properly viewed, imperialism is a "class" phenomenon, with its dynamic center at the corporate level (in the framework of the existing market). The global extension of the U.S. petroleum industry, for example, has less to do with domestic profit margins (though these certainly play a role) than with the global dispersion of the resource itself, and the necessity of controlling the sources of supply in order to maintain monopolistic prices for the finished product (not only abroad but at home as well).

The postwar overseas expansion was stimulated by a combination of factors: these included a domestic profit squeeze, a new wave of corporate mergers; fears of a reconversion crisis and the consequent availability of U.S. government financing; economic nationalism in the underdeveloped world; and the continuing push of the productive forces against national frontiers. To develop commercially the new technologies (many of which received an immense stimulus from the war) required large investments of capital and hence mass markets over which to spread unit costs. At the same time, modern communications and mass media standardized tastes in different countries, while resurgent economic nationalism, often coupled with foreign-currency shortages, induced governments to ensure that international goods which they bought were manufactured on their own soil.

In the course of these developments a new corporate form emerged—the "multinational" or *international* corporation. Carrying out both manufacturing and marketing operations in literally dozens of countries, such corporations, as distinct from even their giant predecessors, no longer merely look to foreign sources for an important share of sales, profits and growth but rather seek "to apply company resources on a global scale to realize business opportunities anywhere in the world." In other words, once placed in "external" markets, international corporations seek to expand their control of these markets as such, for they are locked in mortal struggle with similar giants for control of markets at an *international* level. The predominance of U.S. international corporations within the American political economy, based not least on the fact that *its* prosperity depends on their own, will assure them the necessary leverage over foreign policy to support their operations.

Thus, it is irrelevant that total exports or aggregate "super-profits" from foreign holdings may form only a small fraction of GNP for the expansionist power, though this is often raised to challenge the importance of economic motives and power in the structure of U.S. expansionism. What is significant is the role of the foreign holdings of the giant U.S. corporations in *their* operations, and their own preponderant role in the U.S. domestic economy and polity. The evidence shows that both are overwhelmingly great. In 1964, for example, foreign sources of earnings accounted for about *one quarter* of *all* domestic nonfinancial corporate profits. As for concentration, the hundred largest U.S. corporations, or less than 0.1 percent of all U.S. corporations, owned 55 percent of total net capital assets, and it was among these that the giants of the international field were to be found. Moreoever, concentration does not stop at the national frontier: only forty-five U.S. firms account for almost 60 percent of direct U.S. foreign investment, while 80 percent is held by a hundred and sixty-three firms. Furthermore, it is estimated, on the basis of current growth rates of U.S. overseas companies, that within the next decades some 75 percent of all industrial assets in the "free world" outside the public sector will be controlled by a mere three hundred international firms, of which a hundred and seventy-five will be U.S.-owned.

The postwar expansion of the U.S. corporate stake in the global economy from a relatively modest $7 billion to more than $50 billion in *direct* investments ((70 billion in *total* private foreign investments) undoubtedly played a major part in the growing conservatism of the U.S. corporate ruling class and in Washington's intensified commitment to the international status quo. To assess the impact of this expansion on the overall polarization of global bourgeois and socialist forces, it is also necessary to gauge its effect in the developed and underdeveloped worlds. In particular, it must be asked whether any section of the global bourgeois forces could be expected to come forward to occupy the vanguard position vacated by the United States when it acceded to its role as chief beneficiary and policeman of the international system of property and privilege. For the bankruptcy of the bourgeoisie as a historical force would be irrevocably sealed if it failed to advance those values with which its rise was associated and which continued in the present to provide its legitimating and validating principles. Conversely, a serious commitment to those values by a section of the international bourgeoisie against the inevitable encroachment of the expanding American empire would lead to a new lease on life for the bourgeois democratic revolution and the capitalist system.

Such a challenge to American expansion and domination appeared to have been raised, at least potentially, in the early sixties, by Gaullist France. American investment in Europe had increased from $2 billion in 1950 to a total of over $15 billion a decade and a half later. More than half of this investment, moreover, was in manufacturing and included the fastest growth sectors and most technically advanced industries of the European economy. In France alone, U.S. corporations had come to control almost the whole electronics industry, 90 percent of the production of synthetic rubber, 65 percent of petroleum distribution and 65 percent of farm-machinery production.

The extent of this penetration already indicated the ultimate futility of the Gaullist opposition. It was not merely the U.S. economic foothold that ensured this futility, however, but the balance of international class forces. For potential opposition to U.S. domination had to be tempered by the recognition that the capitalist system could no longer afford a showdown struggle between its leading powers. The European powers' use of their financial strength to reduce the American capital inflow, could not, for example, be carried to the point of precipitating an international monetary crisis without at the same time creating a grave threat to the European ruling classes themselves. As a result of the undiminished, and indeed increasing, strength of the European socialist Left and the presence of an expanding and progressing socialist world camp, any European bourgeoisie would hesitate at the outset to embark on a course of opposition to the United States that would lead to such a point of no return.

Underlying the weakness of the European bourgeoisie and the historic bankruptcy of its cause was the basic fact that, short of an unworkable fascist "solution" (leading to eventual inter-capitalist war), the only possible structural basis for an *independent* European development was a *socialist* one.

Nearly half a century earlier, the Bolshevik theorist Preobrazhensky noted that America had already acquired a dominant role in the world economy, and drew a momentous conclusion: *"American expansion,"* he wrote, *"cannot encounter an unbreakable resistance in any country of the capitalist world so long as the country undergoing attack and pressure remains capitalist."* The reason for this was that American dominance was a function of the commanding superiority of its monopolistic and technically advanced economy in the increasingly integrated world market, and that this very superiority ensured its future triumph in any competition in that market. He wrote: "The very economic structure of the present-day capitalist countries excludes the possibility of serious resistance to American conquest, because the already attained level of the world division of labor, of world exchange, with the existence of the huge and ever-growing economic, technical, and financial superiority of America over all the rest of the world inevitably subjects this world to the value-relations of America. Not a single capitalist country can, without ceasing to be capitalist, break away from the operation of the law of value [i.e., the market] in its changed form. And it is just here that the avalanche of American monopolism falls on it. Resistance is possible only, perhaps, on a political basis, specifically on a military basis, but just because of America's economic superiority this would hardly prove successful. . . ." (And because of the strength of the Left, as well as the deterrent factor of nuclear weapons would hardly be tried).

"A struggle against American monopolism," concluded Preobrazhensky, "is possible only through changes in the whole structure of the given country, that is, through going over to a socialist economy," which would permit the total mobilization of economic resources, "and would not allow American capitalism to get hold of one branch of industry after another, subjecting them to American trusts or banks, as is happening with the 'natural' contact between present-day American capitalism and the capitalism of other capitalist countries. . . . For Europe of today the old freedom of competition is impossible *in any sense*. Europe must choose between capitalist monopoly, externally bound to the monopolism of the United States, and internal socialist monopoly, which would make independence possible." (Emphasis in original.)

Notwithstanding the prematurity of Preobrazhensky's posing of the problem, it is evident that in the postwar decades the very choice which he outlined has been firmly placed on the historical agenda.

That which applies in the realm of economic power to the bourgeoisies of the developed capitalist countries, moreover, applies with immeasurably greater force to those of the underdeveloped world. Yet, it is precisely this section of the global bourgeoisie that in the postwar independence struggles provided one of the few instances of bourgeois revolutionary leadership since 1848. Even though ultimately no effort to achieve economic independence in the underdeveloped world can be successful except on a socialist basis, it is still important to consider what the alignment of such a class would tend to be in the next stages of the historical process.

In fact, the very conquest of political sovereignty, taken together with the triumph of the Russian, Chinese and Cuban revolutions tends, as has in fact already been noted, to sap the revolutionary will of the national bourgeoisie in the underdeveloped world, as the social and economic questions are approached. To these conservatizing influences can be added yet another factor in the new postwar patterns of imperialist investment. These patterns were pioneered by the United States in its neo-colonial system in Latin America, and are associated in the postwar period with the emergence of the international corporation.

Under classic imperialism, investment was largely in extractive industries, and indigenous manufacturing industry was suppressed, while direct control of the state was used to enforce this basic pattern. There was, therefore, an inherent conflict between the development requirements of an indigenous bourgeoisie and the policies of the imperial power, so that the potential growth of the former came to hinge on freedom from foreign rule.

The post-colonial pattern has been significantly different. As a result of the nationalist protectionism of the new formally independent governments, the international corporation has come under pressure to defend its markets by setting up manufacturing industries inside the freshly erected tariff walls in the underdeveloped regions. This has been one of the crucial factors in the postwar economic expansion, and has resulted in a new partnership between the national bourgeoisie and the foreign corporations.

The national bourgeoisie is now needed by foreign capital to mediate with the local environment and the national state, over which the metropolitan power no longer exercises overt control. In return, national capital is allowed a share in the new manufacturing and marketing industries which can amount to as much as 51 percent or more (the so-called "Chileanization," "Indianization," etc., of the economy). In fact, however, the technical and economic superiority of the metropolitan-based corporations still ensures their effective control of these satellite industries, even in the absence of majority shares. Moreover, the conflict between the policies of these monopolistic international firms and the requirements of national development remain basically as intense and unresolvable as before. Consequently, while political decolonization and neo-colonial investment tend to divest the national bourgeoisie of the last remnant of its revolutionary character, real domination of the satellite country (which also takes place through its overall financial, economic and military dependence on the metropolis) continues, and the neo-colony remains caught in the vise of economic stagnation and underdevelopment.

Sooner or later, this post-independence impasse compels recognition of the fact that formal political independence does not really free the satellite country to pursue its national development and consequently that "the interests of the national liberation movement are intimately connected with the needs of social revolution." It is no accident that this was first recognized by the revolutionary movements in Latin America which achieved formal political independence more than a hundred and fifty years ago, and where the Castroist revolution in Cuba has provided the basis for a concerted challenge to the tenets of Stalinism among the international revolutionary forces. In the shaping of this recognition, the Cuban Revolution and the intimately related and abortive Alliance for Progress were pivotal events.

The Cuban Revolution began as an attempt to solve the problems of national development within a bourgeois democratic framework, but quickly found the backbone of the opposition to its reforms (particularly the land reform) to be U.S. corporate interests and, behind them, the U.S. government. In order to carry out the program of bourgeois reforms, therefore, it became necessary to wage a struggle for *national* liberation.

However, partly because the national bourgeoisie refused to

support a head-on collision with the United States and—putting its class interests before its national allegiance—left the revolutionary coalition to go over to the counterrevolution, and partly because to concentrate economic power in the hands of the state was the only possible way to wage such a struggle, the Cubans soon discovered that to be successful, the nationalist revolution must be socialist.

The inability of the Cuban bourgeoisie to carry through a bourgeois nationalist revolution or—what amounts to the same thing—the impossibility of carrying out a bourgeois revolution on the basis of the capitalist, neo-colonial production relationships in Cuba was shown to be a phenomenon of hemispheric significance by the subsequent failure of the Alliance for Progress. For in this Alliance, Washington attempted to put its financial and political resources behind a bourgeois-democratic program of social and economic reform. "Those who possess wealth and power in poor nations," declared President Kennedy, "must accept their own responsibilities. They must lead the fight for those basic reforms which alone can preserve the fabric of their own societies." This program, however, came up against the hard reality that the bourgeoisie was not prepared, in the first place, to relinquish its own privileges, and in the second, to jeopardize its economically and socially dominant position by playing with revolutionary—even "moderate" revolutionary—fire. Even more important, any attempt to carry through really basic reforms fundamentally conflicted with U.S. corporate interests and the U.S. corporate system in Latin America.

In fact, just as a radical bourgeois government, bent on reform, had been overthrown by U.S. agents in Guatemala in pre-Alliance days (1954), so similar Alliance governments were toppled by military coups engineered or supported by the United States, including those in the Dominican Republic (1963) and Brazil (1965). A land reform in Honduras which touched the interests of the U.S.-owned United Fruit Company was frustrated by the U.S. Congress, while in 1965 a revolution to restore the deposed Alliance government in Dominica was crushed by 30,000 U.S. marines. The failure of the Alliance in practice (the program of reforms was abandoned, the minimum growth goals were not even approached) demonstrated that there was no U.S.-backed "democratic" alternative to Castroist revolution: to be successful, the nationalist revolution must be socialist.

This did not mean that the coming Latin American revolution would necessarily be fought under socialist rather than nationalist and bourgeois-democratic banners. It meant, rather, that democracy and self-determination, even in their limited bourgeois forms, could no longer be realized in Latin America under bourgeois conditions of production, i.e., without breaking out of the United States' "free world" system, the system of international capital. Such is the concrete meaning of the "historic bankruptcy" of the bourgeois-democratic revolution in the underdeveloped world in the present epoch.

Nowhere, however, was the imperialist decay and failure of the capitalist sysem more significantly manifested, or the question of its future more fatefully posed, than in the crises besetting its transfigured dominant power. In 1945 the United States had provided inspiration to a demoralized and discredited bourgeois world, which had seen in America's New Deal welfarism, liberal political and egalitarian outlook the promise of a better capitalist future. (The fact that this "egalitarianism" excluded black people was as expressive of the character of America's bourgeois-imperialist social order as was the acceptance of American racism by the liberals of Europe characteristic of their own imperial role and outlook.)

Little more than two decades later, the bitter disillusionment with America's performance and the widespread sense of betrayed hope in the American future were recognized and reflected upon even by the system's committed adherents. "At the present," declared the chairman of the U.S. Senate Foreign Relations Committee in the summer of 1967, "much of the world is repelled by America and what America seems to stand for. Both in our foreign affairs and in our domestic life we convey an image of violence, . . . Abroad we are engaged in a savage and unsuccessful war against poor people in a small backward nation. At home—largely because of the neglect resulting from 25 years of preoccupation with foreign involvement—our cities are exploding in violent protest against generations of social injustice. America, which only a few years ago seemed to the world to be a model of democracy and social justice, has become a symbol of violence and undisciplined power."

As befitted the remarks of a partisan, the statement retained a residue of undaunted optimism. The great unchecked domestic crises in race relations, urban development, education and the general pollution of the human environment are blamed not on a system of irrational and inequitable resource allocation based on the private accumulation of social capital but on "foreign involvement." This is indeed to misunderstand the essence of the system. For the unchecked concentration of financial and corporate power and its expansion beyond local and national boundaries are the very cornerstone of "free enterprise" capitalism. The system is not merely *involved* in global markets and politics; it *is* global. Even if it were possible to make the social decision to surrender markets abroad while retaining capitalist relations at home, such a decision would merely be to choose the existence of a colonial satellite in place of that of an imperial power. Within capitalism there is no way to avoid the toils of imperialist rivalry and competition, no way to elude the political and military conflicts which the imperialist struggle entails.

Moreover, the assumption that it is possible within capitalism to reallocate resources domestically according to social rather than market criteria and on a scale adequate to meet the cumulative social crisis has no foundation in reality. For it is belied by the whole historical experience of capitalist societies and runs counter to the logic of the system itself. Historically, the capitalist state, whether under the formal rule of social democratic radicals or tory conservatives, has never marshaled the funds necessary to even begin a genuine social reconstruction. War and preparation for war have proved the only vast expenditure programs (proportionate to calculated need) that capitalist states have been willing or able to undertake.

As an indication of the larger pattern of fiscal priorities, just before the Vietnam escalation and the subsequent increase of annual government outlays on the war from less than $500 million to more than $30 *billion,* pleas to expand the government's poverty program were rejected on the grounds that no money was available for such an expansion. In the preceding Keynes-oriented Kennedy administration, which expanded the military budget by 20 percent in its first two years, plans to stimulate the flagging economy by increased social expenditure were similarly rejected, under intense corporate pressure, in favor of a tax cut. (This tax cut, moreover, had the net effect of redistributing income to the wealthier classes.) For the vital interests of the corporations require that nondefense government expenditure on social welfare be kept to a minimum and "as long as the levels of control over the productive apparatus are in [their] hands, no [governmental] economic program can hope to succeed without their consent."

So powerful are the structural forces shaping the misallocation of resources in capitalist society and actively preventing remedial federal action that those of its liberal spokesmen who are able to sense in some degree the magnitude of the gathering social crisis are themselves beginning to realize that to solve it within the limits of the existing system is not really possible. Thus, as one well-informed correspondent reported of the New Frontier: ". . . while [Kennedy] and his associates go on talking publicly about the progress they have made, privately they are beginning to fear that given the existing form of American society and the existing balance of political power, the evils they complain about simply cannot be remedied."

One of the crises that had caused the President and his advisers most concern was inevitably the mounting tide of black revolt in the country—a direct consequence of the long-term social and economic oppression of black people, the colonial status of the black ghettos, and the regime of terror under which large sections of the black community have been compelled to live in the United States since reconstruction. The deep-rooted character of this oppression, symbolized by the failure of the ruling class to meet the most basic political and economic demands of the black movement, was starkly illuminated by the alacrity with which it was ready to squander men and resources in its murderous war to preserve the corporate frontier in Asia. Indeed, the basic priorities of America's imperialist and racist social order were unsparingly revealed in the comparative sums allocated, on the one hand, to the domestic "War on Poverty," and on the other, to the war against the peasantry in Vietnam. For every fifty-four dollars scraped together by the federal government (under the pressure of mass protest) to ease the plight of one exploited and oppressed black laborer in America, three hundred and fifty *thousand* dollars were made available to kill a yellow peasant in the deltas of Indochina. More money was being spent annually on ground ammunition alone for use in Vietnam than for the entire poverty program in the United States; and while Washington was willing to shed rivers of blood for its puppet dictatorship in Saigon, hardly an official white finger was raised to defend the lives and freedom of black Americans in the American South. This scale of priorities was itself an incitement to revolt, the index of a system depraved by the immensity of the effort necessary to maintain itself and its class privileges in an era in which it had lost the power to advance the struggle for human justice and liberty within its own institutional framework.

As the first-line official response to the ghetto uprisings resolved itself more and more clearly into the armed occupation of American cities, the symmetry of repression and rebellion on the national and international levels began to forge a unity of consciousness and purpose between the various forces struggling for self-determination and liberation. "We are living in an era of revolution," the American black leader Malxolm X had declared in the last year of his life, "and the revolt of the American Negro is part of the rebellion against the oppression and colonialism which has characterized this era. It is incorrect to classify the revolt of the Negro as simply a racial conflict of black against white, or as a purely American problem. Rather, we are today seeing a rebellion of the oppressed against the oppressor, the exploited against the exploiter."

The more and more visible connection between the national and international structures of exploitation and oppression, and the growing solidarity between the revolutionary forces challenging these structures, underscored both the general character and the historic import of the developing crisis. Rooted in the insoluble social and economic contradictions of the international capitalist system, the crisis found its expression *politically,* as a crisis of the democratic order itself. The increasing resort to militarism and repressive violence and the parallel expansion of the domestic apparatuses of authority and control, on the one hand, reflected the inability of the system to generate the sources of its own renewal while at the same time it posed an active challenge to the very concept of popular sovereignty, i.e., the legitimating principles of bourgeois rule and order.

The truly international foundations of this crisis, which manifested itself so intensely within the American national framework, were expressed in the fact that a major pressure against the constitutional system in the United States came from the exigencies of the war abroad. Thus, in order to carry out the intervention in Vietnam, for which there could be no popular sanction, the President had to present both Congress and the people with a *fait accompli* and launch the overt stage of U.S. aggression (the bombing of the North, the mass landing of U.S. troops in the South) "illegally," without a declaration of war. He had, further, to contain a historically unprecedented resistance to the draft, which struck at the very basis of governmental authority. While the immediate impact of these events was to unsettle the political consensus which had governed and supported U.S. foreign policy since the Second World War, its implications as a reflection of basic forces and long-term trends were far more important.

Thus, historically, one of the main pressures leading toward fascism in the belated capitalist powers had been the incompatibility of parliamentary or even constitutional rule with the requirements of a policy of military imperialism. Prior to the cold war, the liberal imperialist powers, and the United States in particular, had been able to carry out their interventions with only a minimal need for military mobilization. Consequently the potential conflicts between civil and military authority, between the popular sanctioning of policy required by democratic order and wars waged for predatory ends on behalf of a minute, if extremely powerful, section of society were effectively contained. With the strengthening of the socialist world movement and its renewed challenge in the wave of nationalist and Communist revolutions after the Second World War, however, the liberal powers, and especially the United States in its new preeminence, lost this margin of maneuver. In order to repress revolutions internationally, to weaken and retard the development of the existing socialist states, and to sustain domestic demand amid the stagnationist tendencies of the increasingly monopolistic economic system, it became necessary to mobilize permanently on an immense and ever-expanding scale. In addition to causing powerful, new adverse economic pressures (a domestic inflationary spiral, a critical outflow of gold), this mobilization accelerated the corporatist-fascist trend within the economy, bringing the most technologically advanced sectors within the province of a monopolistic complex of military-industrial interests.

At the same time, the growing desperation of the capitalist ruling classes before the prospect of the rising socialist challenge made them even more prone to intervene actively wherever revolution reared its head. The result was the frank embrace of the counterrevolutionary principle by Washington and the open articulation of a vast "counter-insurgency" program, linking the programs in "aid," "information" and "defense" to an expanding apparatus of subversion and intervention. At the heart of this network of institutions was the Central Intelligence Agency, a secretive body employing tens of thousands of agents and utilizing an astronomical, concealed budget to dominate and control the key organizations and agencies of social change both at home and abroad.

Just as the militarization of a large area of the American economic system greatly increased the structural tendencies toward a fascist state, the counter-insurgency program and its expanding clandestine network, operating at all levels of political and cultural life, set up a powerful, parallel momentum toward totalitarian control. For the outlook developed and the techniques employed in maintaining an empire abroad could not be segregated from the approach to social conflict and the maintenance of the corporate empire at home, particularly when the social struggles were not themselves distinct.

Similarly, the liberal-racist ruling coalition, on which U.S. imperialist policy had depended throughout the century, could not be dissolved to clear the way for the drastic reform of domestic racist institutions at a time when the pressure on the overseas empire was so great. The permanence of a fascist political base in the right wings of the Democratic and Republican parties was thus assured. Thus, too, the expansion of the domestic police forces and their arsenals of anti-"riot" weaponry, coupled with the resistance to structural reform, was only the domestic side of the intensified repression in answer to the demand for social change abroad.

These developments would tend to be less portentous if the economic expansion of the domestic system were itself assured. But the domestic economic system does not exist in a vacuum, and the tightening up of alternatives globally was not accidentally matched with a narrowing margin of flexibility at home. Intensified competition from the revived capitalist powers of Western Europe and Japan for markets shrinking before the tremendous expansion of productive forces; intensified pressure from the industrial working classes pushing up wage levels and raising a political barrier to large-scale unemployment; spiraling inflation and mushrooming monetary crisis—all pointed to a period of increased instability for international capitalism, a consequent loss of options in dealing with the cumulative social crises, and hence a mounting pressure to abandon the democratic process and its forms.

Precisely because it expresses the deeper crisis of the social order and the moribund nature of the bourgeois epoch the growing crisis of democratic power in the world capitalist system poses the central issues of the crises in both the national and international realms: on the one hand, the root injustices and irrationalities of a system in which social production and distribution remain beyond social control; on the other, the criminal character and military dangers of foreign policies of overseas expansion, armed repression and global counterrevolution on behalf of immensely powerful financial-corporate oligarchies.

By posing on the national level the central issues of the international conflict, by linking the international struggle for self-determination with the internal quest for social equality and social control, the crisis of democracy increasingly presents itself as the revolutionary crisis of the epoch. The movement for the sovereignty of the people within the imperial nation coincides with the struggle for self-determination in the international sphere. Just as domestically the demand for democratic power is a demand to overthrow the corporate ruling class and to make the productive apparatus responsive to social needs, so internationally the precondition of democratic sovereignty and inter-state coexistence is the dissolution of the government of the international corporations and financial institutions which have expropriated the sovereignty of nations in order to appropriate the wealth of the world.

The struggle which the Bolsheviks began more than half a century ago is still in its early stages—indeed, in a sense, is just beginning. The awakening of the consciousness of the peoples, particularly in the West, to the catastrophe of capitalism's continued rule and domination has been a slow and fitful process. But the contradiction between means and ends in the present era is reaching hitherto unimaginable proportions. More than ever before, for humanity to live under capitalism is to live on borrowed time. For the continuing worldwide oppression of class, nation and race, the incalculable waste and untold misery, the unending destruction and preparation for destruction and the permanent threat to democratic order the characterize the rule of capitalism in this, its most technically advanced, most "enlightened" and most materially wealthy era now threaten human survival itself. In the age of atomic weapons and intercontinental missiles, the predatory system of imperialist rivalry and global exploitation, of military intervention and counterrevolutionary war, faces mankind with the prospect of the ultimate barbarism.

Liberation is no longer, and can be no longer, merely a national concern. The dimension of the struggle, as Lenin and the Bolsheviks so clearly saw, is international: its road is the socialist revolution.

REFERENCES

Anderson, Perry, and Blackburn (eds.). *Towards Socialism*. Ithaca, N.Y.: Cornell University Press, 1965.

Carr, E. H. *A History of Soviet Russia*. Vols. 1-4. Baltimore: Penguin Books, 1951-60.

Cleaver, Eldridge. *Post-Prison Writings*. New York: Random House, 1969.

Debray, Regis. *Revolution in the Revolution*. New York: Monthly Review Press, 1968.

Fanon, Frantz. *The Wretched of the Earth*. New York: Grove Press, 1968.

Gorz, Andre. *Strategy for Labor*. Boston: Beacon Press, 1968.

Gramsci, Antonio. *The Modern Prince*. New York: International Publishers, 1959.

Guevara, Che. *Venceremos*. Edited by John Gerassi. New York: Macmillan, 1969.

Hayden, Tom. *The Trial*. New York: Holt, Rinehart, & Winston, 1970.

Horowitz, David. *Empire and Revolution*. New York: Random House, 1969.

Jacobs, Harold. *Weatherman*. Berkeley, Calif.: Ramparts Press, 1971.

Lenin, V. I. *Two Tactics of the Social Democracy in the Democratic Revolution*. Moscow, FLPH, 1905.

Lin Piao. *Long Live the Victory of People's War*. Peking: Foreign Languages Press, 1968.

Trotsky, Leon. *The Lessons of October* 1923 in *The Essential Trotsky* Allen & Unwin, 1961.